THE COINS

THE COINS

OF THE

GREEK AND SCYTHIC KINGS OF BACTRIA

AND INDIA

IN

THE BRITISH MUSEUM

PERCY GARDNER

GYAN

Published by

Gyan Publishing House
5, Ansari Road
Daryaganj, New Delhi-110002
Phone: 011-47034999, 9811692060
E-mail: books@gyanbooks.com

Distribution Network
gyanbooks.com
India, USA, Canada, UK, Australia

ISBN: 978-93-7133-709-0 (PB)

First Published, 1886

2nd Impression 2025

Printed at: Gyan Press, Delhi.

THE COINS
Author Percy Gardner

CATALOGUE

OF

INDIAN COINS

IN

THE BRITISH MUSEUM.

GREEK AND SCYTHIC KINGS OF BACTRIA AND INDIA.

LONDON:

PRINTED BY ORDER OF THE TRUSTEES.

LONGMANS & CO., Paternoster Row;
B. QUARITCH, 15, Piccadilly; A. ASHER & CO., 13, Bedford Street,
Covent Garden, and at Berlin; TRÜBNER & CO., 57 & 59, Ludgate Hill.

Paris: C. ROLLIN & FEUARDENT, 4, Rue de Louvois.

THE COINS

OF THE

GREEK AND SCYTHIC KINGS OF BACTRIA AND INDIA

IN

THE BRITISH MUSEUM.

BY PERCY GARDNER, Litt. D.

DISNEY PROFESSOR OF ARCHAEOLOGY IN THE UNIVERSITY OF CAMBRIDGE.

EDITED BY

REGINALD STUART POOLE, LL.D.

CORRESPONDENT OF THE INSTITUTE OF FRANCE.

LONDON:

PRINTED BY ORDER OF THE TRUSTEES.

1886.

EDITOR'S PREFACE.

THE present volume contains all the coins which were issued by the Greek and Scythic kings who ruled in India and the neighbouring lands between the time of Alexander the Great and the third century A.D.

The work has been long and laborious, alike to compiler, editor, and printer. The number of unusual characters which it contains has greatly hindered its progress; but the typographical difficulties have not been the only ones. The history of the kings is very obscure, and the types employed on their coins often of a mixed and uncertain character. On the other hand, few fields of numismatics offer richer material, historical, archaeological, and even philological; though philological theories are necessarily excluded from these pages.

Special thanks are due to General Cunningham, R.E., who has allowed the compiler free use of his plates published in recent volumes of the Numismatic Chronicle, and has thus enabled the present work to be rendered far more complete than it could otherwise be: also to Professor Cecil Bendall, who has given valuable philological aid.

The system of transliteration adopted for Prakrit words is that used by Professor Aufrecht in the Sanskritic Catalogue of the Bodleian Library; also in the Catalogue of Books in the British Museum.

I have carefully revised the manuscript of this work, comparing each coin with the corresponding description.

REGINALD STUART POOLE.

CONTENTS.

LIST OF PLATES.

THE COINS

OF THE

GREEK AND SCYTHIC KINGS

OF

BACTRIA AND INDIA.

INTRODUCTION.

In treating of the arrangement of the coins of the Greek and Scythic Kings of Bactria and India, it is necessary to enter briefly into all the known facts of their history. The Kings of the Seleucid and Ptolemaic dynasties succeeded one another in a known order, and the chief events of their reigns have been handed down to us by ancient writers. It was therefore unnecessary to give the facts of their history as an introduction to the lists of the coins issued by them. But in regard to all but two or three of the kings of the farther East, the ancient historians are quite silent; and coins and inscriptions alone save us from ignorance even of their names. Therefore it is necessary in this Introduction to trace the outlines of any history which can now be recovered, and in particular in some detail to set forth the historical facts which may fairly be established by means of the coins. In order to bring the discussion into the narrowest possible limits, it will be necessary (1) to abstain from mere conjecture, however tempting; (2) to avoid full discussion of disputed points, merely indicating where difference of opinion exists, and referring, when possible, to works already published, or monographs in various numismatic journals; (3) to treat in detail only such parts of history as have a numismatic bearing.

Necessity for here examining historical data.

The writers to whom credit is due for the arrangement and decipherment of these coins are, in the first rank, James Prinsep* and General Alexander Cunningham.†

Most important writers.

* *Essays on Indian Antiquities.*

† Coins of the Successors of Alexander, *Numismatic Chronicle*, 1868, &c.

Mr. E. Thomas,* Lassen,† and Wilson,‡ have also done much important work, both historical and numismatic, in the same field. The most recent monograph on the coins is that of von Sallet,§ whose scholarly acquirements and solid numismatic judgment have enabled him to correct on many points the theories of his predecessors. Mr. James Fergusson's and Professor Cowell's researches have also been of the greatest value to the present purpose; and there is much valuable matter in von Gutschmid's article on the Graeco-Parthian Empire in the ninth edition of the *Encyclopædia Britannica*, s. v. *Persia*. When a debt is due to other writers, it will be mentioned in the foot-notes.

I. Historical Outlines.

Alexander the Great: Rulers who issued coin B.C. 330—260.

The numismatics of the Greek rulers of India properly begins with Diodotus. But there are a few coins issued in India or neighbouring countries at an earlier period than his, which are, for convenience, included in this volume. Whether Alexander himself, during his sojourn in India, issued coins in his own name, may perhaps be doubted; but it is at least a plausible conjecture that certain bronze coins,‖ bearing the usual types of Alexander and his name, but of square form, were issued in India, as the custom of issuing square coins already existed in India in Alexander's time, but in no other country. These pieces, then, unfortunately wanting in the British Museum, may be considered as the earliest Greek coins of India.

* Notes to Prinsep's *Essays*.

† *Indische Alterthumskunde*.

‡ *Ariana Antiqua*.

§ *Zeitschrift für Numismatik*, Berlin 1879.

‖ The conjecture is Dannenberg's, *Zeitschr. f. Num.* vi. 166 (note), who, however, gives the coins to Bactria. India is a far more reasonable attribution.

In recent years the region of Balkh (Bactria) has furnished an abundant supply of coins, issued by the immediate successors of Alexander in that district.* Among these are double darics, with Greek letters on the obverse; gold and silver coins of the first three Antiochi, with the types of a seated Apollo and of a horse's head; silver coins of Seleucus I., with types of a chariot of elephants and a horse's head; coins issued during the joint reigns of Seleucus and Antiochus I., bearing the names of both rulers; and gold money of an early king of the Persepolitan class, with Pehlvi legend.

Andragoras.

Among these also have come to light a few coins, in gold and silver, of a king named Andragoras, who is conjectured to have been ruler of Parthia or one of the neighbouring countries in the early part of the third century B.C. The only ancient authority who mentions this king is Justin,† who states Andragoras to have been the name of (1) a Persian noble set up as Satrap of Parthia by Alexander, (2) a Satrap of Parthia overthrown eighty years later by the first Arsaces. It is more probable that the coins published in our catalogue belong to the period of the second of these rulers. The issue of gold coin shows that the ruler who issued them claimed a complete independence; and this is a further reason for assigning him to the time of the break up of the Seleucid empire in the East, about B.C. 250.

Sophytes.

The coins of Sophytes were first published by Cunningham.‡ They are the more interesting because their date and place of issue can be approximately fixed. We learn from several of the historians of Alexander's reign that Sopeithes, or Sophytes, ruled a district on the banks of the Acesines

* P. Gardner, in *Num. Chron.* 1879, p. 1; 1880, p. 181; 1881, p. 8. Cunningham, in *R. A. S. B. Journal*, 1881, p. 151. Especially has a find from the Oxus river enriched the cabinets of collectors.

† Justin, xii. 4, xli. 4. Cf. *Num. Chron.* 1879, p. 1; 1881, p. 8.

‡ *Num. Chron.* 1866, p. 220.

at the time of Alexander's invasion, and was confirmed by the latter in the possession of it. But Sophytes' coins are copied from the issues, not of Alexander, but of Seleucus. It would appear from them that Sophytes renewed with Seleucus, very probably on the occasion of that king's eastern expedition against Sandracottus, the friendship which he had established with Alexander.

After this expedition, for the period of a century, that is to say during the third century before our era, India proper was governed altogether by native rulers; the power of the Seleucidae and Greek kings of Bactria stopping at the Indian Caucasus.

The Bactrian revolt. Diodotus.

The date of the revolt of Bactria against the authority of the Seleucidae, who had inherited all the eastern parts of the empire of Alexander, cannot be accurately fixed. Justin,* however, states that it was contemporary with another revolt of one of the eastern provinces of the Seleucid empire, that of the Parthians under Arsaces; an event which took place in B.C. 248.† About that time, then, Diodotus, Satrap of Bactria, revolted against Antiochus II. of Syria, and succeeded in establishing his independence. He seems to have prepared his subjects for a change of masters by issuing coin bearing the types of Antiochus II. of Syria, but with his own portrait.‡ After his establishment in the kingdom he continued this issue unchanged, only substituting his own name, besides his portrait, for that of the Seleucid king. According to Justin,§ Diodotus soon died, and was succeeded by his son, also named Diodotus, who made a treaty of alliance with Arsaces, the first Parthian king. But it seems clear that all coins which have come down to us bearing the

* xli. 4.

† Gardner, *The Parthian Coinage*, p. 3.

‡ *Br. Mus. Catalogue of Seleucid Coins*, p. 15. Cf. *Num. Chron.* 1881, p. 11.

§ xli. 4. Justin calls Diodotus Theodotus. But Trogus Pompeius seems to have had the name right, *Prol.* lib. xli.

name of Diodotus were issued by one king. We must therefore either suppose that Justin is wrong and has duplicated a single monarch, or that the younger Diodotus continued the issue of his father's money unchanged, or, finally, that the elder Diodotus continued during his lifetime to issue money in the name of Antiochus of Syria, and that our coins with the name of Diodotus were issued by his son, who first ventured to introduce his own name and portrait on the coin. Between these alternatives we cannot venture to decide; in favour of the last, it may be observed that the portrait of Diodotus on his coins is that of a man of not more than middle age; the coins of flat fabric, and bearing an elderly portrait, being now considered forgeries.

Euthydemus. Eastern expedition of Antiochus III.

We learn that Diodotus was superseded in the rule of Bactria by Euthydemus, a native of Magnesia, in Ionia, possibly a Satrap of some neighbouring province, who was in full power at the time when Antiochus the Great made his eastern expedition, in or about B.C. 208. The accurate pages of Polybius* give us a glimpse into his history which is very valuable. Euthydemus being defeated in battle by Antiochus, and unable to oppose him, appealed to his generosity, saying that he was born in Asia Minor, and was not one of those who had revolted against Antiochus II., but, on the contrary, had gained the kingdom after rooting out the descendants of those who had so revolted. He pointed out the grave danger that must arise if he were obliged to call in the aid of the Scythians, who were already hovering on the Chinese frontier of his dominions. Antiochus seems to have been open to conviction: finally, he agreed to acknowledge Euthydemus' independence; and, taking a fancy to Demetrius his son, promised him one of his own daughters in marriage.

* *Hist.* x. *ad fin.*, xi. 34.

After making terms with Euthydemus, Antiochus advanced across the Paropamisus into India, and made a treaty with the Indian king, Sophagasenus, or Subhāgasena, who seems at that time to have been in full possession of the Kabul Valley, the Greek dominion stretching little, if at all, to the south of the Indian Caucasus. Thence Antiochus returned, through Arachosia and Drangiana, to Syria.

Demetrius and Eucratides: conquests to East & South

With the beginning of the second century B.C. we find great changes taking place in the Greek regions of Central Asia. On the death of Euthydemus, his son Demetrius succeeded; and we find, as contemporary and rival of the latter, the great Eucratides, whose career of chequered victory and defeat may be partly traced in historical records. At the same time the Greeks, perhaps in consequence of the constantly increasing pressure from the north of the nomadic tribes of Central Asia, made their way across the Indian Caucasus, and began to wrest from the native Indian princes the districts of Kabul and the Panjab, which had been left under native dominion by the Seleucid kings from Seleucus I. to Antiochus III., and which Diodotus does not seem to have attacked; for coins of Diodotus are not found south of the Indian Caucasus. On the other hand, those of Euthydemus are found as far south as Seistan, and as far east as the Panjab;* and the city of Sagala, in the neighbourhood of Lahore, bore the surname of Euthydemia. Thus the sudden extension of the Greek pale would seem to have been a feature of the later years of Euthydemus. But it appears, from the statements of ancient writers, that the actual conqueror was not Euthydemus but his son Demetrius, who was probably his colleague in the kingdom as well as his successor. Thus Justin† speaks of

* Some were found in the Indus at Attok. See Cunningham, in *Num. Chron.*, 1869, p. 137.

† xli. 6.

Demetrius as king of India, and Strabo* couples him with Menander as a chief agent of Greek conquest in India. What seems most likely is that Demetrius made considerable conquests during his father's lifetime.

We are, however, scarcely justified in saying, as does v. Gutschmid,† that "Demetrius himself marched down the course of the Indus, conquered Pattala and the kingdom of Saraostes (Surāshtra) and Sigerdis, probably the district of the commercial city Barygaza." The careless language of the passage of Strabo in which these places are mentioned as within the Greek pale seems only to imply that some of the Greek kings extended their conquests so far; and it is reasonable to suppose that the rule of Menander was extended farther to south and east than that of Demetrius; to Menander therefore the conquest of the Indus valley may be with more reason ascribed.

Not only did Euthydemus acquire, through his son's activity, territory in India, but he also probably ruled the widest district ever possessed by the Greeks to the north of the Paropamisus, from Margiana to Chinese Tartary. Even into the Celestial Empire the influence and the trade of the Greeks seems at this time to have penetrated. Of this a proof is furnished by a coin brought by Sir D. Forsyth from Kashgar,‡ bearing a Chinese legend and inscribed with the name and titles of a Greek king, possibly Hermaeus. After Euthydemus' death his dominions were broken up by the rivalry between Demetrius and Eucratides, as well as by the rise and usurpations of fresh kings of uncertain origin, such as the first Antimachus.

* *Geog.* xi. 11, 1. Most of Strabo's statements as to early Bactrian history are loose and incorrect. For instance, he speaks of the revolt of Arsaces as subsequent to the rise of Euthydemus.

† In *Encycl. Brit.*, Persia, p. 590.

‡ *Numism. Chron.* 1879, p. 274. That this coin is of iron, is now, I am informed, denied.

Coins of Eucratides with his father and mother.

Of Eucratides also the origin is obscure. We know, however, by a fortunate chance, the names of his father and mother. These are furnished to us by the remarkable coins * which bear on one side the head of Eucratides, and the inscription Βασιλεὺς Εὐκρατίδης; on the other the portraits of his father and mother, Heliocles and Laodice. The very collocation of the inscriptions which appear on the two sides of those coins, Βασιλεὺς Εὐκρατίδης—Ἡλιοκλέους καὶ Λαοδίκης, where we seem almost compelled to understand the word υἱός, shows that in them Eucratides intends to proclaim his parentage. Heliocles does not seem to have been a king at all, for his portrait wears no diadema, but Laodice's head does seem to be bound with the diadema, in the Greek East the invariable sign of royalty. And indeed her appearance on coins in such a connexion would scarcely be explicable unless she were of royal parentage. But we must remain in ignorance whose daughter she was. Von Sallet has proposed an entirely different interpretation of the coins in question. He thinks that they were issued by Eucratides, not in honour of his parents, but on the occasion of the marriage of his son Heliocles (who afterwards succeeded him) with a Laodice, whom Sallet conjectures to have been daughter of Demetrius by the daughter of Antiochus III., whom that monarch betrothed to Demetrius in the course of his Indian campaign. On this hypothesis some recent writers have tried to build further structures of theory. But it is unfitted to bear such a weight. In its favour is the one fact that the name Laodice was usual in (not peculiar to) the Seleucid dynasty of Syria. On the other side are reasons of more weight. The portraits of Heliocles and Laodice on the coins are of elderly, not young persons; and it is not easy to see how Sallet would interpret in the inscriptions which accompany

* See page 19, pl. vi. 9, 10.

the portraits the genitive case in the names of Heliocles and Laodice, unless he understands before them the word υἱός. If any one carefully compares the head of the elder Heliocles (pl. vi. 9), with that of Eucratides (pl. v. 6), and that of the younger Heliocles (pl. vii. 1, 2), he must allow that it resembles Eucratides far more nearly than his son; which may be best accounted for by supposing that the artist constructed the head of the elder Heliocles after his death, on the analogy of that of his son Eucratides.

Wars of Demetrius and Eucratides.

The wars between Demetrius and Eucratides are mentioned by Justin;* but the statements of this writer must be received with great caution, nor can we believe his assertions that the Indian conquests of Eucratides belong to the end of his reign, or that Demetrius ruled until nearly the same time. For the coins seem to contradict them. The coins of Demetrius come in almost all cases from Bactria, those of Eucratides are very commonly found in the Kabul Valley. The coins of Demetrius bear Greek legends only, with rare exception, while the bronze coins of Eucratides are nearly all bilingual, an indication alike of their later date than the money of Demetrius and that they were issued in India. We therefore, must still retain the opinion that Demetrius ruled only during the early part of the reign of Eucratides in Bactria as well as in India, and that Eucratides was for a great part of his reign lord of India as well as of Bactria and Arachosia. Eucratides founded the city of Eucratidia in Bactria; Demetrius, Demetrias in Arachosia, and Euthydemia in India.

Cunningham places the commencement of the career of Eucratides

* "Multa tamen Eucratides bella magna virtute gessit, quibus adtritus cum obsidionem Demetrii regis Indorum pateretur, cum ccc. militibus lx. milia hostium adsiduis eruptionibus vicit. Quinto itaque mense liberatus Indiam in potestatem redegit. Unde cum se reciperet a filio quem socium regni fecerat, in itinere interficitur."—Justin, xli. 6.

Reign of Eucratides.

about B.C. 190, and this date must be approximately right.* His reign began brilliantly, and was continued with chequered fortune; but the wide field over which his coins are found,† and their commonness, seems to testify to his great power. We may also remark his assumption of the title *Βασιλεὺς μέγας* as a clear indication of extensive dominions, and the fact that his types and titles are copied by the kings of Parthia,‡ and by Timarchus, king of Babylon,§ as showing how widely his money circulated. But it appears that towards the end of his reign certain provinces‖ were wrested from him by the Parthians, probably in the time of their great king Mithradates, who came to the throne about B.C. 170. The reign of Eucratides appears to have lasted until the times of two kings, who certainly imitate his money, Plato, whom the date on his unique and remarkable coin shows to have ruled in B.C. 165, and Timarchus of Babylon B.C. 162. Plato would seem to have been a mere ephemeral rival, or a revolted satrap of Eucratides.

Plato.

We must assign to the period of the reign of Eucratides, that is, to the first half of the second century B.C., the coins of the kings Euthydemus II., Pantaleon, Agathocles, and Antimachus I. This assignment, which was first made by von Sallet, is on grounds of style quite incontestable. It is impossible, in view of the art

Euthydemus II. Pantaleon, Agathocles, Antimachus I.

* There does not seem to be any conclusive evidence on the point. v. Sallet quotes the imitation of Eucratides' types by certain early Arsacid kings as a proof that Eucratides' reign began early; but the attribution of the early coins of the Arsacidae is a matter of dispute.

† According to Cunningham, they are found at Balkh, in Bokhara; Seistan, the Kabul Valley, &c., and a few in the Panjab.

‡ For instance, Arsaces VI., Mithradates I. See Gardner, *The Parthian Coinage*, p. 31. Other writers attribute these coins to others of the Arsacidae.

§ *B. M. Cat. Seleucidae*, pl. xv. 2, p. 50.

‖ Τήν τε Ἀσπιώνου καὶ τὴν Τουριούαν ἀφῄρηντο Εὐκρατίδην οἱ Παρθυαῖοι: Strabo xi. 11, ed. Kramer. The names seem corrupt, and have been variously amended.

and fabric of the coins of those kings, to give them, as previous writers, and even Cunningham did, to the earliest days of Bactrian independence. And the evidence of style is further confirmed by the consideration that as all these kings reigned on the south side of the Paropamisus, they cannot be assigned to an earlier period than that of the Indian conquests of Demetrius.

This new light is of the utmost importance in the classification of the earlier Greek kings of India: it entirely destroys an order which was full of difficulties, and puts in its place one which is thoroughly intelligible and satisfactory.

The coins of the younger Euthydemus are certainly subsequent to those of Demetrius, whose types they borrow. There can, therefore, be no reasonable doubt that this king was either the younger son of Euthydemus I., or else the son of Demetrius and grandson of Euthydemus I. As the coins of the younger Euthydemus are not by most writers distinguished from those of the elder, it is not possible to ascertain their find-spots, or to determine the locality of his reign; its date would seem to be about B.C. 170. From the rarity of his coins it may be judged that his reign was soon brought to an end.

Pantaleon and Agathocles strike with almost identical types. They both adopt the metal nickel* for their coins, and they alone use in their legends the square Indian alphabet. They seem, therefore, to have been closely connected, either brothers, or father and son. Coins of both are found in the Kabul Valley and the western Panjab, and those of Agathocles as far south as Kandahar. Pantaleon seems from his portrait to have been the elder of the two, and the rarity of his coins shows his reign to have been ephemeral. Agathocles seems to have ruled more widely and longer, and he has

* See Dr. Flight's analysis in *Num. Chron.* 1868, p. 305.

left us in some of his coins valuable materials for the determination of points in his history.

Medals struck by Agathocles and Antimachus.

Of the greatest importance is a series of coins,* which indeed we may rather term medals, of the weight of Attic tetradrachms, issued by Agathocles in commemoration of his predecessors in the Greek rule of Bactria. These medals reproduce alike the portraits of these predecessors, and, what is still more unusual, their coin-types, so that only by their style and their inscriptions do they differ from the ordinary coins of those monarchs. The inscriptions run thus:—

ΑΛΕΞΑΝΔΡΟΥ ΤΟΥ ΦΙΛΙΠΠΟΥ	ΒΑΣΙΛΕΥΟΝΤΟΣ ΑΓΑΘΟΚΛΕΟΥΣ ΔΙΚΑΙΟΥ
ΑΝΤΙΟΧΟΥ ΝΙΚΑΤΟΡΟΣ	"
ΔΙΟΔΟΤΟΥ ΣΩΤΗΡΟΣ	"
ΕΥΘΥΔΗΜΟΥ ΘΕΟΥ	"

To these we must add the parallel coin of King Antimachus:

ΔΙΟΔΟΤΟΥ ΣΩΤΗΡΟΣ	ΒΑΣΙΛΕΥΟΝΤΟΣ ΘΕΟΥ ΑΝΤΙΜΑΧΟΥ

I have elsewhere† discussed these medals, the true character of which v. Sallet was the first to establish. They prove that Pantaleon and Agathocles, like the younger Euthydemus, belonged to the faction of Euthydemus I. and Demetrius, and were presumably opposed to Eucratides. Agathocles traces his political pedigree through Euthydemus I., Diodotus, and an Antiochus,‡ to

* Pl. iv. 1, 3, xxx. 5, 6.

† *Num. Chron.* 1881, p. 184.

‡ It is disputed which of the three first Antiochi of Syria is the Antiochus Nicator of these coins. None of them seems really to have borne the title: the first was Soter, the second Theos, the third Megas. In favour of Antiochus I., it may be urged that he was the only Antiochus who held undisputed sway in Bactria, and might well be regarded by the Eastern Greeks as full successor of Alexander the Great; also his father Seleucus was called Nicator. In favour of Antiochus II., we have the strong argument that the type of the seated Heraklès which is repeated on the Bactrian coin is copied from coins of Syria given by

Alexander the Great himself. Antimachus claims Diodotus as his predecessor. These facts seem to suggest, what is by no means improbable in itself, that Euthydemus II., Pantaleon, and Agathocles were all sons of Demetrius. And possibly, though this is more speculative, Antimachus, as to whose connexions we have no information, was the representative by descent or otherwise of the house of Diodotus.

Types of Antimachus.

The types of Antimachus' coins add one more to the few known facts of Greek-Indian history. They are, on the silver coins, Poseidon holding trident and palm; and on the bronze, Victory standing on a ship. There is no mistaking the meaning of these types, which clearly allude to a naval victory won by the king. It might seem at first sight that this victory must have been won on the open sea. But Antimachus' rule never extended to the sea: his coins are found both on the north and the south of the Caucasus, but never south of the Panjab. We must therefore suppose that the naval victory was won on the Indus, or one of its great tributaries; and, indeed, it may easily be understood that the Greeks would place so large a river as the Indus under the sway of Poseidon.

Heliocles: two classes of coins.

Eucratides was succeeded by his son Heliocles. The coins of this king are found mostly in Bactria, but also in the Kabul Valley. He is, as Cunningham remarks, the last king who struck to the north of the Indian Caucasus. We may therefore be almost sure that in his reign the nomadic tribes conquered the whole country as far south as the Bamian Pass. The silver coins of Heliocles fall into two classes. The first class consists of coins of the Attic standard of weight, bearing Greek

general consent to Antiochus II. In favour of Antiochus III., the only argument is a passage of Malala (p. 261), where the term Nicator seems to be applied to this king. But this passage is deprived of all weight by the numerous mistakes which it contains. The balance of evidence is greatly in favour of Antiochus I. or II.

legends only. The second class consists of coins of a different weight, which I call the Persian,* which bear bilingual inscriptions and a different portrait of the king. The theory is obvious that the first class was issued by the king while he ruled in Bactria, and the second class at a later period, when he was king only of a corner of India. And it is greatly in favour of this view that the coins of the Bactrian class were largely copied by the barbarous tribes of central Asia, just as the coins of Philip and Alexander were by the Gauls who invaded Macedon about B.C. 290, while those of the Indian class are closely like coins of subsequent Greek kings of the Kabul Valley and India.

Successors of Heliocles.

Down to the reign of Heliocles, which must be assigned to about B.C. 160—120, we are able to trace with certainty, or little less than certainty, the order of succession of the Greek kings of India. But we now arrive on the verge of a period of uncertainty, where the data are very scanty. In fact, our task would become almost hopeless, were it not that the annals of China preserve a general outline of the history of Bactria and India in the account which they give of the wanderings of the nomad nations on the western borders of China, during the second and first centuries B.C. To identify the names of kings and of places as recorded by the Chinese with those which we find on the coins is no easy task, but it is a task which has been attempted, and with some measure of success in the opinion of those best qualified to judge.

Principal information from Chinese sources.

Chinese account of the Yue-chi.

The most recent authority who has examined the Chinese evidence as to the migrations of the Yueh-chi, M. E. Specht,† thus sums it up:—The Yueh-chi were conquered in 201 and 165 B.C. by the Huns, and fled westward, subjugating the Ta-hia of Bactria, and fixing their seat to the north of the Oxus,

* See below, p. lviii.

† *Journal Asiatique*, 8th Ser., vol. ii. p. 348.

where a Chinese ambassador found them in 126 B.C. After that visit they captured Lan-chi, the capital of the Ta-hia. A hundred years later, Khiu-tsiu-kio [Kadphises I.], ruler of the Kushans, one of the Yueh-chi tribes, conquered all the other tribes, invaded the kingdom of the Arsacidae,* seized Kabul and Ki-pin [Cophene], and formed a great kingdom. His son conquered India, and the empire thus founded lasted from the middle of the first to the end of the fourth century.

Who the Ta-hia may be is not clear: they have been identified with the Scythian tribe of the Dahae, but the Chinese description of them—"each town was governed by its magistrate, the population was weak and feared war,"—would not apply to any Scythic race, but would very well apply to the native Bactrians under Greek dominion; and the date at which the Greeks were driven across the Paropamisus, in the reign of Heliocles, would fall not far from B.C. 126.

In the Kabul Valley the Hellenic race held out for a century later, until Kadphises I. led the united tribes of Yueh-chi against them, and, after vanquishing them, ruled the country, at first in conjunction with the last king, Hermaeus, and finally in his place.

The Chinese authorities thus give us two dates of the utmost value for the reconstruction of the history of India and Bactria: the nomad tribes conquered Bactria (Heliocles) about B.C. 125, and India (Hermaeus) about B.C. 25. These dates both suit the numismatic evidence very well. Gen. Cunningham gives Hermaeus to a far earlier period than B.C. 25, assigning him indeed to so early a time as 138—120. But not only does this conflict with historical records, but it is also in collision with numismatic testimony. For Hermaeus was, as all writers agree, the last of the

* About B.C. 31, Phraates, with the help of a Scythian army, expelled Tiridates from the government of Parthia.

Greek kings of Kabul. We are therefore obliged to place between Heliocles and him the reigns of all the twenty Greek kings whose coins have come down to us. To cramp all these reigns into the space of thirty years, B.C. 160—130, is an unreasonable proceeding. Moreover the forms of letters on some of the coins, those of Zoilus, Nicias, and Hermaeus, entirely preclude us from assigning them to so early a period as B.C. 130; they must be quite a century later.

The Chinese writers also authorize the supposition that the Scythian race which wrought the ruin of the Greeks was that of the Yueh-chi, who have been identified with the Tochari of Strabo. And the coins, in this confirming Chinese testimony, show that the tribe of Yueh-chi to which Kadphises belonged was the tribe of Kushan, already mentioned on the last page.

This knowledge is valuable; but it leaves us in ignorance on many points. We are still unaware to what tribes belonged the barbarous rulers of India in this age who did not come in with Kadphises. Maues, Azes, and their successors, who established a kingdom in India, as we shall hereafter see, before the days of Hermaeus, do not appear to have been Yueh-chi; and we are quite in doubt as to the connexions of Gondophares and other rulers.

Before proceeding to speak more in detail of the various groups of kings, we will set forth in the form of a chart the general outlines of our historical and geographical knowledge in regard to them:—

CHART TO SHOW EXTENT OF DOMINIONS AND DATES OF GREEK AND SCYTHIC KINGS.

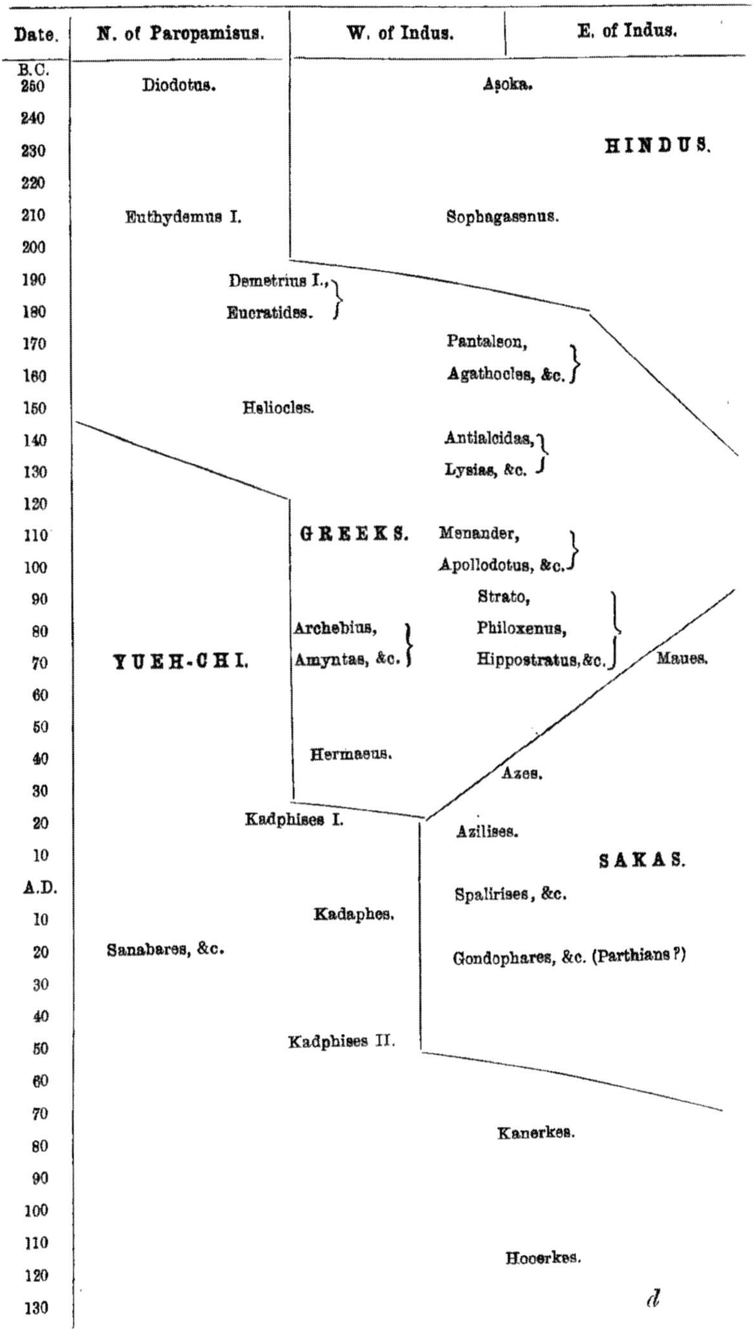

Greek Successors of Heliocles;—arrangement.

Leaving out of account the predecessors of Heliocles, we know already of upwards of twenty kings and of two queens who ruled in the Kabul Valley and the Panjab after about B.C. 160, and before the Indo-Scythic conquest of those regions. The orderly arrangement of these rulers is a matter of the utmost difficulty and even of impossibility. The classification of General Cunningham is based on indications so slight that it cannot resist serious criticism: and indeed its validity depends in a great degree on his arrangement of the early kings, which must now be given up in consequence of the readjustment of Pantaleon and Agathocles. Von Sallet so entirely despairs of any reasonable arrangement that he adopts one which is merely alphabetical. All that has been attempted in the present catalogue is to group the kings roughly in something like chronological order, keeping similar types of coin as far as possible together. By means of the Index any king can easily be found, and that is the chief necessity.

Chronological data.

It will however be well to set forth briefly what certain data we possess for the chronological and geographical assignment of the kings. We will begin with the chronological.

Date of Antialcidas and Lysias.

The only one of these later kings who strikes money on the Attic standard is Antialcidas, who must therefore be either a contemporary or an immediate successor of Heliocles. And as Antialcidas and Lysias strike some coins in common they also must be contemporaries. A common type of Antialcidas is the pilei of the Dioscuri, which seems to connect him with Eucratides; his portrait also resembles that of Heliocles: he would seem therefore not improbably to belong to the Eucratidian dynasty. The connexion of Lysias is obscure.

There are also a few restrikings which help us in the assign-

Evidence of restrikings.

ment of dates to some of the Greek kings of India. Heliocles restrikes some of the coins of Strato I,* and the name and types of Eucratides are stamped on a piece of Antialcidas,† as well as on some coins which I have assigned to Apollodotus I;‡ but it has been doubted whether these coins of Eucratides were really issued during his lifetime.

Types and legends of coins offer few indications.

Any attempt finally to arrange the kings in dynastic lists by means of the types and legends which they use is destined to failure. The kings did not inherit these things, but adopted them according to fancy or convenience. One or two instances will be sufficient to establish this. That Heliocles was son and successor of Eucratides is perhaps the most certain fact in Bactrian history. Yet he does not resemble Eucratides in his title (δίκαιος for μέγας), he does not wear the same helmet, nor use the same types. In the two last respects Demetrius differs from his father Euthydemus. On the other hand, Diodotus, who revolted against Antiochus II., retained the types of the Syrian king. These instances are sufficient to prove that identity of types between two kings is no proof of their relation to one another, nor is divergence of types any proof that they were not related. Still less can we draw any conclusions from the form of a helmet or the adoption of a title.

Perhaps the most suggestive approximation of types is that which appears when we compare the rare coins of Agathocleia, wife of Strato, with those of Euthydemus. They bear on the reverse the same type, Herakles seated, which is not usual in the Bactrian series. It is almost certain that Agathocleia must have been a king's daughter and heiress; otherwise, as we know from the coins

* Strato also restrikes coins of Heliocles.

† Sallet, p. 298.

‡ Cunningham, in *Num. Chron.* 1869, p. 226.

of Greek kings, her name would scarcely have appeared on the coin. That she was descended from Euthydemus is therefore very likely. We have already seen that king Agathocles was probably son of Euthydemus; Agathocleia may well have been his grand-daughter, or otherwise related to him. But in this kind of argument there are obviously the greatest risks; and we will attempt it in no second instance.

A large find of coins of the kings from Heliocles to Hermaeus was discovered some years ago at Sonipat;* and no less than 703 specimens have been weighed by Gen. Cunningham, who has acutely suggested that the order of the reigns may be gathered by a consideration of the amount of weight lost in circulation by the coins of different kings, those kings whose coins are most worn being naturally supposed to be the earliest. The loss is as follows:—

Evidence of Sonipat find.

Heliocles, 5·43 gr.	Philoxenus, 3·77 gr.
Apollodotus, 4·57 gr.	Menander, 3·72 gr.
Strato, 4·56 gr.	Diomedes, 3·39 gr.
Antimachus II., 4·48 gr.	Amyntas, 3·30 gr.
Antialcidas, 4·10 gr.	Hermaeus, 3·20 gr.
Lysias, 3·73 gr.	

In this calculation it is assumed that the normal standard for hemidrachms is 37 grains, and that all kings minted up to that standard. This is, of course, not certain; nevertheless, the results of the test so nearly agree with the testimony of style, that we can scarcely be wrong in regarding the above order as approximately correct; only Antialcidas and Lysias should not be placed so late.

Among all these kings, two only, Apollodotus and Menander, are known to us from other sources. Menander is identified with the Milinda of the Buddhist work

Menander.

* *Num. Chron.* 1872, p. 161.

"Milinda-praṣna," which records not only that he was born at the sub-Caucasian Alexandria, but that he was a just and powerful ruler, and a convert to the Buddhist religion. Strabo* says that he was reported to have crossed the river Hypanis eastward and penetrated as far as the Isamus, but as we are ignorant where the Isamus was, this does not greatly add to our knowledge. Plutarch† records that as a ruler he was noted for justice; and that when he died many cities were anxious to possess his ashes—a curious tale, which is considered by Prinsep to indicate a Buddhist source. The extraordinary abundance and wide distribution of his silver coins is well known. They were current, with those of Apollodotus, at Barygaza, many years after his death,‡ and are still abundantly found over a wide region, including Kabul, Jalalabad, Peshawar, Mathura, and Rampur. They are not brought from Kandahar or Seistan. "From this evidence," says Cunningham,§ "it is certain that Menander could not have possessed any part of Arachosia or Drangiana, and that his dominions to the west of the Indus must have been confined to the Kabul Valley and Eastern Afghanistan."

Apollodotus.

The coins which bear the name of Apollodotus fall into two classes: these are distinguished in the Catalogue. The second class are of later and poorer style; and on them the king usually bears the title of Philopator. General Cunningham says‖ that the Philopator coins are found only in the Panjab and N.-W. India, while the others are found over a much wider area, including the "Upper Kabul Valley in the north, Kandahar and Roh in the west and east, and Sindh in the south." The evidence, on the whole, indicates that there were two kings of the name of Apollodotus, of whom the later, Philopator, was

* xi. 11. 1. † *De Repub. Ger.*, p. 821.
‡ *Periplus maris Erythraei*, c. 47, ed. Müller.
§ *Num. Chron.* 1870, p. 221. ‖ Ibid., 1870, p. 77.

colleague of his father, the earlier, and his successor in some part of his dominions. And this probability will be raised almost to a certainty if we suppose that the restriking of Apollodotus' coins with the name of Eucratides took place in the life-time of the latter; since the coins which bear the legend Philopator cannot be brought within a considerable distance of the reign of Eucratides.

Geographical data; find-spots, and monograms.

We have thus but slight indications, beside those of art and fabric, to help us in determining the dates of the kings from Heliocles to Hermaeus. Nor have we safer data for their geographical assignment. The find-spots of their coins have never been recorded with completeness or accuracy. And the monograms which have been supposed to contain the names of mints have not been satisfactorily read, in spite of the diligent efforts of General Cunningham, whose want of success* in the matter seems to prove that success is not possible, at least in the present state of knowledge on the subject. And the details of the types adopted by various kings help us no more in determining the locality of their rule than in assigning their line of descent.

We can, however, make a few rough divisions of territory. Heliocles and his predecessors minted, as we have seen, in Bactria, his successors only on the south of the Indian Caucasus. And further, it would seem that the Panjab and the Kabul Valley were frequently in different hands. Thus the coins of Archebius and Amyntas seem to be found in Kabul, and not to the east of the Indus; and those of Hermaeus are far commoner in the same district than in the Panjab. On the other hand, the coins of kings Philoxenus, Strato, and

* Gen. Cunningham's readings have not been accepted by the best numismatists. Von Sallet remarks, "Such interpretations and experiments have too weak a basis to serve for historical investigations." See also the remarks of M. Chabouillet in the *Revue Numism.*, 1867, p. 403.

Hippostratus are chiefly found to the east of Jalalabad. A more exact statement could only be made after many years' study on the spot.

The recorded find-spots of coins are however sufficient to give us an idea of the extent of the Greek kingdom in India. Cunningham states that coins of Apollodotus are found as far south as Kandahar and Sindh, and those of Menander as far east as Mathura on the Jamna. And there appear to be proofs in Sanskrit literature* that a Greek ruler (perhaps Menander) besieged Ayodhya and Pāṭali-putra (Oudh and Patna). But these expansions were temporary, and there is no doubt that the only districts which were really Hellenized were the Kabul Valley and the western Panjab.

Coins of Antialcidas, Apollodotus, Menander, Lysias, Antimachus II., Diomedes, Archebius, and Hermaeus, were found by Masson† in the course of a few years at Beghram; and since his time coins of Epander, Dionysius, Zoilus, Amyntas, and other kings have been found in the same region, if not on the same site. The kings mentioned, and probably others of Greek race, must all have reigned in the Kabul Valley.

Ranjabala.

With the Greek kings we have placed one of Indian name, Ranjabala, whose coins resemble those of Strato, and show him to have been nearly contemporary with that king. He may have been a satrap of Strato, who asserted his independence. His coins have been found in the eastern Panjab and at Mathura‡ in company with some of Strato.

* Cunningham, in *Num. Chron.* 1870, p. 224.

† See his important list of coins found at Beghram, in the *Journ. As. Soc. Bengal*, 1836, p. 537.

‡ Cunningham, *J. A. S. B.* 1854, p. 691. In this paper it is suggested that Ranjabala may be identical with Rājapāla, a king of the lunar race of Dehli, and that Zeionises may be Jīvana Rāja of the same dynasty. The reasons against these identifications are, however, very strong.

The barbarous kings who make their appearance in India after the destruction of the Greek kingdoms present even greater difficulties of arrangement than do the Greek kings themselves. Between the eastern expedition of Antiochus III., in B.C. 208, and the era of Kanerkes, which may be taken as fixed* to A.D. 78, there is no absolutely fixed point, and we are reduced to arguments of mere probability.

Scythic Kings.

Difficulties of Chronology.

Of all the coins of the barbarous rulers, those of Maues are the earliest in style. Von Sallet remarks that the copper coins of this king are like those of Demetrius and Apollodotus, and belong to a period not much later than that of those kings. In the forms of Greek letters, and the style of art, his coins are superior not only to those of Hermaeus, but also to those of kings such as Zoilus and Nicias. It is impossible to place King Maues at a later date than the middle of the first century B.C. And it is an interesting fact, vouched for by Cunningham, that his coins are found in the Panjab only, especially the N.W. part of it, and not in Afghanistan. We must suppose that he ruled over some Scythic invaders, who had entered India not through the Kabul Valley, but through Kashmir or Nepal, while the country to the west of Peshawar was ruled by contemporary Greek kings. At present the Passes between Kashmir and Yarkand are but little used, but it is stated that the Karakoram Pass is open all the year round; and the trade between India and Yarkand by that route has of late years greatly increased. And we know that in old times Kashgar was far more thickly peopled than at present. It is also a matter of history that Nepal has more than once been invaded by Chinese armies. It would appear likely that at the time of the conquest of Bactria by the

Maues.

* See below, p. li.

Yueh-chi, as to which something has been said already, about B.C. 130, some tribe of that race or some other Scythic horde passed southward through Kashmir or Nepal; and after imbibing something of Greek civilization, and learning the Greek language, succeeded during the decline of the Greek power after Menander in establishing a kingdom to the east of the Indus, of which Maues was the first ruler.

Azes was, according to general consent, the successor of Maues.

Azes, Azilises.

Von Sallet suggests that he was his son, and reads on coins of Azes, with hesitation, the legend ΥΜΑVΩ, which may stand for *υἱὸς Μαύου*. Azes was certainly of later date than Maues, as the forms of his inscriptions and the art of his coins testify. His money also is not found to the west of Jalalabad; it is therefore likely that he did not greatly extend the dominions of Maues, though the extraordinary number of his coins testifies to his wealth and power. Azes strikes in conjunction with Aspavarma, Azilises, Vonones, and Spalirises, and Vonones in conjunction with Spalahores and Spalagadames. This shows that Azes, Azilises, Vonones, and the Spalirises group, of whom we shall speak presently, all belong to one time and to a single group of kings. But Vonones and Spalirises seem, from the find-spots of their coins, certainly to have reigned in Kabul: they may have ruled there and been tributary to Azes; but how they coexisted with the latest Greek kings and the invaders from Bactria, the kings of the Kadphises line, we are unable to determine.

Of the relations between themselves of the kings composing this

Vonones, Spalirises, &c.

group the legends of their coins enable us to judge in some measure:—

1. *Βασιλέως βασιλέων μεγάλου Ἄζου* = name and titles of the Strategos Aspavarma.

2. *Βασιλέως βασιλέων μεγάλου Ἄζου=Βασιλέως βασιλέων μεγάλου Ἀζιλίσου.**

3. *Βασιλέως βασιλέων μεγάλου Ὀνώνου=Βασιλέως ἀδέλφου δικαίου Σπαλαόρου.*

4. *Βασιλέως βασιλέων μεγάλου Ὀνώνου=Σπαλαόρου υἱοῦ δικαίου Σπαλαγαδάμου.*

5. *Βασιλέως βασιλέων μεγάλου Σπαλιρίσου = Βασιλέως μεγάλου Σπαλιρίσου.*

6. *Βασιλέως μεγάλου Σπαλιρίσου=Βασιλέως μεγάλου Ἄζου.*†

7. *Βασιλέως ἀδέλφου Σπαλιρίσου = Βασιλέως ἀδέλφου δικαίου Σπαλιρίσου.*

8. Σπαλύριος *δικαίου ἀδέλφου τοῦ βασιλέως = Σπαλαόρου υἱοῦ δικαίου Σπαλαγαδάμου.*

9. Vonones and Azes (undescribed coin, said to be in Gen. Cunningham's possession).

The evidence afforded by these legends is valuable, but not so decisive as it might at first sight appear, and capable of being variously construed. Some points, however, are clear. Four kings of the set assume the title King of Kings (Azes, Azilises, Vonones and Spalirises), but they do not do so in succession; Azes seems content to share the title in a friendly way with Azilises and Spalirises, at any rate.† Spalirises was brother of a king, but of which king does not appear. Spalahores is also brother of a king, and he and his son Spalagadames strike in conjunction with Vonones. Spalyris is another brother, and at one time Spalagadames strikes in conjunction with him. As close alliances of this kind scarcely occurred in antiquity, except between members of one family, we may regard it

* These reverse titles are really written in Indian. I give, for convenience, the Greek equivalents.

† This is sufficient proof that the assumption of the title Βασιλεὺς βασιλέων, 'Maharāja adhirāja', does not imply a claim to general supremacy.

as probable, if not certain, that all the kings of the group were related one to the other. In that case it is likely that Azilises, Vonones, Spalirises, Spalahores, and Spalyris were all sons of Azes, and Spalagadames his grandson. Aspavarma was a mere general or satrap of Azes—perhaps, as his name seems to show, of Hindu descent. The kingdom of Maues lasted in the hands of these rulers from before the middle of the first century B.C. at least until A.D. 20 or 30, spreading with time over a larger and larger area. It must have been put down by the growing power of the kings of the Kushan tribe, perhaps by Kadphises II.

Kings with Parthian names.

We have coins of several other kings in India of the same period, who do not appear to have been connected with either the dynasty of Kadphises or that of Azes. The only tie which connects them together is the Parthian character of their names, and in most cases of their coin-types. Some both in name and portrait, Pacores and Arsaces, for instance, are thoroughly Parthian. It is to be observed that under Mithradates and his warlike successors the Parthians had extended their empire into Bactria, and driven back the invading Scythians. Some scions of the royal Arsacid stock, or mere Parthian noblemen, may have gained a footing in India and maintained themselves in opposition to the Scythic kings.

Gondophares and Abdagases.

The most important king of the Parthian class is Gondophares, with whom goes Abdagases, who on his coins calls himself the nephew of Gondophares. The names of these rulers fortunately occur in the legends dating from the third century A.D., which record the visit of S. Thomas to India,* con-

* Cunningham, in *Journ. As. Soc. Bengal*, vol. xxiii. Cf. also Gutschmid, *Rhein. Mus.* 1864, p. 161, and von Sallet in *Zeitschr. f. Num.*, 1880, p. 296. Gutschmid shows that Gaspard, one of the three kings of the Christian legend, is identical with Gondophares.

taining indeed much that is untrustworthy, but also a basis of fact. S. Thomas is represented as converting Gundaphorus, his brother Gad, possibly the Orthagnes mentioned below, and his sister's son Labdanes, which last name seems to be a corruption of Abdagases. Where these rulers lived is not very clear. The legend, however, may furnish some ground for assigning them to the period of S. Thomas, that is, the first century A.D. More trustworthy than an early Christian legend should be the inscription at Takht-i-Bahi, if it could be read with certainty. Professor Dowson renders thus: * "In the 26th year of the great king Gondophares, on the third day of the month Vaiṣākha, (year) one hundred of the Samvatsara." Unfortunately, doubt hangs alike over the reading of name and date, nor can the era be identified, for Samvatsara means merely era. All that we can be sure of is that Gondophares did *not* reign in the hundredth year of the Ṣaka era, by which Kanerkes and his successors (see p. li) date their inscriptions; for the style of his coins forbids us to place them as late as A.D. 178. If the name of the king be rightly read it will prove that Gondophares reigned in the neighbourhood of Peshawar; but even this is not certain.

A silver coin of Gondophares discovered by v. Sallet, and figured in our plate xxxiii. 2, may perhaps give us a clue to his date. It is of the types of Arsacid silver coins, and especially reminds us of a coin of Mithradates II. (B.C. 90 or 80), which has similar types on both sides†—on one the head of the king; on the other the king seated, holding an eagle, crowned by a City, who stands behind him. And this last mentioned type seems not to recur in the Arsacid coinage, so that it would seem likely that Gondophares actually copied it from the coinage of Mithradates. In the inscription of Gondophares' coin we find the epithet *αὐτοκρατώρ*, which is found on the money of only two

* *Journ. R. As. Soc.*, 1875, p. 379.

† Gardner, *Parthian Coinage*, pl. ii. 19.

Arsacid kings—Sinatroces, B.C. 76 to 69, and Phraates IV., A.D. 8—11. This particular coin of Gondophares then would seem to have been struck not later than the middle of the first century A.D. The period mentioned would suit the other coins of Gondophares.

Orthagnes, Arsaces, Zeionises.

That Orthagnes was a brother of Gondophares rests on a reading of his coins proposed by Gen. Cunningham. The supposition has nothing improbable in it; the type of Victory which appears on his coins being also found on those of Gondophares and Abdagases. If it be well founded, it will clearly prove the Parthian origin of the dynasty of Gondophares, Orthagnes connecting him with other Indian kings of Parthian type such as Pacores,* Arsaces θεός and Arsaces δίκαιος. All these rulers must have been contemporary with the great time of the Parthian empire. To the same period will be assigned also Zeionises, who on his coins calls himself by the modest title of Satrap.

Dominions of these kings.

With regard to the seat of the power of these Indo-Parthian kings we have a little information. The coins of Gondophares were found in plenty at Beghram by Masson, and his small rude silver coins in the Panjab; while those of Orthagnes are said by Gen. Cunningham to come from Seistan and Kandahar, and those of Abdagases (with legend Sasasa) from Western Panjab. These facts seem to point to an extensive dominion, and confirm the testimony of the anonymous Egyptian merchant,† who informs us of the existence of a Parthian realm in the neighbourhood of the mouth of the Indus, in the reign of Vespasian.

The silver coins of Sanabares, of which there is a specimen in the

* Not Pacorus. Almost all the names of the kings of this class end in —es; I have therefore kept that ending in doubtful cases, such as Maues and Spalirises.

† *Periplus maris Eryth.*, c. 38. Cf. Mommsen, *Röm. Geschichte*, vol. v., p. 352.

Sanabares. British Museum (pl. xxiii. 10), have been given by v. Sallet to about the year A.D. 80, and have been compared as contemporary with money of the Arsacid king Vologeses III.* of that period. But the portrait of Sanabares, though it resembles that of Vologeses, is still more like that of Mithradates II., the helmet having cheek-pieces like the helmet of the latter monarch, while the style of work is very superior to anything known in Parthia in the days of Vologeses. Mr. Thomas had read on the Museum specimen the date ΓΙΤ, which he interpreted as implying the 313th year of the Seleucid, and first of the Christian era. But this reading is now disputed,† and cannot be insisted on. But if it is given up we should be still inclined to place Sanabares at about the beginning of the Christian era. Sanabares does not use Indian characters in his legends, but either Greek or Pehlvi, and four of the five coins of his in the British Museum came from Persia. It is therefore likely that this king ruled exclusively or principally to the north of the Indian Caucasus.

Epigraphy of these kings. On referring to the coins of the Arsacidae, we find that in that series the square □ and ⊏ come in some twenty years B.C. On the other hand, the square Ш ‡ does not take the place of Ω until 8 A.D. It is quite in keeping with these facts that Maues uses round letters only; Azes, Azilises, Spalirises and their contemporaries, use the square □ with Ω; Gondophares and Abdagases use the forms □ and Ш. We have thus a series of kings covering the period B.C. 50 to A.D. 50. The date of Pacores

* *Zeitschrift f. Num.*, 1879, p. 356. The text reads 'Vologeses I.'; following the erroneous numbering of Prokesch-Osten.

† On other specimens the letters take the form TꓶT &c. They may have no meaning.

‡ In the text this form is used in the legend of King Nicias, who certainly reigned earlier than 8 A.D. But on the actual coins of that king the letter is rounder, and of earlier type.

and Arsaces is not easy to fix, but must fall during this period. It is, however, noteworthy, as von Sallet points out, that the coin of Arsaces θεὸς bears precisely the same types as one of Maues.

The nameless king. The nameless king, who calls himself merely Soter Megas, naturally gives us no clue in his inscription to decide his affinities. Some of his coins are in type and style closely like those of Abdagases; and as he also makes use of the form Ш, he must be of about the same period as that king, A.D. 30–50. His coins are found in great numbers in the Kabul Valley. He may possibly have been a member of the Kadphises dynasty.

Heraüs and the Sakas. After the kings of Parthian character we must mention some others whose types are not dissimilar, yet who appear to be of Scythian race. Among these the most important is Heraüs, whose remarkable coin (pl. xxiv. 7) throws some light over the history of this troubled time. Of late the reading of the legend *Τυραννοῦντος Ἡράου Σάκα κοιράνου* has been disputed, but without solid reason, except as regards the last word. This may with equal exactness and probability be read *κορράνου*; but even if we do thus read it, the presence of the *τυραννοῦντος*, which is quite undisputed, proves that unusual Greek words may be expected at this time, and suggests that *κορράνου* may be a corruption of *κοιράνου*. The reading ΗΡΑΟΥ is allowed by Mr. Thomas; but he now disputes the important word Saka, reading instead of it the unintelligible words ΣΑΝ ΑΒ.* But we must point out that on the Brit. Mus. coin the third letter of the word is not formed like the N's, of which there are four in the inscription, but like a retrograde И, which is on late Parthian and Bactrian coins an ordinary shape of K: see pls. xxv, vi. *passim*. Thus there seems to

* A similar coin in the possession of M. Tiesenhausen seems to read ΣΑИΑΒ ΚΟΡΡΑИΟΥ. See Thomas, *R. A. S. Journal*, 1883, p. 75.

be at present no sufficient reason for doubting that Heraüs calls himself a Saka king; and we thus gain a confirmation of the statement of ancient historians, that that race was prominent in the conquest of India from the Greeks. But Heraüs probably ruled, like other kings of the class, to the north of the Caucasus.

Similar in type of head to Heraüs is Hyrcodes, one of whose ordinary types, that of the half-horse, is taken from silver coins of the early Antiochi of Syria, which circulated in Bactria. Wilson states that most of his coins come from the Bactrian side of the Caucasus; Mr. Thomas,* that they belong to Kerman. At page 119 of the Catalogue will be found a few coins of the same class which seem to bear the names of other kings; but these legends may be mere blundered attempts to produce some more intelligible name.

Hyrcodes and others.

Finally, we have to speak of a well-defined group of kings which takes its rise with that Kozulo Kadphises who appears on coins as colleague and successor of Hermaeus. His date must be the last quarter of the first century B.C.

Kadphises I. and successors.

We do not know to what branch of the widely extended race of Sakas, or nomads, Maues and his successors belonged. But we have reason to think that the group at present discussed were kings of the Yueh-chi, who are identified by Cunningham with the Tochari, and that they belonged to the Kushan branch of that tribe.

We have already seen how Kadphises led the Yueh-chi, about B.C. 25, southward across the Paropamisus and conquered Hermaeus, whom he reduced to a state of vassalage. Under his successors the dominions of the Yueh-chi went on increasing. Probably he was succeeded by the king who bears the very similar name of Kozola

* On a coin probably similar to our pl. xxiv. 13, Mr. Thomas reads Guāth in Pehlvi characters (*Sassanian Inscriptions*, p. 10). Our coin is not sufficiently complete for me to be sure of the reading.

Kadaphes, who on his money calls himself the ruler of the Kushans. The portrait of this ruler on the coins bears so strong a resemblance to that of Augustus that it seems all but certain that he must have reigned at the very beginning of the Christian era. That he succeeded the first Kadphises is very probable, and it is equally probable that he was succeeded by the second, who on his coins calls himself Ooemo Kadphises, and whose reign brings us down to the accession of Kanerkes in A.D. 78. We thus have a succession of princes of the same or nearly the same name extending over 100 years, and it is hard to believe that they do not represent a dynasty which reigned in the Kabul Valley.

Kadaphes, Kadphises II.

We have on a copper-plate from Manikyala (Taxila) a record, wherein a satrap called Liako Kusuluko dates from the 78th year of the great king Moga. It seems not unlikely that the satrap in question may be Kozola Kadaphes, and perhaps still more probable that the great king Moga is Maues. Kadaphes, who probably reigned at the very beginning of the Christian era, may well be placed seventy-eight years later than the accession of Maues, which must be placed not so late as the middle of the first century B.C. But of course it is all but impossible that Maues can have himself reigned seventy-eight years. The reference must be not to the year of his reign, but to an era established by him.

Inscription from Taxila.

The evidence derived from the style and epigraphy of coins seems to show that Kadphises I. and Kadaphes ruled but a part of N.-W. India. When Kadphises came in as an invader from the north, he found Hermaeus ruling in the Kabul Valley, and reduced him to a state of dependence. At the same time Azes was probably ruler of the Panjab; and perhaps some of the later Greek rulers, such as Hippostratus, still held rule on the lower Indus. When Hermaeus died no Greek succeeded him, but Kadphises occupied his place. Kadaphes, or the nameless

Spread of Yueh-chi in India.

king, must have succeeded Kadphises: their contemporaries must have been Azilises, Spalirises and Gondophares. That the coins of Gondophares and of the nameless king are alike found in abundance at Beghram, while those of Kadaphes are not abundant, seems to show that the Yueh-chi did not rapidly extend their dominion in India, but met at first with formidable rivals in the descendants of Azes. Only on the accession of the second Kadphises did the power of the invaders become altogether predominant. It appears that under him and his successors it was supreme in all N.-W. India; and Greeks, Parthians, and the race of Azes alike disappear from history as reflected in the coins.

They become dominant under Kadphises II.

Kadphises II, Ooemo Kadphises, was a wealthy monarch, and the founder of a powerful line of Scythic kings, as to whom inscriptions give us some information. His date is about the middle of the first century A.D. His successors are the kings called on their coins Kanerkes and Hooerkes, and in the records Kanishka and Huvishka. Their rule comprised the whole of N.-W. India and the Kabul Valley.

Successors of Kadphises II., Kanerkes and Hooerkes.

The date of these kings was a matter of uncertainty until the brilliant conjecture of Mr. Fergusson * as to the origin and use of the Ṣaka era settled the matter. Mr. Fergusson's theory is accepted by most Sanskrit scholars, and the numismatic evidence in its favour is so overwhelming, that the numismatist cannot hesitate to join them; in fact, v. Sallet had before the publication of Mr. Fergusson's paper assigned Kanerkes to the same period into which he falls on the theory proposed in that paper, and that on numismatic evidence only. The new theory is that the Saka era starts from the date not of the destruction of the Sakas,

Their date.

* *On the Saka, Samvat and Gupta Eras, J. R. A. S.* 1880, p. 259. Cf. Max Müller, *India—What can it teach us?* p. 291.

but of the establishment of their empire in India under Kanerkes.* It is fixed to A.D. 78. The dates at Mathura and elsewhere are said to be as follows (Thomas: *Ancient Indian Weights*, p. 46, and *Jainism*, p. 10):—

KING.	SAKA YEAR.	YEAR A.D.
Kanerkes,	9, 11, 18, 28	87—106.
Hooerkes,	33, 39, 47, 48, 51	111—129.
Vasu Deva,	44, 83, 87, 98	122—176.

The evidence of finds confirms this assignment of dates. In a tope at Ahin Posh near Jalalabad, Mr. Simpson found together the following gold coins:—

10 coins of Kanerkes, 6 of Kadphises, 1 of Hooerkes.
1 of Domitian, 1 of Trajan, 1 of Sabina.

The reigns of the Roman imperial persons cover the period A.D. 81-136; and this proves that the deposit cannot have been buried until about A.D. 130,† probably in the reign of Hooerkes.

It is true that in the Manikyala tope there were found with coins of Kanerkes some worn consular denarii which belong to the period before Augustus,‡ but it is more than probable that these coins were not buried till a long time after their issue.

It seems to be universally allowed that the Kanerkes and Hooerkes of the coins are the Kanishka and Huvishka of inscriptions, and that these were successive kings of the Kabul Valley and the Panjab.

Vasu Deva.

But the Vasu Deva of the inscriptions, who is supposed to correspond to the Bazodeo of the coins, is a more mysterious personage. He overlaps in the dates Huvishka,

* Or, perhaps, Kadphises II.; as it is Kadphises who begins the issue of Indo-Scythic gold coins: and Kanerkes' earliest date is the year 9.

† Sabina came to the throne in 128. The coin of her issue, now preserved in the British Museum, is not as stated by previous writers "much worn," but seems to have greatly suffered, whether in ancient or modern times, by being exposed to heat. The coin of Trajan is worn. Cf. *J. R. A. Soc.* 1880, p. 266.

‡ *Journ. As. Soc. Bengal*, iii. p. 34.

and appears to have reigned for no less a period than fifty-four years. Indeed, if one inscription be rightly read, he sometimes dates from year 5 of the era,* which will give to his reign the impossible length of 94 years. Prof. Dowson therefore suggests that Vasu Deva may have been the name given by their Indian subjects to kings of the Kanerkes dynasty. In favour of this view it may be remarked that the words Vasu Deva occur in Sanskrit letters on coins of various periods and classes; and the supposed Greek equivalent **BAZOΔHO** occurs only on Indo-Scythic coins of semi-barbarous fabric.

The coins of Vasu Deva are succeeded by a large variety of copies, some of fairly good style, others of barbarous work, neither class bearing intelligible legends. Some of these, in copper, were usually given to an imaginary king Ooer Kenorano, such being their legend. Von Sallet has, however, conjectured that as there are no gold coins with the legend Ooer Kenorano, and no copper bearing the legend Ooerke Korano, the copper coins above mentioned must have been struck by king Hooerkes. This conjecture is strongly confirmed by the discovery in the Museum series of coins† in all respects similar to those reading Ooer Kenorano but reading clearly Ooerke Korano. But in fact the difference between the two legends is almost evanescent, **N** in the one taking the place of **K** in the other; however, in the inscriptions of this class these two letters are constantly confounded.‡

The gold coins which repeat barbarously the legends and types of Vasu Deva become eventually of thin fabric and cup-like shape, like some of the issues of Byzantium of the ninth and subsequent centuries. But they must be earlier than that period, and are perhaps copied from the concave coins of the class struck at Persepolis during Parthian supremacy.

* Cunningham, *Archaeological Reports*, iii. 30. Dowson, *J.R.A.S.* vii. p. 381.
† Pages 156-8. ‡ See above, p. xlvii.

The whole class of Indo-Scythic gold coins appears as a most remarkable phenomenon amid the coins of India, especially as gold coins are entirely wanting in the Greek-Indian issues after the time of Eucratides. The line of descent of the new issue must be traced not through the gold money of Alexander, which perhaps still circulated in southern Asia, but through the Roman aurei which were first issued in abundance by Augustus, and which at the beginning of the Christian era made their way into India, where they have been found in conjunction with coins of Kadphises and Kanerkes. In weight the Indo-Scythic coins nearly correspond to the Roman.

II. Inscriptions.

The inscriptions on the coins contained in this volume are of the following kinds:—

Greek language.

(1) Greek language in Greek characters. On the coins of earlier kings, from Diodotus to Demetrius, Greek legends only are employed. After that time we usually find Greek on one side of the coin only. It is, however, quite evident that the Greek letters and the Greek language were generally understood in northern India and in Kabul as late as the second century of our era. This fact, clearly established by the testimony of coins, confirms the otherwise not trustworthy testimony of Philostratus, who represents that Apollonius of Tyana, when he visited India, had no difficulty in making himself generally understood by speaking Greek. In the Hindu revival under the Guptas the Greek language was probably swept away with other traces of Greek culture. Notable is the use by some of the later rulers of poetical Greek words like *κοίρανος*, *τυραννέων* and *ἀνίκητος*.

Indian language.

(2) Indian language in native characters. These last are of two sorts. The square letters of the so-called Indian Pali are used by Pantaleon and Agathocles only; the

more cursive characters, called Arian Pali, are used by all the other kings down to the latest times. In the case of the edicts of Aṣoka, the Arian characters are used only in the Kabul Valley, and the Indian characters elsewhere; and this fact shows, what is proved in many other ways, how completely the Greek and Scythian power in India centred in the Kabul Valley.

The language which I have called by the general name of Indian is a debased form of Sanskrit or Pali. To fix authoritatively the readings of words in this language is impossible except to a Pali scholar. I have therefore given, in nearly all cases, the readings of previous writers, unless they seemed to me to conflict with the clear testimony of the coins; in which case (a very rare one) I have ventured on innovation. In the cases where it was necessary to decide between various authorities, I have sometimes had the advantage of the advice of Mr. Cecil Bendall, who has kindly allowed me to profit by his wider knowledge of Sanskrit. Still more have I regarded any philological criticism of the forms presented by the coin-legends as lying outside my task. Such criticism might well form a supplement to M. Senart's valuable papers on the language of the Aṣoka edicts in vols. xv. and xvi. of the *Journal Asiatique*, but in a numismatic work it would be altogether out of place. And this is clearly a task which could only be attempted with advantage by a highly-trained Sanskritist.

The system here adopted in transliteration of Pali inscriptions is the same as is used in other Museum Catalogues, and nearly identical with that used by Prof. M. Williams in his Lexicon and Grammar.

Forms of Indian letters.

To the letters in which these inscriptions are written I have paid closer attention, palæography being perhaps more nearly related to archæology than to philology. To determine their forms requires care and a practised eye rather than wide linguistic knowledge. I have drawn up a table of Arian Pali letters used on the coins, after careful comparison of the authoritative tables drawn up by Gen. Cunningham (see p. lxx). All the letters in the table have been cut upon types; so that printing in this alphabet will in future be comparatively easy. With the square or Indian Pali characters I have not concerned myself, as they occur on so few coins.

Scythic language. (3) Scythic language in Greek characters. These are the inscriptions on coins of the late kings of the Kanerkes group, such as PAO, NANO, KOZOVΛO, KOPANO, and more especially the names of deities on the reverses. These words, so far as at present identified, are of non-Scythic origin, borrowed from the languages of India, Persia, and Greece, and only bearing the Scythian stamp in their termination O, and in modifications of the forms of words.

Lists of Greek, Scythic and Indian words will be found in the *Index of Inscriptions;* and renderings of the last-mentioned in the table at p. lxxii.

III.—Monograms.

In the field of coins of all periods is a prodigious number of monograms and detached letters, sometimes Greek and sometimes of the Arian Pali class. If these could be read and interpreted, there can be no doubt that they would afford us most valuable information. But they present the greatest difficulties.

Difficulties of interpretation. Gen. Cunningham has well remarked, in regard to some of the Greek monograms, that their constant recurrence during successive reigns proves that they cannot denote monetary magistrates, but must stand for mints. There is reason in this; but when the writer goes further, and tries to identify the various mints which they respectively represent, we, like most students of these coins both in England and abroad, are unable to follow him. While therefore we must acknowledge the possibility that many of the Greek monograms may stand for the names of mints, we must stop short at that point. Nor does there seem any probability that we shall advance further, until the find-spots of Bactrian and Indian coins are far more exactly recorded than they have hitherto been. The monograms and letters of the Pali alphabet do not recur in the same way as the Greek, but vary far more; and it does not seem probable that they stand for mints. They may stand for the names of magistrates, for the date or number of the issue, or they may have been used for some other purpose which has not yet been guessed. Perhaps, in these circumstances, it may seem superfluous to record them, as has been done in this Catalogue; but it is impossible to be sure that valuable information will not some day be extracted from them.

IV. Types.

The types which appear on the coins described in the present volume are most interesting from the point of view of art and mythology; but it is to be regretted that they furnish us with but little historical information. We have already noted the futility of trying to determine the genealogy or the dominions of the Greek kings by means of the types of their coins; and the same holds true, in scarcely less degree, in regard to the kings of Scythic race. It is a remarkable fact that throughout the period of which we treat there seem to have been in N.-W. India artists capable of designing original types for coins, so that the necessity for a slavish copying of foreign coins, which gives valuable material to the historian, does not seem to have arisen.

Types of Greek kings.

In the types used by Greek kings we find great variety, and they open to us quite a new chapter of Greek art, affording fresh proof of the remarkable originality of the artists of the Hellenistic age. In regard to their style, we may note two points :—(1) The extraordinary realism of their portraiture. The portraits of Demetrius (pl. ii. 9), of Antimachus (v. 1), and of Eucratides (v. 7), are among the most remarkable which have come down to us from antiquity, and the effect of them is heightened in each case by the introduction of a peculiar and strongly-characteristic head-dress, which is rendered with scrupulous exactness of detail. (2) The decidedly Praxitelean character of the full-length figures of deities on the reverses. The figures of Herakles (pl. ii. 9, iii. 3), of Zeus (iv. 4, vii. 2), of Poseidon (v. 1), of Apollo (v. 4, ix. 10), are all in their attitudes characteristic of the school of Praxiteles. The types of Greek deities which we find are sometimes more distinctive than the style in which they are rendered. Thus, on coins of Demetrius, Artemis is sometimes radiate (pl. iii. 1), on coins of Agathocles (iv. 4) Zeus bears in his hand the three-headed Hekate, Herakles crowns himself with a wreath, Pallas appears in short skirts, and many other such strange forms of Greek deities appear.

To search out the reasons of these variations of type, reasons to be found probably in many instances in the influence of local Indian or Persian legend or belief, would be a very attractive task, and not hopeless, considering the data furnished us by the legends of the gold Indo-Scythic coins, as to which we shall presently have to speak.

Semi-Hellenic types.

The earliest of the clearly Indian types to make its appearance is a dancing-girl, wearing long hanging earrings and oriental trousers, on the money of Pantaleon (iii. 9) and Agathocles (iv. 9). As we come to a later period, non-Hellenic types, or types in which there is a non-Hellenic element, gradually make their way on the coins. On coins of Philoxenus (xiii. 9) and Telephus (xxxii. 7) we find a radiate figure of a sun-god standing, holding a long sceptre. On those of Amyntas (xiv. 11) and Hermaeus (xv. 8) we find the head of a deity wearing Phrygian cap, whence issue rays. But when we reach the issues of King Maues (pls. xvi., xvii.), we find a wealth of most remarkable and original barbaro-Hellenic figures; a figure resembling Tyche (xvi. 3), holding in one hand a patera, in the other a wheel, who seems to be the original of the still more outlandish figure of Azes' coins (xviii. 10, 11); a radiate Artemis, with veil flying round her head (xvi. 4); a draped goddess, bearing a crescent on her head, and standing between two stars; and several others. Still more original is the type (xvi. 9), where a seated Zeus grasps in his extended hand, not, as usual, a Victory (vii. 9) or a thunderbolt (vii. 5), but a being who seems an impersonation of the thunderbolt, and stands in the midst of it; as well as the type (xvii. 2) where a nymph, perhaps a Maenad, stands grasping two stems of vine. Maues' successors, Azes and Azilises, use types of the same class. A careful consideration of these facts will convince us that by some means or other Maues and his race secured the services of artists who had been instructed by Greeks, but were not restricted by Greek traditions. In fact, in these coins we have the sole remaining relics of an interesting school of art, one of many which existed in Asia in the first century B.C., and which have passed away almost without leaving any memorial. It would further seem that kings, who were the patrons of art, and understood the Greek language, must have been considerably softened and refined by contact with civilized neighbours.

Hindu types.

The first of Indian deities to claim a place on the coins is Ṣiva, who seems to make his appearance on the coins of Gondophares (pl. xxii. 8, 9), though it must be confessed that this figure may with equal plausibility be called a Poseidon, for the characteristic marks of Ṣiva are absent. But on coins of Kadphises II. the bull, which appears beside the deity, sufficiently proves him to be Ṣiva; and on the money of Kanerkes and his successor he appears in more and more native form, four-armed, and bearing the numerous symbols associated with him in local belief. It is probable that the goddess who appears on the coins of Azes as standing on a lotus, and holding a flower (xix. 5), is either Pārvatī, the dread wife of Ṣiva, or Lakshmī, the goddess of fortune: the supposed lion, which seems on the coin to lie under her left elbow, may be after all only a lump of oxide. These, and the dancer on the coins of Pantaleon and Agathocles, are the only strictly Hindu types to be found on coins before the time of the great Yueh-chi dynasty, when other deities come in, as will be seen by the list given below.

Parthian types.

To speak of Parthian types on coins at all may seem a misnomer, since there are no original Parthian types in existence, if we except representations of the king himself: in these matters the Parthians were imitators of the Greeks. But there are, notwithstanding, certain types of deities, and a certain style of art, which we learn to associate with the coins of Parthia; and when we can trace these on coins issued in India, a presumption arises that the king who issued them was of Parthian stock. For example, the portraits of Parthian kings, bearded, and wearing the diadema, have quite a distinct aspect; and we find this aspect in the portraits of Gondophares, Pacores, Orthagnes, and Sanabares. The type which represents a City crowning the king, which occurs on the money of Phraates IV. and subsequent kings of Parthia, is used by Zeionises (pl. xxiii. 4); and Nike, who is continually present on Parthian coins, is quite a feature also on our pl. xxiii., which contains coins of the kings of this group. Indeed, some of their coins, such as xxiii. 10 and 11, are altogether of Parthian type.

In view of their types, the gold coins of the conquering Yueh-chi

Types on gold of Yueh-chi.

kings are of surpassing interest. The obverse presents us with a figure of the king clad in helmet and armour, which are closely like those borne by the first Arsaces of Parthia on his coins. The reverses are extremely varied, and present us with a multitude of types borrowed from several different mythologies. Had these coins been anepigraphous, their interpretation would have baffled all ingenuity; but fortunately the names of the various deities represented are written beside them in Greek characters, only somewhat disguised by being crushed into Scythian forms. On these types two important papers have been published, one by Mr. Thomas* and one by Dr. Hoffmann.† Though the present writer does not pretend to the linguistic knowledge of either of these scholars, he ventures to discuss their results from the numismatic point of view and that of comparative archaeology.

On these gold coins the following types appear:—

(*a.*) Greek and Semi-Greek Deities.

Inscriptions.	*Types.*
HΛIOC	Radiate sun-god, holds sceptre.
CAΛHNH	Male moon-deity, holds sceptre.
NANAIA	Female deity holding sceptre, which ends in the fore-part of a horse.

These types occur in the series of coins issued by king Kanerkes with Greek legends only. The names of the deities are given in Greek, not Scythic. Nevertheless, in the types there are clear signs of barbarism. The figure of Helios is identical with that on bilingual coins inscribed with the name of

* *Jainism, or the Early Faith of Asoka; J. R. A. S.* 1877.

† *Abhandlungen f. d. Kunde des Morgenlandes*, vol. vii. (1881), no. 3, p. 139 sqq.

Inscriptions.	*Types.*
	Mioro, and the figure of Nanaia with that on the coins inscribed **NANA**; while the type of 'Salene' is borrowed from the coins inscribed **MAO**, and is male instead of female. Nanaia, though a deity of Persian origin,* was clearly regarded by the die-cutter as Greek, perhaps as identical with Artemis, but there is much that is oriental in her figure.
NANA, NANA PAO [OΔIIO]	Female deity holding sceptre, as above; over her forehead, crescent. The **PAO** is evidently only a suffix. The crescent of course indicates a lunar deity. **NANO** and **OKPO** are combined on a coin published by Prokesch-Osten. *Arch. Zeit.* 1849, pl. x. 8.
HPAKIΛO	Herakles; holds club and apple.
⊢PO	Artemis clad in long chiton; holds bow and arrow. The type is unmistakeable, but the legend is puzzling. Mr. Thomas reads it **ZЄPO** 'Ceres' (?), but that brings us no nearer to Artemis. I venture to suggest that the word **MEIPO** (see p. lxiii) is intended, for we find in other instances that inappropriate legend sometimes accompanying types which were, as we may conjecture, unintelligible to the die-cutter.
PAO PHOPO	War-god, standing; holds spear and shield. The word **PAO**, evidently meaning king or royal, may be detached from the legend. The remainder, **PHOPO**, cannot be with certainty explained, but it seems most likely that it is a mere twisting of the Greek **APHΣ**, and that the intention is to portray the Greek war-god. The type suits Ares perfectly.

* A long dissertation on her by Hoffmann, l. c., p. 130.

Inscriptions.	*Types.*
ΡΙΟΜ	Pallas, or Roma; holds spear and shield. Mr. Thomas reads ΡΙΑΗ, 'Rhea' (?). But ΡΙΟΜ, or even ΡωΜ, is nearer to the actual legend, and the types of Pallas and Roma can scarcely be distinguished; I am therefore inclined to find here an impersonation of the great city, such impersonation being usual in contemporary Roman coins.
ϹΑΡΑΠΟ	Sarapis, holds sceptre; modius on head.
ωΡΟΝ [ωΡΟΗ ?]	Deity, wearing modius, holds sceptre. I am disposed to identify this figure with the Greek Uranus, though he may almost as well stand for the Indian Varuna.

(β.) Persian Deities.

ΑΘΡΟ, ΑΘΟΡΟ	Fire-god, holding hammer and tongs. Male figure, holding wreath and tongs. This is the Iranian fire-god, called by Mr. Thomas Atars; but his form is copied from that of the Greek Hephaestus.
ΑΡΑЄΙΧΡΟ	Sun-god, with hand raised. (Persian ?) The origin of the name is obscure: it may even be a mere corruption of ΑΡΔΟΧΡΟ.
ΛΡΟΟΑϹΓΟ	Male deity, holding wreath, horse beside him. The first letter has usually been corrected to Α. Hoffmann, however, observes that as it stands the name is near to the Persian word Luhrasp. It is not certain that we have here a sun-god, the horse, his only marked attribute, being not necessarily solar.
ΜΑΝΑΟ-ΒΑΓΟ	Moon-god, four-armed, seated on throne.

Inscriptions.	*Types.*
	Mr. Thomas interprets the legend 'Mâonh Bago,' a particular form of the Iranian moon-deity. Hoffmann recognizes the deity as Bahman (Manō Vohū).
ΜΑΟ	Moon-god, holds sceptre, wreath, ankus, &c. Mao is a Zend name for the moon-god.
ΜΙΙΡΟ, ΜΕΙΡΟ, ΜΙΟΡΟ, [ΟΝΙΟ]	Radiate sun-god, holds sceptre, wreath, &c. [In one case the inscription accompanies a figure of Nanaia.] The form ΜΙΘΡΟ does not, so far as I know, occur. The deity intended seems therefore rather to be the Iranian sun-god Mihira, than his Graeco-Roman counterpart Mithras.
ΝΑΝΑ	See above, under Greek deities.
ΟΑΝΙΝΔΑ	Victory, holding wreath and sceptre. The Zend word *Vanaṅt* stands for the star of victory (Hoffmann). Mr. Thomas considers the legend to refer to Anandates, a Persian deity mentioned by Strabo.* But he was a male deity, and of his character we know nothing.
ΟΑΔΟ	Wind-god running. "Zend, 'wind-god,' *vātō*" (Hoffmann). The type is very characteristic, and decidedly original.
ΟΡΛΑΓΝΟ	War-god; holds spear and sword. The legend has been read ΟΡΔΑΓΝΟ, and supposed by Mr. Thomas to refer to Agni. Hoffmann considers the deity to be the Persian war-god Varhran, or Bahram.
ΦΑΡΡΟ	Deity holding fire, sceptre, sword, &c., some-

* 'Ωμανοῦ καὶ 'Αναδάτου, Περσικῶν δαιμόνων, page 512 (c).

Inscriptions. *Types.*

times wears winged helmet, or stands on a fire; sometimes holds the caduceus of Hermes, and even his purse.

The Persian word *far* or *farr* signifies fire, and that the deity is a fire-god is evident. Hoffmann calls him the god of victory, *hvarenaṅh*, "Hoheits und Sieges-glanz."

(γ.) Indian Deities.

ΑΡΔΟΧΡΟ [ΔΟΧΡΟ] — Female deity, holding a cornucopiae.

The type is nearer to that of the Greek Tyche than to any other figure. The legend has been regarded as a transcription of Ardha-ugra, half or consort of Ṣiva, Pārvatī. And that ΟΚΡΟ stands for Ṣiva is certain, as we shall presently see: but there still remains for explanation the aspirate Χ for Κ, as well as the curious circumstance that the cruel and relentless Pārvatī should appear in so mild and propitious a form. Hoffmann considers the deity intended to be the Persian Ashis, daughter of Ahuro, goddess of fortune. Others suppose her to be Lakshmī, the Indian goddess of fortune, who closely corresponds to Tyche.

ΜΑΑϹΗΝΟ — War-god Skanda, holding standard and sword.

There can be little doubt that the legend represents the Sanskrit Mahāsena, 'ruler of a great army,' an epithet of both Ṣiva and Skanda. The

Inscriptions.	*Types.*
	figure so nearly resembles that of Skanda in the present series, that it is safe to identify it with him. Later, Mahāsena reappears, in somewhat different form.
OKPO	Ṣiva, standing with trident and bull; his hair in form of a shell.
	Ṣiva having four hands, in which he holds a vase, an Indian thunderbolt,* a trident, and a goat: sometimes a wreath or a Greek thunderbolt: he is sometimes phallic.
	There has been a quite unnecessary doubt as to the identification of this figure; Hoffmann calls it Ahuro, and von Sallet "Pantheon aus Zeus, Poseidon, Herakles," &c. No doubt there is a Greek element in the type, but the attributes prove beyond any doubt that Ṣiva (Ugra) is intended. The thunderbolt, trident, and goat, are all attributes of that deity as he appears in Hindu pictures, and the special arrangement of the hair and the phallic nature also belong to him especially. On some of the late coins Ṣiva has three faces.
CKANΔO KOMAPO, BIZAΓO	Two figures of armed deities; one holds standard and sword, one sword and spear.
	These figures also can be unhesitatingly identified as Skanda, the Hindu god of war, who bears the epithet of Kumāra, the prince, and Viṣākha, who is called in the Mahābhārata† a son and impersonation of Skanda.

* On p. 132 this attribute has been called a drum. Its form is that of a drum, but the occurrence of the Greek thunderbolt in the hand of Siva shows that it is the Indian counterpart of that weapon.

† i. 2588, iii. 14384, &c.

Inscriptions.	*Types.*
CKANΔO KOMAPO, MAACHNO, BIZAΓO	Two figures, as before; between them a deity, who is apparently horned. In this remarkable group we find again Skanda Kumāra, and Viṣākha: the third figure appears to be Mahāsena, who is here differentiated from Ṣiva.
ωPON	See above, under 'Greek Deities.'

(δ) *Buddha.*

Inscriptions.	*Types.*
BOΔΔO,	Figure of Buddha, standing, preaching.
OΔYO BOY CAKAMA,]ΓO BOYΔΔO	Buddha seated cross-legged (Pl. xxxii. 14). These coins are most interesting as giving us the earliest known artistic representation of Buddha. The second and longer legend seems to be a transcript of Advaya Buddha Ṣākyamuni.* On a British Museum specimen CAKAMA is clear; the old reading CAMANA, with its interpretation Ṣramana, must therefore be given up.

Style of types.

The style in which these various figures are represented is remarkable, and points clearly to a local school. There are a few set schemes according to which all the figures are arranged. Nanaia (xxvi. 10) is in exactly the same attitude as Ardochro (xxvi. 6). The sun-god (xxvii. 9) finds his close parallel in the moon-god (xxvii. 22). Pallas, or Roma (xxviii. 40) differs from Ares (xxviii. 17) only in the length of her chiton. This being the case, it is evidently futile to seek the originals of the types of these coins, as one might be tempted to do, on the Roman aurei of the Cæsars. Thus the Roma (xxviii. 20) is closely like Pallas on an aureus of Galba, and the Victory (xxviii. 13) nearly resembles

* The word advaya is due to a suggestion of Mr. Bendall; the full form would be advaya-vādin, 'he who speaks of the one (knowledge).'

Victory on an aureus of Otho; yet we have no right in these and similar cases to assume that the Roman coin is the prototype, and the Indian coin the copy. Rather both coin-types are copies of a conventional and widely current mode of representing the deities. Within the limits set by their conventional notions as to attitudes and drapery the artists employed by the Scythic kings move freely; they vary attributes continually, and in the case of Ṣiva even develop a type quite different from anything to which they can have been accustomed in a Greek school.

V. Weights.

The purāṇa.

It is maintained by Gen. Cunningham that the earliest Greek coins of India, those of Sophytes, are struck not on the Attic standard, but on a native standard which is based on the rati or grain of *abrus precatorius*. Of these grains, 32 weigh, according to Cunningham, 58⅓ English gr., according to Thomas 56 gr. We thus reach a unit, the purāṇa, followed in the early punched silver coins of India; and that the money of Sophytes follows the same standard is likely enough, though if so it is rather over-weight.

Use of Attic standard.

Apart from these specimens, all the earlier coins of the kings of Greek descent which were issued in India and to the north of the Caucasus, are struck on the Attic standard (drachm, 67·5 grains) which Alexander made universal in the regions which he conquered, and which was maintained by the Seleucid kings who succeeded him in Asia.

The earliest monarch to strike on another standard is Eucratides; and in the reigns of his successors, Heliocles and Antialcidas, the Attic standard is gradually given up, the new standard advancing in conjunction with the custom of using on the coins Indian transcripts of the Greek legends.

This new standard appears to be identical with that called by metrologists the Persian, the standard on which coins were struck in all parts of the Persian Empire, notably the sigli stamped with the figure of the Persian king, which must have freely circulated in the northern parts of India, which paid tribute to the Persians. The standard used by the Indians for the silver coins, which they issued before the Greek conquest, is as we have already remarked different. The present standard therefore would seem not to be native to India, but an importation from Persia.

Persian standard.

In the Persian standard the unit or drachm weighs 84-86 grains: if therefore the lower standard of the Greek kings of India be Persian, we must call the heavier pieces, which weigh as a maximum 160 grains, didrachms; and the smaller pieces, which weigh up to 40 grains, hemidrachms. Hitherto the larger pieces have usually been treated as didrachms, and the smaller as hemidrachms, of Attic standard, which is clearly wrong. But Sallet also appears to be wrong in supposing that the larger pieces are tetradrachms, and the smaller drachms of a standard reduced from the Attic. For the change from the Attic standard to that which I call the Persian takes place suddenly, and is evidently due not to any sinking of standard, but to the adoption for purposes of convenience of a different weight for coins.

All gold coins before the Indo-Scythic period follow the Attic standard, somewhat debased. The Indo-Scythic gold money, as we have already observed, p. liii, follows the standard of the aurei of Rome.

Gold standard.

The following table gives approximately the normal or standard weights of coins in the various metals issued in India by Greek and Scythic kings.

PERCY GARDNER.

NORMAL WEIGHTS OF COINS.

GOLD.

	Grains.	Grammes.
Stater of Attic Standard	132·	8·55
Drachm of Attic Standard	66·	4·27
Indo-Scythic distater	248·	16·07
„ stater	124·	8·03
„ quarter-stater	31·	2·01

SILVER.

	Grains.	Grammes.
Tetradrachm of Attic Standard	264·	17·10
Drachm of Attic Standard	66·	4·27
Hemidrachm of Attic Standard . . .	33·	2·13
Obol of Attic Standard	11·	·71
Didrachm of Persian Standard	160·	10·36
Hemidrachm of Persian Standard	40·	2·59
Drachm of Indian Standard	58·	3·75

NICKEL.

	Grains.	Grammes.
Didrachm of Attic Standard	132·?	8·55
Drachm of Attic Standard	66·	4·27

THE ARIAN PALI ALPHABET, ON COINS.

Value.	Forms.	Value.	Forms.	Value.	Forms.
a	1 2 3*	*gaṃ*		*ṭhe*	
aṃ	1 [2]†	*gu*	1 2	§*ḍa*	[ ]
‡*ā* (medial) or *ṃ*	•	*go*		*ḍha*	[ ]
i		*gha*		*ta*	1 2 3
iṃ		*cha*	1 2	*ti*	1 2
u		*chha*	1 [2]	*te*	
e		*ja*	1 2 3	*tra*	1 2
o	[ ]	*ji*	1 2	*tṣa*	[ ]
ka		*ju*		*tsa*	
ki		*jña*	[ ]	*tha*	[ ]
ku		*jha*		§*da*	1 2 3 4 5
ke		*jhaṃ*		*di*	1 2 3
kra		*jho*		*du*	
kri		*ña*	[1 2]	*de*	1 2
kre	1 2	*ṭa*	[ ]	*do*	
kha	1 2	*ṭha*	[ ]	*dra*	
khu		*ṭhi*		*dha*	
khsa	[ ]	*ṭhu*		*dhra*	
ga	1 2 3			§*na*	1 2 3

* Bottom strokes occur in the case of many letters, such as *a*, *ga*, *ja*, *na*, and *da*; it is therefore sometimes impossible to say whether a letter is intended to be followed by *u* or *r*, or to be only casually varied.

† Forms in square brackets are not found on coins in the British Museum, but are cited as occurring elsewhere on the authority of General Cunningham.

‡ In the Journal Asiatique (xv. 308) M. Senart maintains that this sign has no phonetic value; General Cunningham, with hesitation, assigns to it the value of *a* long: *aṃ* seems on the coins to be sometimes undistinguishable from *ā* and sometimes from *u*.

§ I cannot distinguish on the coins between *na* and *ṇa*, *da* and *ḍa*; the forms of *da*, and , are used interchangeably on the coins of Menander.

THE ARIAN PALI ALPHABET, ON COINS.

Value.	Forms.	Value.	Forms.	Value.	Forms.
ni		*mo*		*vri*	
pa		*ya*		*ṣa*	
pi		*yi*		*ṣi*	
pu		*yu*		*ṣva*	
pra		*ye*		*sha*	
pri		*ra*		*shka*	
pha		*raṃ*		*shni*	
phi		*ri*		*sa*	
phre		*ru*		*saṃ*	
phsa		*rkhe*		*si*	
ba		*rte*		*su*	
bi		*rma*		*so*	
bu		*rva*		*sta*	
bra		*rṣa*		*sti*	
bha		*la*		*stra*	
bhra		*li*		*spa*	
ma		*lu*		*ha*	
mā		*lo*		*hi*	
maṃ		*va*		*hu*	
mi		*vi*		*he*	
me		*vu*		*ho*	

TABLE OF TRANSLITERATIONS AND RENDERINGS OF PRAKRIT LEGENDS.

Indian.	Greek equivalent.	English rendering.
	INDIAN PALI.	
Akathukleyasa	ΑΓΑΘΟΚΛΕΟΥΣ	
Paṃtalevasa	ΠΑΝΤΑΛΕΟΝΤΟΣ	
Rajine	ΒΑΣΙΛΕΩΣ	King (*genitive*).
	ARIAN PALI.	
Akathukreyasa*	ΑΓΑΘΟΚΛΕΟΥΣ	
Amitasa	ΑΜΥΝΤΟΥ	
Aṃtialikidasa	ΑΝΤΙΑΛΚΙΔΟΥ	
Aṃtimakhasa	ΑΝΤΙΜΑΧΟΥ	
Apadihatasa	ΑΝΙΚΗΤΟΥ	Invincible (*gen.*).
Apaladatasa	ΑΠΟΛΛΟΔΟΤΟΥ	
Aparajitasa	ΑΝΙΚΗΤΟΥ	Invincible (*gen.*).
Apratihatasa		Invincible (*gen.*).
Apratihatachakrasa		Invincible with the discus (*gen.*).
Apulaphanasa	ΑΠΟΛΛΟΦΑΝΟΥ *sic*	
Arkhebiyasa	ΑΡΧΕΒΙΟΥ	
Artemidorasa	ΑΡΤΕΜΙΔΩΡΟΥ	
Ashshakasa	ΑΡΣΑΚΟΥ	
Avadagaṣasa	ΑΒΔΑΓΑΣΟΥ	
Ayasa	ΑΖΟΥ	
Ayalishasa *or* Ayilishasa	ΑΖΙΛΙΣΟΥ	

* The distinction between long and short *a* is not preserved in this table, as the two forms seem to be used almost indiscriminately.

Indian.	Greek equivalent.	English rendering.
Bhradaputrasa	ΑΔΕΛΦΙΔΕΩΣ	Brother's son (*gen.*).
Bhrata	ΑΔΕΛΦΟΣ	Brother.
Cha		And (*enclitic*).
Chhatrapasa	ΣΑΤΡΑΠΟΥ	Satrap (*gen.*).
Devatratasa		Protected by the gods (*gen.*).
Dhramaṭhidasa		Steadfast in the law (*gen.*). *See below*, sachadhramaṭhidasa.
Dhramikasa	ΔΙΚΑΙΟΥ	Just (*gen.*), for dharmikasa.
Diyamedasa	ΔΙΟΜΗΔΟΥ	
Dianisiyasa	ΔΙΟΝΥΣΙΟΥ	
Epadrasa	ΕΠΑΝΔΡΟΥ	
Evukratidasa *or* Eukratidasa	ΕΥΚΡΑΤΙΔΟΥ	
Gudapharasa *or* Gadapharasa	ΓΟΝΔΟΦΑΡΟΥ *or* ΥΝΔΟΦΕΡΡΟΥ	
Heliyakreyasa	ΗΛΙΟΚΛΕΟΥΣ	
Heramayasa	ΕΡΜΑΙΟΥ	
Hiduja same		Just to those born on the Indus. Same is Sk. samaḥ (*nom.*). Bendall.
Himakapiṣasa	ΟΟΗΜΟ ΚΑΔΦΙΣΟΥ	
Hipastratasa	ΙΠΠΟΣΤΡΑΤΟΥ	
Jayadharasa	ΝΙΚΗΦΟΡΟΥ	Victorious (*gen.*).
Jayaṃtasa *or* Jayatasa		Conquering: a secondary formation from the participle, common in all Prakrits and vernaculars. Bendall.
Jhoilasa	ΖΩΙΛΟΥ	
Jihuniasa	ΖΕΙΩΝΙΣΟΥ	

Indian.	Greek equivalent.	English rendering.
Kaliyapaya	ΚΑΛΛΙΟΠΗ	
Kaphsasa	ΚΑΔΑΦΕΣ	
Kariṣiye nagara devata		God of the city of Kārisi. Cunningham.
Kasasa	ΚΑΔΦΙΣΟΥ	
Kujula *or* Kuyula	ΚΟΖΟΥΛΟ *or* ΚΟΖΟΛΑ	
Kushana *or* Khushana	ΚΟΡΟΝ *or* ΧΟΡΑΝ	Kushan (tribe).
Lisiasa *or* Lisikasa	ΛΥΣΙΟΥ	
Mahachhatrapasa		Satrap (*gen.*).
Maharajasa	ΒΑΣΙΛΕΩΣ	King (*gen.*).
Maharajabhrata *or* Maharajabhraha	ΒΑΣΙΛΕΩΣ ΑΔΕΛΦΟΣ	Brother of the king.
Mahatasa *or* Mahatakasa	ΜΕΓΑΛΟΥ	Great (*gen.*): Pali, mahanta.
Mahiṣvarasa		Great prince (*gen.*).
Menadrasa	ΜΕΝΑΝΔΡΟΥ	
Moasa	ΜΑΥΟΥ	
Nikiasa	ΝΙΚΙΟΥ	
Pakurasa	ΠΑΚΟΡΟΥ	
Palanakramasa	ΕΥΕΡΓΕΤΟΥ	Perhaps for Sk. pālanakshamasa, 'able to protect' (*gen.*). *Ksh* not being a Prakrit combination of letters, we have not been able to find an example of it in Arian Pali. Bendall.
Philasinasa *or* Philusinasa	ΦΙΛΟΞΕΝΟΥ	
Pratichhasa	ΕΠΙΦΑΝΟΥΣ	Illustrious: — for pratīkshiyasa (*gen.*). Bendall.
Putrasa	ΥΙΟΥ	Son (*gen.*).

Indian.	Greek equivalent.	English rendering.
Rajabalasa, Raṃjabulasa, &c.	ΡΑΞΥ	
Rajadirajasa *or* Rajarajasa	ΒΑΣΙΛΕΩΣ ΒΑΣΙΛΕΩΝ	King of kings (*gen.*).
Sachadhramaṭhidasa		Steadfast in true law:—for satyadharmasthitasya (*gen.*). Bendall.
Sagaba		Brother:—for sagarbha. Cunningham.
Saṃpriyapita		To whom his father is very dear. This seems to be a rendering of the Greek φιλοπατώρ. Cunningham.
Sarvaloga iṣvarasa		Prince of all the world (*gen.*).
Sasasa		
Spalagadamasa		
Spalahorasa		
Spaliriṣasa	ΣΠΑΛΙΡΙΣΟΥ	
Stratasa	ΣΤΡΑΤΩΝΟΣ	
Strategasa		General (*gen.*), Greek στρατηγός.
Teliphasa	ΤΗΛΕΦΟΥ	
Ṭheuphilasa	ΘΕΟΦΙΛΟΥ	
Tradatasa	ΣΩΤΗΡΟΣ	Saviour:—perhaps for a Prakrit trāṇadatasa (*gen.*), cf. Sk. trāṇakartṛi. Bendall.
Vrishabha	ΤΑΥΡΟΣ	Bull.
Yavugasa *or* Yauasa	ΖΑΟΟΥ	Yueh? (*gen.*).

CORRIGENDA.

Page 68, no. 4, & p. 69, nos. 9, 10—The object described in the text as a whip over the king's shoulder seems to be merely the falling ends of the regal diadema, greatly exaggerated. On the coins of Azes and succeeding kings this view is adopted.

Pp. 103, 105—The first letter in the name of Gondophares (𐨒) is transliterated sometimes as *ga* and sometimes as *gu*. It may stand for either, or even *gaṃ*

GREEK AND SCYTHIC

KINGS OF BACTRIA AND INDIA.

ANDRAGORAS, KING OF PARTHIA?

B.C. *cir.* 300.

Gold.

No.	Wt.	Metal. Size.	Obverse.	Reverse.
1	131·9	AV ·7	Bust of Zeus r., wearing taenia; drapery round neck. behind, [monogram].	ΑΝΔΡΑΓΟΡ[ΟΥ Warrior r., in quadriga driven by Nike, and drawn by four horned horses, galloping. [Pl. I. 1.]

Silver.

No.	Wt.	Metal. Size.	Obverse.	Reverse.
2	255·8	AR 1·15	Head of a City r., wearing turreted crown. behind, [monogram].	ΑΝΔΡΑΓΟΡΟΥ Pallas standing l., clad in chiton and peplos; holds owl in r., l. rests on shield which is adorned with Gorgon's head; behind her, spear. [Pl. I. 2.]

No.	Wt.	Metal. Size.	Obverse.	Reverse.

SOPHYTES, KING IN INDIA.

B.C. *cir.* 300.

Silver.

No.	Wt.	Metal. Size.	Obverse.	Reverse.
1	58·3	Æ ·6	Head of the king r., in close-fitting helmet, bound with wreath; wing on cheek-piece, on section of neck, M.	ΣΩΦΥΤΟΥ Cock r.; above, caduceus. [Pl. I. 3.]

No.	Wt.	Metal. Size.	Obverse.	Reverse.
			DIODOTUS I., KING OF BACTRIA.	
			Revolted *cir.* B.C. 250.	
			(*a*) *Gold.*	
			Head of the king r., diad.	ΒΑΣΙΛΕΩΣ ΔΙΟΔΟΤΟΥ Zeus striding to l., hurling thunderbolt; aegis on l. arm; at his feet, eagle l.
1	130·3	AV ·75		to l., wreath. [Pl. I. 4.]
2*	128·3	AV ·75		,, ,, [Pl. I. 5.]
			(*β*) *Silver.*	
			Head of the king r., diad.	ΒΑΣΙΛΕΩΣ ΔΙΟΔΟΤΟΥ Zeus striding to l., hurling thunderbolt; aegis on l. arm; at his feet, eagle l.
3	257·1	AR 1·15		to l., wreath. [Pl. I. 6.]
4	255·7	AR 1·05		,, crescent. [Pl. I. 7.]
5	235·2	AR 1·		,, mon.
6	62·3	AR ·7		to l., Μ. [Pl. I. 8.]
			(*γ*) *Bronze.*	
			Head of Zeus r., laur.	ΒΑ ΣΙΛΕΩΣ ΔΙΟΔΟΤΟΥ Artemis, clad in short chiton, running r.; holds torch in both hands, quiver at shoulder; beside her, hound running r.
7		Æ ·85		[Pl. I. 9.]

* The gold coins bearing an elderly head of Diodotus, and on the reverse the symbols of wreath and spear-head, are regarded as forgeries. They are very common, and all from one die.

No.	Wt.	Metal. Size.	Obverse.	Reverse.
			EUTHYDEMUS I., KING OF BACTRIA.	
			(Successor of Diodotus II., *cir.* B.C. 220.)	
			(α) *Gold.*	
			Head of the king r., diad.	ΒΑΣΙΛΕΩΣ ΕΥΘΥΔΗΜΟΥ Herakles, bearded, naked, seated l. on rock; in r., club, which also rests on rock.
1	129·	AV ·75		to l., [monogram]. [Pl. I. 10.]
			(β) *Silver; middle-aged portrait.*	
			Head of the king r., diad.	ΒΑΣΙΛΕΩΣ ΕΥΘΥΔΗΜΟΥ Herakles, bearded, naked, seated l. on rock; in r., club, which also rests on rock.
2	254·6	AR 1·1		to r., [monogram]. [Pl. I. 11.]
3	256·5	AR 1·		" "
4	244 2	AR 1·1		" "; below, N. [I. O. C.]
5	258·2	AR 1·		to l., [monogram]. [Pl. II. 1.]
6	252·5	AR 1·15		" [monogram]. [I. O. C. Pl. II. 2.]
7	255·	AR 1·1		" "
8	257·7	AR 1·15		" " [Pl. II. 3.]
9	211·2	AR 1·		(barbarous.)

No.	Wt.	Metal. Size.	Obverse.	Reverse.
			Head of the king r., diad.	ΒΑΣΙΛΕΩΣ ΕΥΘΥΔΗΜΟΥ Herakles, bearded, naked, seated l. on rock, on which is spread lion's skin; in r. hand, club, which rests on his knee.
10	252·4	Æ1·15		to r., ₨. (traces of rock under club.) [Pl. II. 4.]
11	249·	Æ1·		" " (semi-barbarous.)
12	186·5	Æ1·		" " "

(γ) *Silver; elderly portrait.*

No.	Wt.	Metal. Size.	Obverse.	Reverse.
			Head of the king r., diad.	ΒΑΣΙΛΕΩΣ ΕΥΘΥΔΗΜΟΥ Herakles, bearded, naked, seated l. on rock, on which is spread lion's skin; in r. hand, club, which rests on his knee.
13	256·7	Æ1·1		to r., ₨. [Pl. II. 5.]
14	60·8	Æ·65		to r., ₨. [Pl. II. 6.]

(δ) *Bronze.*

No.	Wt.	Metal. Size.	Obverse.	Reverse.
			Head of bearded Herakles r., bare.	ΒΑΣΙΛΕΩΣ ΕΥΘΥΔΗΜΟΥ Free horse r., prancing.
15		Æ·85		
16		Æ·85		[I. O. C. Pl. II. 7.]
17		Æ·85		[I. O. C.]
			Head of Zeus r., laur.	ΒΑΣΙΛΕΩΣ ΕΥΘΥΔΗΜΟΥ Free horse r., prancing.
18		Æ·7		to r., ₨. [I. O. C. Pl. II. 8.]

DEMETRIUS, KING OF INDIA.

(Son and successor of Euthydemus I.)

(*a*) *Silver.*

No.	Wt.	Metal. Size.	Obverse.	Reverse.
			Bust of the king r., diad., wearing elephant's scalp.	ΒΑΣΙΛΕΩΣ ΔΗΜΗΤΡΙΟΥ Young Herakles, facing; holds in l. hand, club and lion's skin; with r. hand, crowns himself with ivy-wreath.
1	259·5	Æ 1·3		to l., [monogram]. [Pl. II. 9.]
2	260·7	Æ 1·2		„ „ [I. O. C.]
3	263·	Æ 1·35		„ Φ.
4	220·2	Æ 1·15 (plated)		„ „ [I. O. C.]
5	235·5	Æ 1·25		„ Σ; to r., A. (semi-barbarous.)
6	61·	Æ ·85		to l., [monogram]. [I. O. C. Pl. II. 10.]
7	55·5	Æ ·8		„ [monogram]; to r., [monogram]. [I. O. C.]
8	52·8	Æ ·8	(countermark: Σ, and Herakles crowning himself.)	„ Δ. „
9	9·	Æ ·5	(head, not bust.)	to l., [monogram]. [Pl. II. 11.]
10	9·	Æ ·5		„ „
11	10·5	Æ ·5		„ „ [I. O. C. Pl. II. 12.]
12	10·	Æ ·45		„ Φ.

No.	Wt.	Metal. Size.	Obverse.	Reverse.
			(β) Bronze.	
			Bust of Herakles r., bearded, crowned with ivy; lion's skin round neck, club over shoulder.	ΒΑΣΙΛΕΩΣ ΔΗΜΗΤΡΙΟΥ Artemis, radiate, facing, wearing short chiton; holds in l. hand, bow; with r. hand, draws arrow from quiver at her shoulder.
13		Æ 1·		to l., .
14		Æ 1·		„ „ [I. O. C. Pl. III. 1.]
			Gorgon-head, on round shield.	ΒΑΣΙΛΕΩΣ ΔΗΜΗΤΡΙΟΥ Trident.
15		Æ 1·35		to l., .
			Head of elephant r., bell hung round neck.	ΒΑΣΙΛΕΩΣ ΔΗΜΗΤΡΙΟΥ Caduceus.
16		Æ 1·15		to l., . [I. O. C. Pl. III. 2.]

EUTHYDEMUS II., KING OF INDIA.

(Son and successor? of Demetrius.)

(α) *Silver.*

No.	Wt.	Metal. Size.	Obverse.	Reverse.
			Bust of the king r., diad.	ΒΑΣΙΛΕΩΣ ΕΥΘΥΔΗΜΟΥ Young Herakles, facing, ivy-crowned; holds in r. hand, wreath of ivy; in l. hand, club and lion's skin.
1	260·7	AR 1·35		to l., [monogram]. [Pl. III. 3.]
2	65·1	AR ·75		to l., [monogram].
3	63·5 (plated)	AR ·75		" " [Pl. III. 4.]

(β) *Nickel.*

No.	Wt.	Metal. Size.	Obverse.	Reverse.
			Head of Apollo r., laur.	ΒΑΣΙΛΕΩΣ ΕΥΘΥΔΗΜΟΥ Tripod-lebes.
4	118·2	NI ·95		to l., [monogram]. [Pl. III. 5.]

(γ) *Bronze.*

No.	Wt.	Metal. Size.	Obverse.	Reverse.
			Head of Apollo r., laur.	ΒΑΣΙΛΕΩΣ ΕΥΘΥΔΗΜΟΥ Tripod-lebes.
5		Æ 1·1		to l., [monogram]. [Pl. III. 6.]
			Head of bearded Herakles r., bare.	ΒΑΣΙΛΕΩΣ ΕΥΘΥΔΗΜΟΥ Free horse r., prancing.
6		Æ ·9		[Pl. III. 7.]

No.	Wt.	Metal. Size.	Obverse.	Reverse.
			PANTALEON, KING OF INDIA. (Son and successor ? of Demetrius.)	
			(α) *Nickel.*	
1	110·2	NI·95	Bust of young Dionysos r., wearing ivy-wreath; thyrsos over shoulder.	ΒΑΣΙΛΕΩΣ ΠΑΝΤΑΛΕΟΝΤΟΣ Panther to r., l. fore-paw raised. to l., ΕΥΊ
			(β) *Bronze, round.*	
2		Æ ·95	Bust of young Dionysos r., wearing ivy-wreath; thyrsos over shoulder.	ΒΑΣΙΛΕΩΣ ΠΑΝΤΑΛΕΟΝΤΟΣ Panther to r., l. fore-paw raised. to l., A. [Pl. III. 8.]
			(γ) *Bronze, square.*	
3		Æ ·95	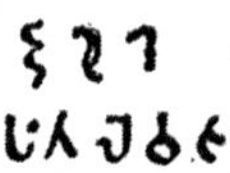 (*Rājine Paṃtalevasa**). Female figure l. with long pendants from her ears, clad in oriental dress with trousers; holds in her r. hand a flower.	ΒΑΣΙΛΕΩΣ ΠΑΝΤΑΛΕΟΝΤΟΣ Maneless lion r., in incuse square. [Pl. III. 9.]
4		Æ ·85		
5		Æ ·9		[I. O. C.]

* I repeat General Cunningham's reading of this inscription and those on the coins of Agathocles. The Indian inscription in the text is a facsimile taken from the inscriptions on the coins: some of the forms of letters seem abnormal.

AGATHOCLES, KING OF INDIA.

(Son and successor ? of Demetrius.)

(*a*) *Silver; with portraits of his predecessors.*

No.	Wt.	Metal. Size.	Obverse.	Reverse.
			ΑΛΕΞΑΝΔΡΟΥ ΤΟΥ ΦΙΛΙΠΠΟΥ Head of Alexander as Herakles r., in lion's skin.	**ΒΑΣΙΛΕΥΟΝΤΟΣ ΑΓΑΘΟΚΛΕΟΥΣ ΔΙΚΑΙΟΥ** Zeus seated l. on throne with back; holds eagle and long sceptre.
1	251·2	AR 1·4		to l., . [Pl. IV. 1.]
			ΔΙΟΔΟΤΟΥ ΣΩΤΗΡΟΣ Head of Diodotus r., diad.	**ΒΑΣΙΛΕΥΟΝΤΟΣ ΑΓΑΘΟΚΛΕΟΥΣ ΔΙΚΑΙΟΥ** Zeus striding to l., hurling thunderbolt, aegis on l. arm; at his feet, eagle l.
2	263·5	AR 1·3		to l., wreath; to r., . [Pl. IV. 2.]
			ΕΥΘΥΔΗΜΟΥ ΘΕΟΥ Head of Euthydemus I. r., diad.	**ΒΑΣΙΛΕΥΟΝΤΟΣ ΑΓΑΘΟΚΛΕΟΥΣ ΔΙΚΑΙΟΥ** Herakles, bearded, naked, seated l. on rock; in r. hand, club, which rests on a rock.
3	261·2	AR 1·2		to r., ⊕. [Pl. IV. 3.]

(*β*) *Silver; with his own portrait.*

No.	Wt.	Metal. Size.	Obverse.	Reverse.
			Bust of the king r., diad.	**ΒΑΣΙΛΕΩΣ ΑΓΑΘΟΚΛΕΟΥΣ** Zeus, facing, clad in himation; holds in r. hand, three-headed Hekate who bears two torches; in his l. hand, long sceptre.
4	240·8	AR 1·2		to l., ⊕. [Pl. IV. 4.]
5	63·6	AR ·8		[Pl. IV. 5.]

No.	Wt.	Metal. Size.	Obverse.	Reverse.
			(γ) Nickel.	
6	117·5	NI 1·	Bust of Dionysos r., wearing ivy-wreath, thyrsos over shoulder.	ΒΑΣΙΛΕΩΣ ΑΓΑΘΟΚΛΕΟΥΣ Panther r., touching a vine with his raised paw. to l., Φ. [Pl. IV. 6.]
7	63·5	NI ·65		below, K. [Pl. IV. 7.]
			(δ) Bronze, round.	
8		Æ ·9	Bust of Dionysos r., wearing ivy-wreath, thyrsos over shoulder.	ΒΑΣΙΛΕΩΣ ΑΓΑΘΟΚΛΕΟΥΣ Panther r., touching a vine with his raised paw. to l., R. [I. O. C. Pl. IV. 8.]
			(ε) Bronze; square; bilingual.	
9		Æ ·9	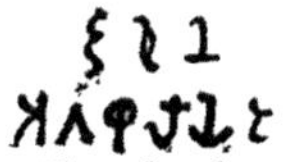 (*Rājine Akathukleyasa*). Female figure l. with long pendants from her ears, clad in oriental drapery with trousers; holds in her r. hand a flower.	ΒΑΣΙΛΕΩΣ ΑΓΑΘΟΚΛΕΟΥΣ Maneless lion r., in incuse square.
10		Æ 1·05		
11		Æ 1·05		
12		Æ 1·		[I. O. C. Pl. IV. 9.]
13		Æ ·8		
14		Æ ·95		

No.	Wt.	Metal. Size.	Obverse.	Reverse.
			(ζ) *Bronze; square; Indian legend.*	
15		Æ ·75	(*Akathukreyasa*). Buddhist stupa, surmounted by star.	(*Hiduja Same*). Tree in a square railed enclosure. letters? in field. [Pl. IV. 10.]

ANTIMACHUS, KING OF INDIA.

(Descendant and successor of Diodotus?).

(*a*) *Silver.*

No.	Wt.	Metal. Size.	Obverse.	Reverse.
			Bust of the king r., diad., wearing causia.	ΒΑΣΙΛΕΩΣ ΘΕΟΥ ΑΝΤΙΜΑΧΟΥ Poseidon, facing, wearing himation and wreath; holds in r. hand, trident; in l., palm, bound with fillet.
1	262·3	AR 1·35		to r., Ⓝ. [Pl. v. 1.]
2	260·5	AR 1·15		„ „
3	252·3	AR 1·2		„ [monogram].
4	59·	AR ·8		to r., Ⓝ.
5	31·5	AR ·6		to r., [monogram]. [Pl. v. 2.]
6	10·6	AR ·45		to r., [monogram]. [I. O. C. Pl. v. 3.]

EUCRATIDES, KING OF BACTRIA AND INDIA.

(Contemporary of Antiochus IV. and Demetrius I. of Syria.)

(α) *Silver ; type, Apollo.*

No.	Wt.	Metal. Size.	Obverse.	Reverse.
			Bust of the king r., diad.: fillet-border.	ΒΑΣΙΛΕΩΣ ΕΥΚΡΑΤΙΔΟΥ Apollo l., clad in chlamys and boots; holds arrow and bow.
1	257·2	Æ 1·2		to l., [monogram].
2	256·5	Æ 1·3		" [monogram].
3	261·	Æ 1·3		" " [I. O. C. Pl. v. 4.]
4	261·	Æ 1·3		" " [I. O. C.]
5	58·5	Æ ·7	(border of dots.)	to l., KI. [I. O. C. Pl. v. 5.]

(β) *Silver ; type, The Dioscuri.*

No.	Wt.	Metal. Size.	Obverse.	Reverse.
			Bust of the king r., diad.: fillet-border.	ΒΑΣΙΛΕΩΣ ΕΥΚΡΑΤΙΔΟΥ The Dioscuri charging r., holding long lances and palms.
6	258·5	Æ1·25		below, [monogram]. [Pl. v. 6.]
7	259·	Æ1·25		" [monogram]. [I. O. C.]

No.	Wt.	Metal. Size.	Obverse.	Reverse.
			Bust of the king r., diad., and wearing helmet in the shape of a causia, adorned with ear and horn of bull, and crest; fillet-border.	ΒΑΣΙΛΕΩΣ ΜΕΓΑΛΟΥ ΕΥΚΡΑΤΙΔΟΥ The Dioscuri charging r., holding long lances and palms.
8	261·2	AR 1·35		below .
9	258·2	AR 1·35		„ . [Pl. v. 7.]
10	259·6	AR 1·3		„ .
11	258·8	AR 1·2		„ .
12	258·7	AR 1·35		„ „
13	258·2	AR 1·3		„ . [Pl. v. 8.]
14	244·5	AR 1·35		to l., . [I. O. C.]
15	57·5	AR ·8		below, . [Pl. v. 9.]
16	62·3	AR ·75	(border of dots.)	„ „
17	59·5	AR ·75	(„)	„ N. (semi-barbarous.)
18	55·3	AR ·75	(„)	to l., . (ΒΑΣΙΛΕΩΣ written ΣΙΛΕΩΣ). [I. O. C.]

No.	Wt.	Metal. Size.	Obverse.	Reverse.
			(γ) Silver; type, Pilei of Dioscuri.	
			Bust of the king r., diad.	ΒΑΣΙΛΕΩΣ ΕΥΚΡΑΤΙΔΟΥ The pilei of the Dioscuri, laur., surmounted by stars; and two palms.
19	9·9	AR ·45		below, . [I. O. C.]
20	9·1	AR ·45		„ .
21	9·9	AR ·45		„ .
22	10·8	AR ·5		„ . [I. O. C. Pl. v. 10.]
23	9·5	AR ·45		„ „ [I. O. C.]
24	10·	AR ·45		„ K.
25	9·2	AR ·45		„ .
26	7·3 (broken)	AR ·4		„ . [I. O. C.]
			Bust of the king r., diad. and helmeted.	ΒΑΣΙΛΕΩΣ ΕΥΚΡΑΤΙΔΟΥ Similar type.
27	9·9	AR ·45		below, .
28	10·1	AR ·45		„ „ [Pl. v. 11.]
29	10·	AR ·45		„ „
30	6· (broken)	AR ·4		„ ΠΓ. [I. O. C.]

No.	Wt.	Metal. Size.	Obverse.	Reverse.
			(δ) *Bronze; round; type, Dioscuri.*	
			Bust of the king r., diad. and helmeted: fillet-border.	ΒΑΣΙΛΕΩΣ ΜΕΓΑΛΟΥ ΕΥΚΡΑΤΙΔΟΥ The Dioscuri charging r., holding long lances and palms.
31		Æ ·95		below, .
32		Æ 1·05		„ „
33		Æ ·9		„ . [I. O. C.]
34		Æ ·8		„ . [I. O. C. Pl. VI. 1.]
			Similar.	Same inscr. One of the Dioscuri charging r., holding long lance.
35		Æ ·6		[Pl. VI. 2.]
			(ε) *Bronze; square; type, Dioscuri.*	
			ΒΑΣΙΛΕΩΣ ΜΕΓΑΛΟΥ ΕΥΚΡΑΤΙΔΟΥ Bust of the king r., diad. and helmeted.	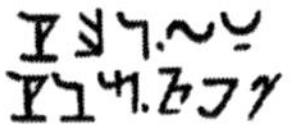 (*Māhārajasa Evukrātidasa* or *Eükrātidasa*). The Dioscuri charging r., holding long lances and palms.
36		Æ ·85		to l., ; to r., E. [I. O. C. Pl. VI. 3.]
37		Æ ·75		„ „ „ „ [I. O. C.]
38		Æ ·9		„ „ „ „
39		Æ ·8		„ .

No.	Wt.	Metal. Size.	Obverse.	Reverse.
			ΒΑΣΙΛΕΩΣ ΜΕΓΑΛΟΥ ΕΥΚΡΑΤΙΔΟΥ Bust of the king r., diad. and helmeted.	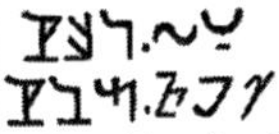 (*Māhārajasa Evukrātidasa* or *Eükrātidasa*). The Dioscuri charging r., holding long lances and palms.
40		Æ ·95		to r., .
41		Æ ·9		„ .
42		Æ ·9		„ .
43		Æ ·95		„ „
44		Æ ·85		„ .
45		Æ ·85		„ . [I. O. C.]
46		Æ ·85		„ . „
47		Æ ·9		„ .
48		Æ ·9		„ .
49		Æ ·85		„ .
50		Æ ·8		„ . ( for ).
51		Æ ·9		„ . [I. O. C.]
52		Æ ·9		„
53		Æ ·7		to r., . [I. O. C.]
54		Æ ·65		„ .
55		Æ ·7		[I. O. C. Pl. vi. 4.]

No.	Wt.	Metal. Size.	Obverse.	Reverse.
			ΒΑΣΙΛΕΩΣ ΜΕΓΑ-ΛΟΥ ΕΥΚΡΑΤΙΔΟΥ Head of the king r., diad., without helmet.	(*Māharajasa Evukrātidasa*). The pilei of the Dioscuri surmounted by stars, and two palms.
56		Æ ·6		
57		Æ ·6		[I. O. C. Pl. VI. 5.]
			(ζ) *Bronze; square; type, Nike.*	
			ΒΑΣΙΛΕΩΣ ΜΕΓΑ-ΛΟΥ ΕΥΚΡΑΤΙΔΟΥ Bust of the king r., diad. and helmeted.	(*Māharajasa Evukratidasa*). Nike l., bearing wreath and palm.
58		Æ ·65		to l., .
59		Æ ·75		„ „ [I. O. C. Pl. VI. 6.]
60		Æ ·7		„ „
			Similar? (obscure coin).	Same inscr.? Nike r., bearing wreath and palm.
61		Æ ·65		
			ΜΕΓΑΛΟΥ ΒΑΣΙΛ-ΕΩΣ ΕΥΚΡΑΤΙΔΟΥ Bust of the king l., helmeted, striking with spear.	Same inscr. Nike r., bearing wreath and palm.
62		Æ ·9		to r., . [I. O. C. Pl. VI. 7.]

(η) *Bronze; square; type, Zeus.*

No.	Wt.	Metal. Size.	Obverse.	Reverse.
			ΒΑΣΙΛΕΩΣ ΜΕΓΑΛΟΥ ΕΥΚΡΑΤΙΔΟΥ Bust of the king r., diad. and helmeted.	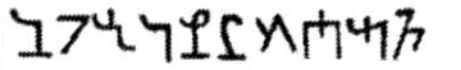 (*Karisiye nagara devata?**). Zeus seated l. on throne; holds wreath and palm; in front, forepart of elephant r.; behind, conical object.
63		Æ ·7		to r., . [Pl. vi. 8.]

EUCRATIDES, WITH HELIOCLES AND LAODICE.

(Father and mother of Eucratides.)

Silver.

No.	Wt.	Metal. Size.	Obverse.	Reverse.
			ΒΑΣΙΛΕΥΣ ΜΕΓΑΣ ΕΥΚΡΑΤΙΔΗΣ Bust of Eucratides r., diad. and helmeted.	ΗΛΙΟΚΛΕΟΥΣ ΚΑΙ ΛΑΟΔΙΚΗΣ Busts jugate r. of Heliocles, with bare head; and Laodice, diad.
1	251·4	AR 1·25	(fillet-border).	to l., . (fillet-border). [I. O. C. Pl. vi. 9.]
2	61·1	AR ·8		to l., . [Pl. vi. 10.]

* This is the conjectural reading of Gen. Cunningham, who interprets, 'the god of the city of Kariei.' These coins are sometimes restruck upon money of Apollodotus: it seems, however, not improbable that they may have been issued after the death of Eucratides. *See* Introduction.

PLATO. B.C. 166.

(Contemporary of Eucratides.)

(a) *Silver.*

No.	Wt.	Metal. Size.	Obverse.	Reverse.
1	249·	Æ 1·3	Bust of the king r., diad. and wearing helmet adorned with ear and horn of bull, and crest: fillet-border.	ΒΑΣΙΛΕΩΣ ΕΠΙΦΑΝΟΥΣ ΠΛΑΤΩΝΟΣ Helios r., radiate, clad in chiton and chlamys; in quadriga. to r., M; in ex., ΡΜΖ.* [Pl. VI. 11.] (year 147 of the Seleucid era.)

* The Ρ can scarcely be considered a certainty, but a down stroke is visible, which seems to prove that a third letter existed.

HELIOCLES.

(Son or brother of Eucratides.)

(a) *Silver; Greek inscription; Attic weight.*

No.	Wt.	Metal. Size.	Obverse.	Reverse.
			Bust of the king r., diad.: fillet-border.	ΒΑΣΙΛΕΩΣ ΗΛΙΟΚΛΕΟΥΣ ΔΙΚΑΙΟΥ Zeus, laur., facing, clad in himation; holds winged thunderbolt and long sceptre.
1	261·2	AR 1·3		to l., ΚΡ. [Pl. VII. 1.]
2	258·	AR 1·25		„ „ [I. O. C.]
3	259·7	AR 1·25		„ Σ. [Pl. VII. 2.]
4	249·8	AR 1·15		„ Ⓐ.
5	246 6	AR 1·4		in ex., ΠΓ.
6	240·8	AR 1·3		to l., ΕΔ. [I. O. C.]
7	205·1	AR 1·05 (plated)		„ Ꝏ.
8	58·9	AR ·8		in ex., ΠΓ. [Pl. VII. 3.]
9	56·7	AR ·8		„ Δ or Λ.
10	56·8	AR ·8		to l., Ⓐ. (inscr. semi-barbarous.) [I. O. C.]

No.	Wt.	Metal. Size.	Obverse.	Reverse.
			(β) Barbarous copies in bronze.	
			Rude copy of bust of Heliocles r., diad.: fillet-border.	Barbarous degradation of— ΒΑΣΙΛΕΩΣ ΗΛΙΟΚΛΕΟΥΣ ΔΙΚΑΙΟΥ Zeus, facing; holds thunderbolt and long sceptre.
11		Æ 1·2		
12		Æ 1·1		[I. O. C.]
13		Æ 1·2		[I. O. C.] (restruck on type next described.)
			Similar.	ΒΑΣΙΛΕΩΣ ΗΛΙΙΛΕΥΣ ΔΙΙΑΙΥ (varied). Horse trotting l.
14		Æ 1·1		
15		Æ 1·1		
16		Æ 1·15		[I. O. C.]
17		Æ 1·1		[I. O. C.]
18		Æ ·75		[Pl. VII. 4.]
19		Æ ·7		
20		Æ ·7		[I. O. C.]
21		Æ ·6		

(ANOTHER HELIOCLES?).

(γ) *Silver; Indian inscription; Persian weight.*

No.	Wt.	Metal. Size.	Obverse.	Reverse.
			ΒΑΣΙΛΕΩΣ ΔΙΚΑΙΟΥ ΗΛΙΟΚΛΕΟΥΣ Bust of the king r., diad.	[Kharoshthi legend] (*Māhārajasa dhramikasa Heliyakreyasa*). Zeus, laur., facing, clad in himation; holds winged thunderbolt and long sceptre.
22	146·4	AR 1·05		to l., [monogram]. [I. O. C. Pl. VII. 5.]
23	34·5	AR ·65		to l., Σ. [I. O. C. Pl. VII. 6.]
24	34·2	AR ·65		" "
25	26·3	AR ·65		" [symbol].

(δ) *Bronze; square.*

No.	Wt.	Metal. Size.	Obverse.	Reverse.
			ΒΑΣΙΛΕΩΣ ΔΙΚΑΙΟΥ ΗΛΙΟΚΛΕΟΥΣ Bust of the king r., diad.	[Kharoshthi legend] (*Māhārajasa dhramikasa Heliyakreyasa*). Elephant l.
26		Æ ·85		below, [monogram].
27		Æ ·85		" "

No.	Wt.	Metal. Size.	Obverse.	Reverse.
			ΒΑΣΙΛΕΩΣ ΔΙΚΑΙΟΥ ΗΛΙΟΚΛΕΟΥΣ Bust of the king r., diad., bearded.	𐨨𐨱𐨪𐨗𐨯 𐨢𐨿𐨪𐨨𐨁𐨐𐨯 𐨱𐨅𐨫𐨁𐨩𐨐𐨿𐨪𐨅𐨩𐨯 (*Māhārajasa dhramikasa Heliyakreyasa*). Elephant l.
28		Æ ·8*		below, Σ.
29		Æ ·85		above, monogram. (inscr. ends *kre-sa-sa*). [I. O. C. Pl. VII. 7.]
			ΒΑΣΙΛΕΩΣ ΔΙΚΑΙΟΥ ΗΛΙΟΚΛΕΟΥΣ Elephant r.	Same inscr. Indian bull r.
30		Æ ·8		[I. O. C. Pl. VII. 8.]
31		Æ ·95		to l., monogram.

* Restruck on a coin of Strato, the characters 𐨟𐨿𐨪𐨟𐨯 remaining on the reverse from previous striking.

No.	Wt.	Metal. Size.	Obverse.	Reverse.
			ANTIALCIDAS.	
			(a) Silver; Attic weight.	
1	257·2	Æ1·35	Bust of the king r., diad.: fillet-border.	ΒΑΣΙΛΕΩΣ ΝΙΚΗΦΟΡΟΥ ΑΝΤΙΑΛΚΙΔΟΥ Zeus, laur., seated l. on throne; holds in r., Nike, who bears wreath and palm; in l., long sceptre; in field l., forepart of elephant with bell round neck, who raises his trunk. to r., [monogram]. [I. O. C. Pl. VII. 9.]
			(β) Silver; Indian weight.	
2	34·5	Æ·65	ΒΑΣΙΛΕΩΣ ΝΙΚΗΦΟΡΟΥ ΑΝΤΙΑΛΚΙΔΟΥ Bust of the king r., diad.	[Kharoshthi] (*Māhārajasa jayadharasa Aṃtialikidasa*). Zeus seated l. on throne; holds in r. hand, palm and wreath; in l., sceptre; to l., small elephant upwards, who grasps the wreath in his trunk. to r., [monogram]. [Pl. VII. 10.]
			Same inscr. Bust of the king r., diad.	Same inscr. Zeus seated l. on throne; holds in r. hand, Nike; in l., sceptre; to l., forepart of elephant, who raises his trunk.
3	36·4	Æ·65		below throne, [monogram]. (elephant r.)
4	38·	Æ·7		to r., [monogram]. „ [I. O. C.]
5	37·9	Æ·65	(king wears causia).	below throne, [monogram]. „ [Pl. VII. 11.]

No.	Wt.	Metal. Size.	Obverse.	Reverse.
			ΒΑΣΙΛΕΩΣ ΝΙΚΗΦΟΡΟΥ ΑΝΤΙΑΛΚΙΔΟΥ Bust of the king r., diad.	[Kharoshthi] (*Mahārajasa jayadharasa Aṃtialikidasa*). Zeus seated l. on throne; holds in r. hand, Nike; in l., sceptre; to l., forepart of elephant, who raises his trunk.
6	33·3	AR ·65	(king helmeted).	to r., [monogram]. (elephant r.)
7	34·5	AR ·7	"	in field r. ~~below~~ throne, [monogram]. "
8	37·2	AR ·65	"	to r., [monogram]. " [I. O. C.]
9	35·8	AR ·65	"	" " (elephant facing). [Pl. VII. 12.]
10	37·8	AR ·65	"	" " (elephant l.) [I. O. C.]
11	37·6	AR ·65	(king wears causia).	" " "
12	37·6	AR ·7	"	" " " [I. O. C. Pl. VII. 13.]

No.	Wt.	Metal. Size.	Obverse.	Reverse.
			Same inscr. Bust of the king r., diad.	Same inscr. Zeus seated l. on throne; holds in r. hand, Nike; in l., sceptre; to l., forepart of elephant l., who carries off the wreath of Nike.
13	36·5	AR ·6	(king wears causia).	below throne, [monogram].
14	33·9	AR ·6	"	" "
15	33·1	AR ·65		" [monogram]. [Pl. VII. 14.]

No.	Wt.	Metal. Size.	Obverse.	Reverse.
			(γ) Bronze; round.	
			ΒΑΣΙΛΕΩΣ ΝΙΚΗΦΟΡΟΥ ΑΝΤΙΑΛΚΙΔΟΥ Bust of Zeus r., with hand hurling thunderbolt.	𐨨𐨱𐨪𐨗𐨯 𐨗𐨩𐨢𐨪𐨯 𐨀𐨎𐨟𐨁𐨀𐨫𐨁𐨐𐨁𐨡𐨯 (*Māhārajasa jayadharasa Aṃtialikidasa*). Laureate pilei of the Dioscuri, surmounted by stars; between them, two palms.
16		Æ ·9		to r., [monogram].
17		Æ ·85		to l., „ [Pl. VIII. 1.]
18		Æ ·85		„ „
			(δ) Bronze; square.	
			ΒΑΣΙΛΕΩΣ ΝΙΚΗΦΟΡΟΥ ΑΝΤΙΑΛΚΙΔΟΥ Bust of Zeus r., bare-headed; thunderbolt over l. shoulder.	𐨨𐨱𐨪𐨗𐨯 𐨗𐨩𐨢𐨪𐨯 𐨀𐨎𐨟𐨁𐨀𐨫𐨁𐨐𐨁𐨡𐨯 (*Māhārajasa jayadharasa Aṃtialikidasa*). Laureate pilei of the Dioscuri, surmounted by stars; between them, two palms.
19		Æ ·75		to l., [monogram]; to r., Σ. [Pl. VIII. 2.]
20		Æ ·8		„ [monogram]; „ „
21		Æ ·75		„ [monogram]; „ „
22		Æ ·8		„ „ „ „ [I. O. C.]
23		Æ ·7		„ [monogram]
24		Æ ·75		„ „ „
25		Æ ·75		„ „

No.	Wt.	Metal. Size.	Obverse.	Reverse.
			ΒΑΣΙΛΕΩΣ ΝΙΚΗΦΟΡΟΥ ΑΝΤΙΑΛΚΙΔΟΥ Bust of Zeus r., laur., with hand hurling thunderbolt.	*(Mahārajasa jayadharasa Amtialikidasa)*. Laureate pilei of the Dioscuri, surmounted by stars; between them, two palms.
26		Æ ·75		to l.,
27		Æ ·75		„ „
28		Æ ·7		„
29		Æ ·7		„ „ [Pl. VIII. 3.]
30		Æ ·85		above, „
			Same inscr., blundered. Aegis.	Same inscr., blundered. Palm and wreath.
31		Æ ·85		below, . [I. O. C. Pl. VIII. 4.]

LYSIAS.

(a) *Silver.*

No.	Wt.	Metal. Size.	Obverse.	Reverse.
			ΒΑΣΙΛΕΩΣ ΑΝΙΚΗΤΟΥ ΛΥΣΙΟΥ Bust of the king r., diad.	𐨨𐨱𐨪𐨗𐨯 𐨀𐨤𐨡𐨁𐨱𐨟𐨯 𐨫𐨁𐨯𐨁𐨐𐨯 (*Māhārajasa apadihātasa Lisikasa*). Young Herakles, facing; holds in l. hand, club, palm, and lion's skin; with r. hand crowns himself with vine-leaves.
1	30·8	Æ ·65		to l., [monogram]; to r., Σ. [Pl. VIII. 5.]
2	37·4	Æ ·7	(king wears elephant's scalp).	" " " " (palm not visible.)
3	37·9	Æ ·7	" "	" " " " [I. O. C. Pl. VIII. 6.]
4	34·4	Æ ·7	" "	" [monogram]. [I. O. C.]
5	36·	Æ ·7	" "	" [monogram]. "
6	33·5	Æ ·65	(king helmeted).	" [monogram]; " "
7	36·4	Æ ·65	"	" [monogram]. (king's name written 𐨫𐨁𐨯𐨁𐨀𐨯, *Lisiasa.*) [Pl. VIII. 7.]

(β) *Bronze; round.*

No.	Wt.	Metal. Size.	Obverse.	Reverse.
			ΒΑΣΙΛΕΩΣ ΑΝΙΚΗΤΟΥ ΛΥΣ[ΙΟΥ Bust of bearded Herakles r.; club and palm over shoulder.	𐨨𐨱𐨪𐨗𐨯 𐨀𐨤𐨡𐨁𐨱𐨟𐨯 𐨫𐨁𐨯𐨁𐨐𐨯 (*Māhārajasa apadihātasa Lisikasa*). Elephant r., walking.
8		Æ ·95		below, [monogram]. [Pl. VIII. 8.]

No.	Wt.	Metal. Size.	Obverse.	Reverse.
			(γ) *Bronze; square.*	
			ΒΑΣΙΛΕΩΣ ΑΝΙΚΗΤΟΥ ΛΥΣΙΟΥ Bust of bearded Herakles r.; lion's skin round neck, and club over shoulder.	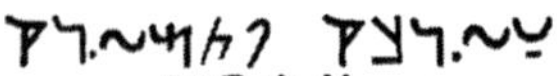 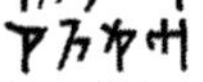 (*Māhārajasa apadihātasa Lisikasa*). Elephant r., walking.
9		Æ ·75		below,  Σ. [Pl. VIII. 9.]
10		Æ ·8		„ „ „
11		Æ ·75		„ „ „
12		Æ ·7		above, .
13		Æ ·75		below, .
14		Æ ·85		„ . (king's name written 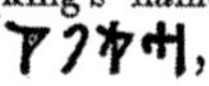, *Lisiasa*.)

DIOMEDES.

(α) Silver; type, Dioscuri, standing.

No.	Wt.	Metal. Size.	Obverse.	Reverse.
			ΒΑΣΙΛΕΩΣ ΣΩΤΗΡΟΣ ΔΙΟΜΗΔΟΥ Bust of the king r., diad.	 (*Maharajasa tradatasa Diyamedasa*). The Dioscuri, facing, holding lances.
1	34·8	AR ·65		to r., . [Pl. VIII. 10.]
2	35·	AR ·65	(king helmeted).	to l., " [Pl. VIII. 11.]

(β) Silver; type, Dioscuri, mounted.

No.	Wt.	Metal. Size.	Obverse.	Reverse.
			ΒΑΣΙΛΕΩΣ ΣΩΤΗΡΟΣ ΔΙΟΜΗΔΟΥ Bust of the king r., diad.	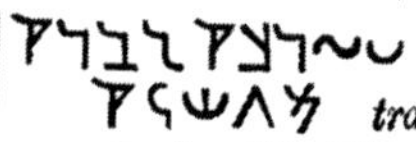 (*Maharajasa tradatasa Diyamedasa*). The Dioscuri, charging r., holding long lances and palms.
3	33·5	AR ·65		below, . [Pl. VIII. 12.]
4	33·1	AR ·65	(king helmeted).	" " [Pl. VIII 13.]

(γ) Bronze; square.

No.	Wt.	Metal. Size.	Obverse.	Reverse.
			ΒΑΣΙΛΕΩΣ ΣΩΤΗΡΟΣ ΔΙΟΜΗΔΟΥ The Dioscuri, facing, holding lances.	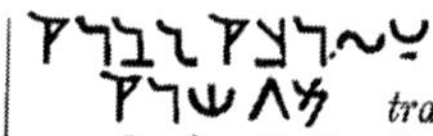 (*Māhārajasa tradatasa Diyamedasa*). Indian bull r.
5		Æ ·8		below, . [Pl. VIII. 14.]
6		Æ ·85		" Σ .
7		Æ ·85		" Σ.
8		Æ ·75		" "

No.	Wt.	Metal. Size.	Obverse.	Reverse.
				ARCHEBIUS.
				(*a*) *Silver.*
			ΒΑΣΙΛΕΩΣ ΔΙΚΑΙ-ΟΥ ΝΙΚΗΦΟΡΟΥ ΑΡΧΕΒΙΟΥ Bust of the king r., diad.	[Kharoshthī legend] (*Māhārajasa dhramikasa jayadharasa Arkhebiyasa*). Zeus, facing, clad in himation; holds long sceptre in l. hand, and hurls thunderbolt with r.
1	139·	AR 1·05		to l., [monogram]. [I. O. C. Pl. IX. 1.]
2	36·	AR ·7		to r., [monogram]. [Pl. IX. 2.]
3	36·3	AR ·65	(king helmeted).	” ” [Pl. IX. 3.]
			ΒΑΣΙΛΕΩΣ ΔΙΚΑΙ-ΟΥ ΝΙΚΗΦΟΡΟΥ ΑΡΧΕΒΙΟΥ Bust of the king l., diad., wearing aegis and thrusting with spear.	[Kharoshthī legend] (*Māhārajasa dhramikasa jayadharasa Arkhebiyasa*). Zeus, facing, clad in himation; holds long sceptre in l. hand, and hurls thunderbolt with r.
4	147·6	AR 1·	(king helmeted).	to l., [monogram]. [I. O. C. Pl. IX. 4.]
5	34·4	AR ·7		to l., [monogram]; to r., [monogram]. [I. O. C. Pl. IX. 5.]
				(*β*) *Bronze; round.*
			ΒΑΣΙΛΕΩΣ ΔΙΚΑΙ-ΟΥ ΝΙΚΗΦΟΡΟΥ ΑΡΧΕΒΙΟΥ Nike l., holding wreath and palm.	[Kharoshthī legend] (*Māhārajasa dhramikasa jayadharasa Arkhebiyasa*). Owl r.
6		Æ 1·		to r., [monogram]. [Pl. IX. 6.]

No.	Wt.	Metal. Size.	Obverse.	Reverse.
			(γ) *Bronze; square.*	
			ΒΑΣΙΛΕΩΣ ΔΙΚΑΙ-ΟΥ ΝΙΚΗΦΟΡΟΥ ΑΡΧΕΒΙΟΥ Elephant r.	(*Māhārajasa dhramikasa jayadharasa Arkhe-biyasa*). Owl r.
7		Æ 1·		below, . [Pl. IX. 7.]
8		Æ ·9		„ . [I. O. C.]

No.	Wt.	Metal. Size.	Obverse.	Reverse.
			APOLLODOTUS I.	
			(α) Silver; round; Attic weight.	
			ΒΑΣΙΛΕΩΣ ΑΠΟΛ-ΛΟΔΟΤΟΥ ΣΩΤΗ-ΡΟΣ Elephant r., band round body.	[Kharoshthi inscription] (*Māhārajasa Apaladatasa tradatasa*). Indian bull r.
1	31·1	AR ·6		[Pl. IX. 8.]
2	30·8	AR ·6		[I. O. C.]
			(β) Silver; square; Indian weight.	
			ΒΑΣΙΛΕΩΣ ΑΠΟΛ-ΛΟΔΟΤΟΥ ΣΩΤΗ-ΡΟΣ Elephant r., band round body.	[Kharoshthi inscription] (*Māhārajasa Apaladatasa tradatasa*). Indian bull r.
3	37·9	AR ·65	below, [monogram].	below, Δ. ([Kharoshthi inscription] in inscr.) [Pl. IX. 9.]
4	37·8	AR ·65	„ „	„ C. „
5	37·8	AR ·65	„ „	„ ω. „
6	37·7	AR ·6	„ [monogram].	„ A.
7	38·	AR ·6	„ „	„ „ [I. O. C.]
8	36·3	AR ·65	„ „	„ A.
9	37·5	AR ·65	„ [monogram].	„ [monogram].
10	38·	AR ·65	„ M.	(Ŏ on bull's hump.)
11	37·9	AR ·6	„ „	„ [I. O. C.]
12	18·3	AR ·5	below, ΞΕ.	[I. O. C.]

No.	Wt.	Metal. Size.	Obverse.	Reverse.
			(γ) *Bronze; square.*	
			ΒΑΣΙΛΕΩΣ ΑΠΟΛΛΟΔΟΤΟΥ ΣΩΤΗΡΟΣ Apollo, laur., facing; holds in r. hand, arrow; in l., bow.	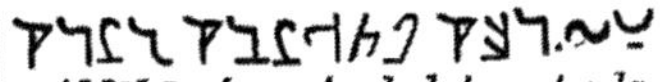 (*Māhārajasa Apaladatasa tradatasa*). Tripod on stand, in square of dots.
13		Æ ·9		[Pl. IX. 10.]
14		Æ ·95		[I. O. C.]
15		Æ ·85		to r., .
16		Æ ·85	to l., .	„ .
17		Æ ·95		„ .
18		Æ ·9		„ „ [I. O. C.]
19		Æ ·9		„ „
20		Æ ·9		„ .
21		Æ ·9		„ . [I. O. C.]
22		Æ 1·		„ . „
23		Æ ·9		„ . „
24		Æ ·75		„ „ [Pl. IX. 11.]

No.	Wt.	Metal. Size.	Obverse.	Reverse.
			ΒΑΣΙΛΕΩΣ ΑΠΟΛΛΟΔΟΤΟΥ ΣΩΤΗΡΟΣ Apollo, laur., facing; holds in r. hand, arrow; in l., bow.	(*Māhārajasa Apaladatasa tradatasa*). Tripod on stand, in square of dots.
25		Æ ·9		[I. O. C.]
26		Æ ·85	to l., ΕΙ.	to l., [monogram].
27		Æ ·95	„ „	„ „
28		Æ ·9	„ [monogram].	„ [monogram].
29		Æ ·9		to r., [monogram].
30		Æ ·9		„ Α ΕΡ (?)
31		Æ ·8		to l., [monogram]. [I. O. C. Pl. IX. 12.]
32		Æ ·7		to r., Μ.
33		Æ ·7	(inscr. blundered.)	„ „ [I. O. C.]
34		Æ ·75		„ Μ.
35		Æ ·9	(„)	„ „ [I. O. C.]
36		Æ ·75		to l., „
37		Æ ·65	(„)	to r., Μ.
38		Æ ·7		„ [monogram].

(δ) *Bronze; square; perhaps of Apollodotus.*

No.	Wt.	Metal. Size.	Obverse.	Reverse.
			Indian bull r., in square of dots.	Tripod, in square of dots.
39		Æ ·5		[I. O. C. Pl. IX. 13.]

APOLLODOTUS II., PHILOPATOR.

(a) *Silver.*

No.	Wt.	Metal. Size.	Obverse.	Reverse.
			ΒΑΣΙΛΕΩΣ ΜΕΓΑΛΟΥ ΣΩΤΗΡΟΣ ΚΑΙ ΦΙΛΟΠΑΤΟΡΟΣ ΑΠΟΛΛΟΔΟΤΟΥ Bust of the king r., diad.	(*Maharajasa tradatasa Apaladatasa*). Pallas l., holding in l. hand aegis, and with r. hurling thunderbolt.
1	128·5	Æ1·15		to l., . [Pl. x. 1.]
			ΒΑΣΙΛΕΩΣ ΣΩΤΗΡΟΣ ΚΑΙ ΦΙΛΟΠΑΤΟΡΟΣ ΑΠΟΛΛΟΔΟΤΟΥ Similar bust.	Similar.
2	37·2	Æ ·75		to l., . [Pl. x. 2.]
3	37·3	Æ ·65		to l., uncertain letter; to r., . [Pl. x. 3.]
4	36·1	Æ ·7		to r., .
5	36·	Æ ·7		" .
6	36·8	Æ ·7		" .
			ΒΑΣΙΛΕΩΣ ΣΩΤΗΡΟΣ ΑΠΟΛΛΟΔΟΤΟΥ Similar bust.	Similar.
7	35·4	Æ ·65		to l., ; to r., .
8	37·8	Æ ·6		[I. " O. C." Pl. x. 4.]

No.	Wt.	Metal. Size.	Obverse.	Reverse.
			(β) Bronze; round.	
			ΒΑΣΙΛΕΩΣ ΣΩΤΗΡΟΣ ΑΠΟΛΛΟΔΟΤΟΥ Apollo r., clad in chlamys and boots, holding with both hands an arrow; a quiver at his shoulder.	(*Maharajasa tradatasa Apaladatasa*). Tripod.
9		Æ 1·25	to l., .	to l., ; to r., .
10		Æ 1·05	„ „	„ „ „ „ [Pl. x. 5.]
			(γ) Bronze; square.	
			ΒΑΣΙΛΕΩΣ ΣΩΤΗΡΟΣ ΑΠΟΛΛΟΔΟΤΟΥ Apollo facing, clad in chlamys and boots; quiver behind shoulder; holds in l. hand, bow; in r., arrow, which rests on the ground.	(*Maharajasa tradatasa Apaladatasa*). Tripod.
11		Æ 1·		to l., ; to r., . [Pl. x. 6.]
			Same inscr. Apollo r., clad in chlamys and boots; holds with both hands an arrow; a quiver at his shoulder.	Same inscr. Tripod.
12		Æ 1·1		to l., ; to r., club. (*flan* of coin round). [Pl. x. 7.]
13		Æ ·95		mons. obscure.
14		Æ ·8		to l., ; to r., . (type within square of dots.)
15		Æ ·8		to r., . [I. O. C. Pl. x. 8.]

No.	Wt.	Metal. Size.	Obverse.	Reverse.
			ΒΑΣΙΛΕΩΣ ΣΩΤΗΡΟΣ ΚΑΙ ΦΙΛΟΠΑΤΟΡΟΣ ΑΠΟΛΛΟΔΟΤΟΥ Apollo r., clad in chlamys and boots; holds in r. hand, arrow; in l., bow.	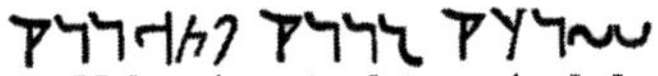 (*Maharajasa tradatasa Apaladatasa*). Tripod.
16		Æ ·8	(type within square of fillet-pattern.)	to r., mon. (type within square of fillet-pattern).
17		Æ ·8	,,	,, . ,,
			ΒΑΣΙΛΕΩΣ ΣΩΤΗΡΟΣ ΚΑΙ ΦΙΛΟΠΑΤΟΡΟΣ ΑΠΟΛΛΟΔΟΤΟΥ Similar type.	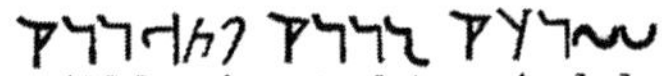 (*Maharajasa tradatasa Apaladatasa*). Tripod.
18		Æ ·65		to r., . [Pl. x. 9.]
19		Æ ·6		,, ,,
			Similar type, within square of fillet-pattern.	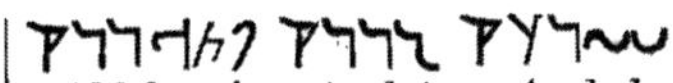 (*Maharajasa tradatasa Apaladatasa*). Diadema.
20		Æ ·6		

No.	Wt.	Metal. Size.	Obverse.	Reverse.
				STRATO I.
				(a) *Silver.*
			ΒΑΣΙΛΕΩΣ ΕΠΙΦΑΝΟΥΣ ΣΩΤΗΡΟΣ ΣΤΡΑΤΩΝΟΣ Bust of the king r., diad.	(*Māhārajasa pratichhasa* tradatasa Stratasa*). Pallas l., holding with l. hand aegis, and with r. hurling thunderbolt.
1	133·3	AR 1·05	(king wears helmet.)	to l., [monogram]. [Pl. x. 10.]
2	31·3	AR ·7		to l., [monogram].
3	36·2	AR ·7		„ [monogram]. [Pl. x. 11.]
4	33·3	AR ·65		„ „
			ΒΑΣΙΛΕΩΣ ΣΩΤΗΡΟΣ ΣΤΡΑΤΩΝΟΣ Bust of the king r., diad.	(*Māhārajasa tradatasa Stratasa*). Similar type.
5	35·8	AR ·7	(king helmeted.)	to l., [monogram]. [Pl. x. 12.]
6	35·5	AR ·6		„ [monogram]; to r., [monogram]. (semi-barbarous.)
7	37·6	AR ·65		„ [monogram]; „ [monogram]. „ [I. O. C. Pl. x. 13.]
8	35·4	AR ·6		„ [monogram]; „ „ [monogram]. „
9	†34·4	AR ·6	inscr. ....ΡΟΝΟΣΑ ...ΝΟΣ	„ „ „ „ [monogram]. „ [Pl. x. 14.]
10	32·2	AR ·65		„ [monogram]; „ „ [monogram]. „ [I. O. C.] (last line of inscr. *padayashasa* ?).

* Or *cha*, *prachchhasa*.

† This is one of the coins sometimes wrongly given to an imaginary king, Rosastonos.

No.	Wt.	Metal. Size.	Obverse.	Reverse.
			ΒΑΣΙΛΕΩΣ ΣΩΤΗΡΟΣ ΔΙΚΑΙΟΥ ΣΤΡΑΤΩΝΟΣ Bust of the king r., diad.	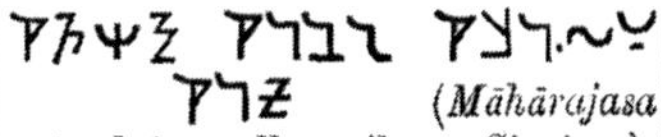 (*Māhārajasa tradatasa dhramikasa Stratasa*). Pallas r., holding in l. hand aegis, and with r. hurling thunderbolt.
11	32·7	AR ·65		to l, . [Pl. XI. 1.]
			(β) Bronze; round.	
			ΒΑΣΙΛΕΩΣ ΕΠΙΦΑΝΟΥΣ ΣΩΤΗΡΟΣ ΣΤΡΑΤΩΝΟΣ Bust of Apollo r., laur.; hair in queue.	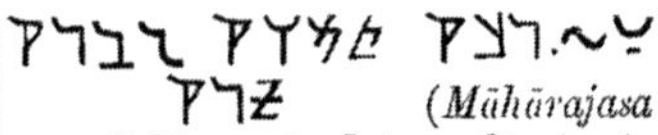 (*Māhārajasa pratichhasa tradatasa Stratasa*). Bow and quiver, with strap.
12		Æ 1·		to l., . [Pl. XI. 2.]
			(γ) Bronze; square; type, Apollo.	
			ΒΑΣΙΛΕΩΣ ΕΠΙΦΑΝΟΥΣ ΣΩΤΗΡΟΣ ΣΤΡΑΤΩΝΟΣ Apollo, facing; holds in r. hand, arrow; in l., bow.	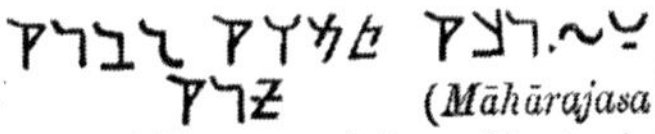 (*Māhārajasa pratichhasa tradatasa Stratasa*). Tripod-lebes, on stand.
13		Æ ·95		to l., ; to r., . [I. O. C. Pl. XI. 3.]
14		Æ ·9		„ . [I. O. C.]
15		Æ ·9		„ .
16		Æ ·85		„ ; to r.,  and mon. [I. O. C.]

No.	Wt.	Metal. Size.	Obverse.	Reverse.
			(δ) *Bronze; square; type, Nike.*	
			ΒΑΣΙΛΕΩΣ ΣΩΤΗΡΟΣ ΣΤΡΑΤΩΝΟΣ Bust of bearded Herakles r.; over shoulder, club bound with taenia.	(*Māhārajasa tradatasa Stratasa*). Nike r., holds wreath and palm.
17		Æ ·8		to r., [monogram]. [I. O. C. Pl. XI. 4.]
18		Æ ·85		„ Σ. [I. O. C.]
19		Æ ·8		„ „
			ΒΑΣΙΛΕΩΣ ΣΩΤΗΡΟΣ ΔΙΚΑΙΟΥ ΣΤΡΑΤΩΝΟΣ Similar type.	(*Maharajasa tradatasa dhramikasa Stratasa*). Similar type.
20		Æ ·9		to r., [monogram]. [Pl. XI. 5.]

AGATHOCLEIA, WITH STRATO.

(*a*) *Bronze; square.*

No.	Wt.	Metal. Size.	Obverse.	Reverse.
			ΒΑΣΙΛΙΣΣΗΣ ΘΕΟΤΡΟΠΟΥ ΑΓΑΘΟΚΛΕΙΑΣ Bust of the Queen r., helmeted.	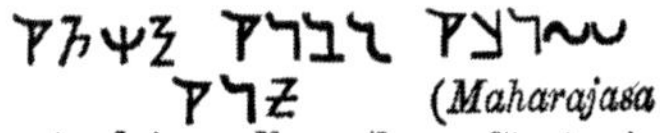 (*Maharajasa tradatasa dhramikasa Stratasa*). Herakles seated l. on rock; holds in r. hand, club, which rests on knee (type of Euthydemus).
1		Æ ·8		to l., . [Pl. xi. 6.]
2		Æ ·8		" " [I. O. C.]

MENANDER.

(*a*) *Silver.*

No.	Wt.	Metal. Size.	Obverse.	Reverse.
			ΒΑΣΙΛΕΩΣ ΣΩΤΗΡΟΣ ΜΕΝΑΝΔΡΟΥ Bust of the king r., diad.	𐨨𐨱𐨪𐨗𐨯 𐨟𐨿𐨪𐨟𐨪𐨯 𐨨𐨅𐨣𐨡𐨿𐨪𐨯 (*Māhārajasa trādatasa Menadrāsa*). Pallas l., holding in l. hand aegis, and with r. hurling thunderbolt.
1	150·9	Æ 1·05		to l., Σ; to r., [monogram]. [I. O. C.]
2	148·6	Æ 1·		,, ,, ,, ,,
3	149·	Æ 1·		,, [monogram]. [Pl. xi. 7.]
4	142·7	Æ 1·	(king helmeted).	,, ,, ,, Σ. [I. O. C.]
5	149·8	Æ 1·1	,,	,, ,, ,, ,, [Pl. xi. 8.]
6	38·1	Æ ·6	(king helmeted).	to r., [monogram].
7	37·	Æ ·7	,,	,, [monogram].
8	37·5	Æ ·7	,,	,, [monogram].
9	34·8	Æ ·6	,,	to l., ,,
10	37·8	Æ ·65	,,	to r., [monogram].
11	38·	Æ ·65	,,	,, ,, [Pl. xi. 9.]

No.	Wt.	Metal. Size.	Obverse.	Reverse.
			ΒΑΣΙΛΕΩΣ ΣΩΤΗΡΟΣ ΜΕΝΑΝΔΡΟΥ Bust of the king r., diad.	 (*Māhārajasa trādatasa Menadrāsa*). Pallas l., holding in l. hand aegis, and with r. hurling thunderbolt.
12	37·8	Æ ·7	(king helmeted).	to r., .
13	37·8	Æ ·7	„	„ „
14	39·	Æ ·7		[I. O. C.]
15	34·8	Æ ·65		to l., .
16	33·6	Æ ·7		to r., „
17	37·6	Æ ·7		„ .
18	37·4	Æ ·7		„ .
19	38·	Æ ·65		„ .
20	34·1	Æ ·75		to l., .
21	37·5	Æ ·65		„ „; to r., .
22	36·	Æ ·65		„ .
23	37·7	Æ ·65		„ „ [I. O. C.]
24	37·3	Æ ·65		„ .
25	37·	Æ ·7		to r., „ [Pl. xi. 10.]

No.	Wt.	Metal. Size.	Obverse.	Reverse.
			ΒΑΣΙΛΕΩΣ ΣΩΤΗΡΟΣ ΜΕΝΑΝΔΡΟΥ Bust of the king r., diad.	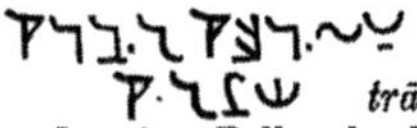 (*Māhārajasa trādatasa Menadrāsa*). Pallas l., holding in l. hand aegis, and with r. hurling thunderbolt.
26	36·3	Æ ·65		to l., ; to r., Γ. [I. O. C.]
27	39·	Æ ·7		,, ,, ,, Ε.
28	38·3	Æ ·7		,, Σ; ,, .
29	38·	Æ ·75		to r., .
30	38·7	Æ ·7		,, ,,
			Same inscr. Bust of the king l., wearing aegis and thrusting with spear.	Similar.
31	36·6	Æ ·7		to l., .
32	37·1	Æ ·65		to r., .
33	37·3	Æ ·65		,, .
34	37·8	Æ ·7		,, .
35	38·	Æ ·75		,, .

No.	Wt.	Metal. Size.	Obverse.	Reverse.
			ΒΑΣΙΛΕΩΣ ΣΩΤΗΡΟΣ ΜΕΝΑΝΔΡΟΥ Bust of the king l., wearing aegis and thrusting with spear.	(*Mahārajasa trādatasa Menadrāsa*). Pallas r., holding in l. hand aegis, and with r. hurling thunderbolt.
36	38·2	AR ·7		to l., .
37	38·	AR ·7		„ „
38	37·8	AR ·65		„ .
39	37·7	AR ·7		to r., . [I. O. C. Pl. xi. 11.]
40	38·2	AR ·65		„ „
41	37·8	AR ·65		to l., .
42	37·9	AR ·7		„ .
43	38·2	AR ·65		„ .

(β) *Bronze; square; with portrait.*

No.	Wt.	Metal. Size.	Obverse.	Reverse.
			ΒΑΣΙΛΕΩΣ ΣΩΤΗΡΟΣ ΜΕΝΑΝΔΡΟΥ Bust of the king l., diad., wearing aegis and thrusting with spear.	(*Mahārajasa tradatasa Menadrāsa*). Pallas r., holding in l. hand aegis, and with r. hurling thunderbolt.
44		Æ ·85		to r., .
45		Æ ·8		„ „
46		Æ ·9		„ . [I. O. C. Pl. xi. 12.]

No.	Wt.	Metal. Size.	Obverse.	Reverse.
			(γ) Bronze; square; with head of Pallas.	
			ΒΑΣΙΛΕΩΣ ΣΩΤΗΡΟΣ ΜΕΝΑΝΔΡΟΥ Bust of Pallas r., wearing crested helmet.	(*Māhārajasa tradatasa Menadrasa*). Horse r., prancing.
47		Æ 1·1		below, .
			Similar.	Same inscr. Nike r.; holds wreath and palm.
48		Æ ·9		to r., . [I. O. C.]
49		Æ ·8		,, . [I. O. C. Pl. XI. 13.]
50		Æ ·75		,, .
51		Æ ·85		,, .
52		Æ ·7		,, ,,
53		Æ ·8		,, .
54		Æ ·7		,, ,,
55		Æ ·8		,, .
			Similar.	Same inscr. Nike l.; holds wreath and palm.
56		Æ ·75		to l., ; to r., **B**. [I. O. C.]
57		Æ ·8		,, ; ,, ,, [Pl. XII. 1.]
58		Æ ·75		,, **B**. [I. O. C.]

No.	Wt.	Metal. Size.	Obverse.	Reverse.
			ΒΑΣΙΛΕΩΣ ΣΩΤΗΡΟΣ ΜΕΝΑΝΔΡΟΥ Bust of Pallas r., wearing crested helmet.	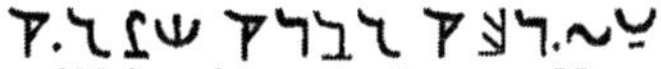 (*Māhārajasa tradatasa Menadrāsa*). Round buckler; Gorgon-head in the midst.
59		Æ ·85		below, . [Pl. XII. 2.]
60		Æ ·85		„ .
61		Æ ·85		to l., .
62		Æ ·9		„ „ [I. O. C. Pl. XII. 3.]
			Similar.	Same inscr. Owl r.
63		Æ ·8		to r., . [I. O. C. Pl. XII. 4.]

(δ) *Bronze; square; Apolline types.*

No.	Wt.	Metal. Size.	Obverse.	Reverse.
			ΒΑΣΙΛΕΩΣ ΣΩΤΗΡΟΣ ΜΕΝΑΝΔΡΟΥ Ox-head, facing.	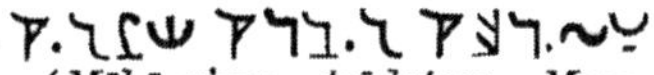 (*Māhārajasa trādatasa Menadrāsa*). Tripod-lebes.
64		Æ ·9		to l., .
65		Æ ·9		„ „
66		Æ ·9		„ ; to r., . [Pl. XII. 5.]

No.	Wt.	Metal. Size.	Obverse.	Reverse.
			(ε) Bronze; square; Herakleian types.	
			ΒΑΣΙΛΕΩΣ ΣΩΤΗΡΟΣ ΜΕΝΑΝΔΡΟΥ Elephant's head r., bell round neck.	(*Māhārajasa trādatasa Menadrāsa*). Club upwards.
67		Æ ·65		to l., [monogram]; to r., Α.
68		Æ ·55		„ „ „ „ [Pl. XII. 6.]
69		Æ ·6		„ Α; „ [monogram].
70		Æ ·6		„ „ „ „ [I. O. C.]
71		Æ ·55	below, Α.	to r., [illegible].
72		Æ ·55	„ Ο.	„ [monogram].
			(ζ) Bronze; square; type, wheel.	
			ΒΑΣΙΛΕΩΣ ΣΩΤΗΡΟΣ ΜΕΝΑΝΔΡΟΥ Wheel.	(*Māhārajasa trādatasa Menadrāsa*). Palm.
73		Æ ·5		to r., mon. [I. O. C. Pl. XII. 7.]
			(η) Bronze; square; with title δικαιός.	
			ΒΑΣΙΛΕΩΣ ΔΙΚΑΙΟΥ ΜΕΝΑΝΔΡΟΥ Pallas l., holds patera? and spear, against which leans shield.	(*Māhārajasa dhramikasa Menadrāsa*) Maneless Indian lion l.
74		Æ ·85		below, [monogram].

EPANDER.

(a) *Bronze.*

No.	Wt.	Metal. Size.	Obverse.	Reverse.
1		Æ ·9	ΒΑΣΙΛΕΩΣ ΝΙΚΗ-ΦΟΡΟΥ ΕΠΑΝΔΡΟΥ Nike advancing r.; holds wreath and palm.	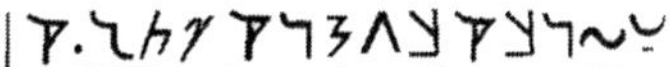 (*Māharajasa jayadharasa Epa-drāsa*). Indian bull r. below,  . [I. O. C. Pl. XII 8.]

DIONYSIUS.

(a) *Silver.*

No.	Wt.	Metal. Size.	Obverse.	Reverse.
1	38·	AR ·7	ΒΑΣΙΛΕΩΣ ΣΩΤΗ-ΡΟΣ ΔΙΟΝΥΣΙΟΥ Bust of the king r., diad.	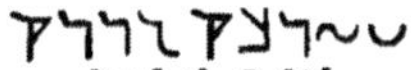 (*Maharajasa* 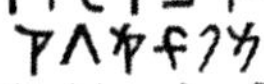 *tradatasa Dianisiyasa*). Pallas l.; holding in l. hand, aegis; and with r., hurling thunderbolt. to r., . [I. O. C. Pl. XII. 9.]

(β) *Bronze.*

No.	Wt.	Metal. Size.	Obverse.	Reverse.
2		Æ ·85	ΒΑΣΙΛΕΩΣ ΣΩΤΗ-ΡΟΣ ΔΙΟΝΥΣΙΟΥ Apollo r., clad in chlamys and boots; holds in both hands an arrow; a quiver at his back.	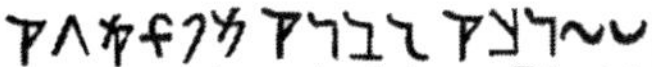 (*Maharajasa tradatasa Dianisi-yasa*). Tripod. to l., ; to r., . [I. O. C.]
3		Æ ·8		mons. obscure.

No.	Wt.	Metal. Size.	Obverse.	Reverse.
			ZOILUS.	
			(*a*) *Silver; with title* δικαιός.	
			ΒΑΣΙΛΕΩΣ ΔΙΚΑΙ-ΟΥ ΖΩΙΛΟΥ Bust of the king r., diad.	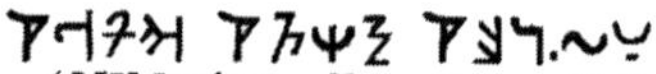 (*Māhārajasa dhramikasa Jhoïlasa*). Herakles facing, crowned with ivy; holds in r. hand, wreath; in l., club and lion's skin.
1	37·4	Æ ·7		to l., . [Pl. XII. 10.]
2	38·5	Æ ·65		„ . [I. O. C.]
			(*β*) *Silver; with title* σωτήρ.	
			ΒΑΣΙΛΕΩΣ ΣΩΤΗ-ΡΟΣ ΖΩΙΛΟΥ Bust of the king r., diad.	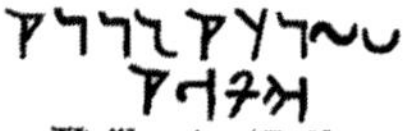 (*Maharajasa tradatasa Jhoïlasa*). Pallas l.; holding in l. hand, aegis; and with r., hurling thunderbolt.
3	34·8	Æ ·65		to l., ; to r., . [I. O. C. Pl. XII. 11.]
4	37·4	Æ ·65	Z in inscr.	„ ; „ „ [I. O. C.]
5	37·6	Æ ·8	„	„ ; „ „ „
6	36·6	Æ ·6	„	„ ; „  .
7	34·4	Æ ·7	„	„ „ .
8	38·2	Æ ·7	„	„ . [I. O. C.]

No.	Wt.	Metal. Size.	Obverse.	Reverse.
			(γ) *Bronze; round.*	
			ΒΑΣΙΛΕΩΣ ΣΩΤΗ-ΡΟΣ ΖΩΙΛΟΥ Apollo r., clad in chlamys and boots; holds in both hands an arrow; a quiver at his back; in field l., small elephant.	(*Maharajasa tradatasa Jhoïlasa*). Tripod.
9		Æ 1·25		to l., ; to r., . [Pl. xii. 12.]
			Elephant r.	Similar.
10		Æ ·75		to l., ; to r., . (double-struck).
			(δ) *Bronze; square.*	
			ΒΑΣΙΛΕΩΣ ΣΩΤΗ-ΡΟΣ ΖΩΙΛΟΥ Apollo r., clad in chlamys and boots; holds in both hands an arrow; a quiver at his back.	(*Maharajasa tradatasa Jhoïlasa*). Tripod.
11		Æ 1·	to l., .	to l., ; to r., . [Pl. xii. 13.]

APOLLOPHANES.

(a) *Silver.*

No.	Wt.	Metal. Size.	Obverse.	Reverse.
			ΒΑΣΙΛΕΩΣ ΣΩΤΗΡΟΣ ΑΠΟΛΛΟΦΑΝΟΥ (*sic*) Bust of the king r., helmeted; diadem tied round the helmet.	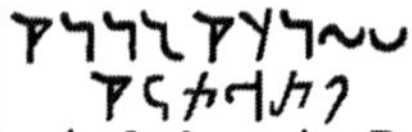 (*Maharajasa tradatasa Apulaphanasa*). Pallas l.; holding in l. hand, aegis; and with r. hurling thunderbolt.
1	36·3	Æ ·65		to l., ; to r., . [Pl. XIII. 1.]
2	37·8	Æ ·65		" " " " [I. O. C.]

ARTEMIDORUS.

(a) *Bronze; square.*

No.	Wt.	Metal. Size.	Obverse.	Reverse.
			ΒΑΣΙΛΕΩΣ ΑΝΙΚΗ[ΤΟΥ ΑΡ]ΤΕΜΙΔΩΡΟΥ Artemis, facing; holds in l., bow, and with r., draws arrow from quiver at her back.	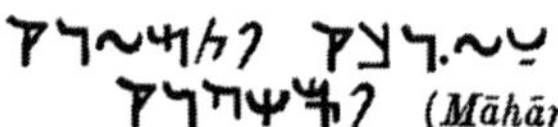 (*Māhārajasa apadihatasa Artemidorasa*). Humped bull r.
1		Æ ·8		below, . [Pl. XIII. 2.]

No.	Wt.	Metal. Size.	Obverse.	Reverse.
			ANTIMACHUS II., NICEPHORUS.	
			(a) Silver.	
			ΒΑΣΙΛΕΩΣ ΝΙΚΗΦΟΡΟΥ ΑΝΤΙΜΑΧΟΥ Nike l.; holds palm and wreath.	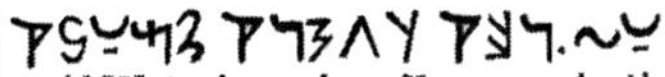 (*Māhārajasa jayadharasa Aṃtimākhasa*). The king, wearing causia, diadem, and chlamys, on horseback r.
1	37·6	AR ·65	to l., .	[Pl. XIII. 3.]
2	37·5	AR ·65	” ”	
3	37·8	AR ·65	” .	
4	38·4	AR ·7	” ”	[I. O. C.]
5	37·8	AR ·7	” .	
6	37·5	AR ·6	” ”	
7	37·8	AR ·65	” ”	[I. O. C.]
8	38·3	AR ·65	” .	
9	36·7	AR ·7	” ”	
			(β) Bronze; square.	
			ΒΑΣΙΛΕΩΣ ΝΙΚΗΦΟΡΟΥ ΑΝΤΙΜΑΧΟΥ Aegis: in the midst, Gorgon-head.	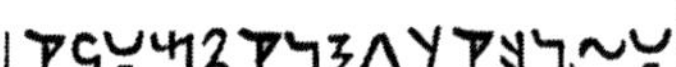 (*Māhārajasa jayadharasa Aṃtimākhasa*). Wreath and palm.
10		Æ ·8		below, . [Pl. XIII. 4.]

No.	Wt.	Metal. Size.	Obverse.	Reverse.
			PHILOXENUS.	
			(*a*) *Silver; round.*	
			ΒΑΣΙΛΕΩΣ ΑΝΙΚΗ-ΤΟΥ ΦΙΛΟΞΕΝΟΥ Bust of the king r., diad.	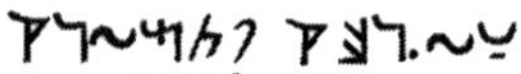 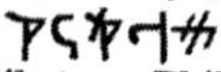 (*Māhārajasa apadihatasa Philasinasa*). King, helmeted and diad., on horseback r.; horse prancing.
1	151·4	Æ1·05		below, . ( for  in inscr.).
2	150·8	Æ1·2		„ . [Pl. XIII. 5.]
3	149·	Æ1·05	(king helmeted).	„ Σ . [Pl. XIII. 6.]
			(*β*) *Silver; square.*	
			ΒΑΣΙΛΕΩΣ ΑΝΙΚΗ-ΤΟΥ ΦΙΛΟΞΕΝΟΥ Bust of the king r., diad.	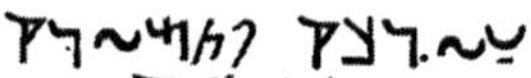 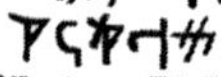 (*Māhārajasa apadihatasa Phila*sinasa*). King, helmeted and diad., on horseback r.; horse prancing.
4	36·8	Æ ·65		below, . [I. O. C. Pl. XIII. 7.]
5	33·3	Æ ·65		„ Σ . [I. O. C.]
6	35·	Æ ·7		„ .
7	27·3	Æ ·6	(king helmeted).	„ . [I. O. C. Pl. XIII. 8.]
8	25·	Æ ·7	„	„ . (plated).
9	26·	Æ ·6	„	„ . „ [I. O. C.]

* Sometimes *lu* for *la*.

No.	Wt.	Metal. Size.	Obverse.	Reverse.
			(γ) *Bronze; square.*	
			ΒΑΣΙΛΕΩΣ ΑΝΙΚΗΤΟΥ ΦΙΛΟΞΕΝΟΥ Sun-god, facing, radiate, clad in chiton, himation, and boots; holds in l. hand long sceptre; r. extended.	[Kharoshthi] (*Māhārajasa apadihatasa Phila*sinasa*). Nike r.; holds wreath and palm.
10		Æ ·8		to r., [monogram]. [Pl. XIII. 9.]
			Same inscr. A City l.; in l. hand cornucopiae; r. extended.	Same inscr. Indian bull r.
11		Æ ·85	to l., [monogram].	below, Σ.
12		Æ ·8	„ „	„ „
13		Æ ·8	„ [monogram].	„ Ί. [I. O. C. Pl. XIII. 10.]
14		Æ ·8	„ „	[I. O. C.]
15		Æ ·8	„ „	
16		Æ ·9	„ mon.	„ Φ. „
17		Æ ·8	„ Π.	„ Σ. „

* Sometimes *lu* for *la*.

NICIAS.

(a) *Bronze; square.*

No.	Wt.	Metal. Size.	Obverse.	Reverse.
1		Æ ·8	ΒΑСΙΛΕШС СШΤΗΡΟС ΝΙΚΙΟΥ Head of the king r., diad.	(or [illegible]) [illegible] (*Maharajasa* or *Maharayasa tradatasa Nikiasa*). King, diad. and wearing chlamys, on horseback r.; horse prancing. [Pl. XIII. 11.]
2		Æ ·9	ΒΑΣΙΛΕΩΣ ΣΩΤΗΡΟΣ ΝΙΚΙΟΥ Similar head.	[illegible] (*Maharajasa tradatasa Nikiasa*). Dolphin twined round anchor. [Pl. XIII. 12.]

HIPPOSTRATUS.

(a) *Silver; type, City.*

No.	Wt.	Metal. Size.	Obverse.	Reverse.
			ΒΑΣΙΛΕΩΣ ΣΩΤΗΡΟΣ ΙΠΠΟΣΤΡΑΤΟΥ Bust of the king r., diad.	[Kharoshthi legend] (*Maharajasa tradatasa Hipastratasa*). City l., wearing modius; holds in l. hand, cornucopiae; r. advanced.
1	146·	Æ1·1		to l., [monogram]; to r., [monogram]. [Pl. XIV. 1.]
2	147·7	Æ1·15		„ „ „ „

(β) *Silver; type, King on horseback.*

No.	Wt.	Metal. Size.	Obverse.	Reverse.
			ΒΑΣΙΛΕΩΣ ΜΕΓΑΛΟΥ ΣΩΤΗΡΟΣ ΙΠΠΟΣΤΡΑΤΟΥ Bust of the king r., diad.	[Kharoshthi legend] (*Maharajasa tradatasa mahātasa jayaṃtasa Hipastratasa*). King, diad. and helmeted, wearing chlamys, on horseback r.; horse prancing.
3	139·5	Æ 1·2		below, [monogram].
4	147·	Æ 1·1		to l., [monogram]; to r., [monogram]; below, [monogram]. [Pl. XIV. 2.]
5	144·	Æ1·05		„ „ „ „ „ [monogram]. [I. O. C.]
6	34·6	Æ ·75		to l., [monogram]; to r., [monogram]; below, [monogram]. [Pl. XIV. 3.]
			Similar.	Similar, horse walking.
7	143·2	Æ1·1		to l., [monogram]; to r., [monogram]; below, [monogram]. [Pl. XIV. 4.]
8	144·8	Æ1·05		„ „ „ „ „ „
9	143·	Æ1·1		„ „ „ „ „ [monogram]. [I. O. C.]

No.	Wt.	Metal. Size.	Obverse.	Reverse.
10	143·	AR 1·15	ΒΑΣΙΛΕΩΣ ΣΩΤΗΡΟΣ ΙΠΠΟΣΤΡΑΤΟΥ Bust of the king r., diad.	(*Maharajasa tradatasa jayaṃtasa Hipastratasa*). King, diad. and helmeted, wearing chlamys, on horseback r.; horse prancing. below, . [I. O. C. Pl. XIV. 5.]

(γ) *Bronze; square.*

No.	Wt.	Metal. Size.	Obverse.	Reverse.
11		Æ 1·05	ΒΑΣΙΛΕΩΣ ΣΩΤΗΡΟΣ ΙΠΠΟΣΤΡΑΤΟΥ Triton, facing, his body ending in fish's tails; holds dolphin and rudder.	(*Maharajasa tradatasa Hipastratasa*). City l., turreted; holds in l. hand, palm; r. advanced. to l., ; to r., [illegible].
12		Æ 1·		" " " "
13		Æ 1·		" " " " [I. O. C. Pl. XIV. 6.]
14		Æ ·9	Same inscr. Apollo r., clad in chlamys; holds arrow in both hands; quiver at shoulder.	Same inscr. Tripod. to l., ; to r., [illegible]. [Pl. XIV. 7.]
15		Æ ·85	Same inscr. Pallas, helmeted, seated l. on throne; holds in r., taenia; in l., spear.	(*Maharajasa tradatasa jayaṃtasa Hipastratasa*). Horse l., in square of fillet-pattern. to l., .
16		Æ ·8		" " [I. O. C. Pl. XIV. 8.]
17		Æ ·85		" "

AMYNTAS.

(α) *Silver; type, Pallas.*

No.	Wt.	Metal. Size.	Obverse.	Reverse.
			ΒΑΣΙΛΕΩΣ ΝΙΚΑΤΟΡΟΣ ΑΜΥΝΤΟΥ Bust of the king r., diad., helmeted.	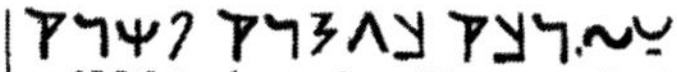 (*Māhārajasa jayadharasa Amitasa*). Pallas l.; holding in l. hand, aegis; and with r. hurling thunderbolt.
1	127·2	AR 1·		to l., . [Pl. xiv. 9.]

(β) *Silver; type, Zeus.*

No.	Wt.	Metal. Size.	Obverse.	Reverse.
			ΒΑΣΙΛΕΩΣ ΝΙΚΑΤΟΡΟΣ ΑΜΥΝΤΟΥ Bust of the king r., diad.	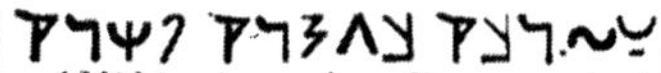 (*Māhārajasa jayadharasa Amitasa*). Zeus seated l. on throne; in r. hand, Nike; in l., palm and sceptre.
2	33·4	AR ·65		to l., .
3	36·2	AR ·65		to r., „ [I. O. C. Pl. xiv. 10.]

(γ) *Bronze; square.*

No.	Wt.	Metal. Size.	Obverse.	Reverse.
			ΒΑΣΙΛΕΩΣ ΝΙΚΑΤΟΡΟΣ ΑΜΥΝΤΟΥ Bearded bust r., radiate, in Phrygian cap; sceptre over shoulder.	(*Māhārajasa jayadharasa Amitasa*). Pallas standing l., her r. hand advanced; in her l., spear and shield.
4		Æ ·8		to l., .
5		Æ ·8		„ . [I. O. C. Pl. xiv. 11.]

HERMAEUS.

(*a*) *Silver.*

No.	Wt.	Metal. Size.	Obverse.	Reverse.
			ΒΑΣΙΛΕΩΣ ΣΩΤΗΡΟΣ ΕΡΜΑΙΟΥ Bust of the king r., diad.	(*Māhārajasa tradatasa Heramayasa*). Zeus, laur., seated l. on throne with back; his r. hand advanced; in his l., sceptre.
1	150·7	Æ 1·		to r., . [I. O. C. Pl. xv. 1.]
2	148·6	Æ 1·		„ .
3	144·1	Æ 1·		„ .
4	143·3	Æ 1·		„ . [I. O. C. Pl. xv. 2.]
5	35·4	Æ ·65		to r., .
6	34·7	Æ ·65		„ „ [I. O. C.]
7	33·8	Æ ·65		„ .
8	33·	Æ ·65		„ „ „
9	36·	Æ ·65		„ .
10	36·	Æ ·7		„ .
11	36·5	Æ ·65		„ . [Pl. xv. 3.]
12	36·3	Æ ·7		„ . [I. O. C.]

No.	Wt.	Metal. Size.	Obverse.	Reverse.
	–		ΒΑΣΙΛΕΩΣ ΣΩΤΗΡΟΣ ΕΡΜΑΙΟΥ Bust of the king r., diad.	(*Māhārajasa tradatasa Heramayasa*). Zeus, laur., seated l. on throne with back; his r. hand advanced; in his l., sceptre.
13	32·8	Æ ·65		to r., [monogram].
14	34·5	Æ ·6		„ „ [I. O. C.]
15	37·3	Æ ·65		to l., [monogram].
16	35·	Æ ·65		„ [monogram]; to r., [monogram]. [I. O. C.]
17	36·3	Æ ·6		„ „ „ „
18	37·5	Æ ·6		„ [monogram].
19	50·	Æ ·7 (plated)		„ „
			ΒΑΣΙΛΕΩΣ ΣΩΤΗΡΟΣ ΕΡΜΑΙΟΥ Similar type.	Similar.
20	140·6	Æ 1·1		to l., [monogram]; to r., [monogram] ϛ. [Pl. xv. 4.]
21	144·6	Æ 1·		„ [monogram]; „ ᴗ.
22	34·9	Æ ·65		to l., [monogram]; to r., [monogram].
23	29·4	Æ ·65		„ [monogram].
			ΒΑΣΙΛΕΩΣ ΣΩΤΗΡΟΣ ΕΡΜΑΙΟΥ Bust of the king r., diad. and helmeted.	Similar.
24	37·7	Æ ·65		to l., [monogram]. [Pl. xv. 5.]

No.	Wt.	Metal. Size.	Obverse.	Reverse.
			(β) Bronze; round; with portrait.	
			ΒΑΣΙΛΕΩΣ ΣΩΤΗΡΟΣ ΕΡΜΑΙΟΥ Bust of the king r., diad.	𐨨𐨱𐨪𐨗𐨯 𐨟𐨿𐨪𐨟𐨟𐨯 𐨱𐨅𐨪𐨨𐨩𐨯 (*Maharajasa tradatasa Heramayasa*). Zeus, laur., seated l. on throne with back; his r. hand advanced; in his l., sceptre.
25		Æ ·95		to l., [monogram]; to r., Ȥ.
26		Æ 1·		„ „ , uncertain Indian letter. [I. O. C. Pl. xv. 6.]
27		Æ ·95		„ „ „ uncertain Indian letter.
28		Æ ·85		„ „ „ ፖ. [I. O. C.]
29		Æ ·95		„ „ „ uncertain Indian letter.
30		Æ ·9		„ „ „ Ψ. [I. O. C.]
31		Æ ·95		„ „ „ Ƴ.
32		Æ 1·05		„ „ „ „
33		Æ 1·		„ „ „ Ћ.
34		Æ ·95		„ „ „ „
35		Æ ·95		„ „ „ Ψ.
36		Æ 1·		„ „ „ ς. [I. O. C.]
37		Æ ·95		„ [monogram]; „ ∾.

No.	Wt.	Metal. Size.	Obverse.	Reverse.
			ΒΑΣΙΛΕΩΣ ΣΩΤΗΡΟΣ ΕΡΜΑΙΟΥ Bust of the king r., diad.	[Kharoshthi inscription] (*Maharajasa tradatasa Heramayasa*). Zeus, laur., seated l. on throne with back; his r. hand advanced; in his l., sceptre.
38		Æ ·9		to l., [monogram]; to r., [letter]. [I. O. C.]
39		Æ ·9		" " " [letter].
40		Æ ·9		" " " [letter]. "
41		Æ ·6		to l., [monogram]; to r., [letter].
42		Æ ·6		" " " [letter]. [I. O. C.]
43		Æ ·7		" " " [letter]. [Pl. xv. 7.]
44		Æ ·6		" [monogram]; " [letter]. [I. O. C.]

(γ) *Bronze; round;* **ΣV** *inserted after* **Σ[Ω]ΤΗΡΟΣ**.*

No.	Wt.	Metal. Size.	Obverse.	Reverse.
			ΒΑΣΙΛΕΩΣ ΣΤΗΡΟΣ ΣV ΕΡΜΑΙΟΥ Bust of the king r., diad.	[Kharoshthi inscription] (*Maharajasa mahatasa Heramayasa*). Type as last, degraded.
45		Æ ·8		to l., (?); to r., [monogram].
46		Æ ·7		" [letter] "
47		Æ ·8		" " "
48		Æ ·75		" " "
			Similar.	Inscr. various. Nike l.; holds wreath and palm.
49		Æ ·65		inscr. [Kharoshthi inscription]. to r., [monogram].
50		Æ ·6	(obscure).	" [Kharoshthi inscription]. to l., [monogram]; to r., [monogram].

* Other coins with the same obverse inscription and type, but bearing on the reverse the name of Kadphises and the type of Herakles, are described among the coins of Kadphises I., below.

No.	Wt.	Metal. Size.	Obverse.	Reverse.
			(δ) *Bronze; square; without portrait.*	
			ΒΑΣΙΛΕΩΣ ΣΩΤΗΡΟΣ ΕΡΜΑΙΟΥ Bearded male bust r., radiate, wearing Phrygian cap.	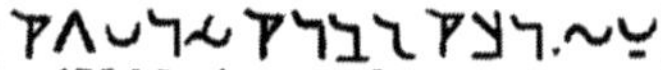 (*Māhārajasa tradatasa Heramayasa*). Horse r., trotting.
51		Æ ·8		below, .
52		Æ ·75		„ „
53		Æ ·75		„ . [I. O. C.]
54		Æ ·75		„ „ „
55		Æ ·75		„ „ [I. O. C. Pl. xv. 8.]
			HERMAEUS AND CALLIOPE.	
			(a) *Silver.*	
			ΒΑΣΙΛΕΩΣ ΣΩΤΗΡΟΣ ΕΡΜΑΙΟΥ ΚΑΙ ΚΑΛΛΙΟΠΗΣ Busts jugate r. of the King and Queen, both diad.	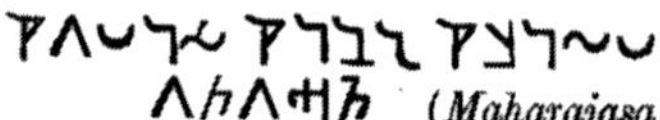 (*Maharajasa tradatasa Heramayasa Kaliyapaya*). King, helmeted and diad., r. on horseback; horse prancing, bow and lance on his back.
1	36·2	AR ·65		below, . [Pl. xv. 9.]
2	33·2	AR ·6		„ „ [I. O. C. Pl. xv. 10.]

RANJABALA.

(a) Silver.

No.	Wt.	Metal. Size.	Obverse.	Reverse.
1	38·	Æ ·55	BACIΛЄI BACIΛЄωC CωTHPOC PAΙY Bust of the king r., diad.	(*Apratihata-chakrasa chhatrapasa Rajabulasa*). Pallas l.; holding in l. hand aegis, and with r., hurling thunderbolt. to l., ; to r., . [Pl. xv. 11.]
2	36·8	Æ ·55	Blundered inscr. Same type.	. . . (*Chhatrapasa Apra . . . chakrasa Rajabulasa*). Same type. to l., ; to r., . [Pl. xv. 12.]
3	36·6	Æ ·55	(both sides blundered).	„ „ „ „
4	36·4	Æ ·55	(inscr. BA MOC-CωTHPOCPA).	„ „ „ „
5	36·	Æ ·55		„ „ „ „ . (name, *Ramjabulasa*).
6	30·8	Æ ·55		„ ; „ .
7	35·7	Æ ·5		„ ; „ . (Inscr., . . . *mahachhatrapasa*, &c.)
8	35·8	Æ ·5		„ ; „ . „

MAUES.

(*a*) *Bronze ; round ; Greek legend only.*

No.	Wt.	Metal. Size.	Obverse.	Reverse.
			Head of elephant r. ; bell round neck.	**ΒΑΣΙΛΕΩΣ ΜΑΥΟΥ** Caduceus.
1		Æ 1·15		to l., [monogram]. [I. O. C. Pl. XVI. 1.]
2		Æ 1·15		" "

(*β*) *Silver ; type, Zeus.*

No.	Wt.	Metal. Size.	Obverse.	Reverse.
			ΒΑΣΙΛΕΩΣ ΒΑΣΙΛΕΩΝ ΜΕΓΑΛΟΥ ΜΑΥΟΥ Zeus standing l., clad in himation; r. hand extended; in l., long sceptre.	(*Rajadirajasa mahatasa Moasa*). Nike r. ; holds wreath and palm bound with fillet.
3	151·	AR 1·15		to r., [monogram]. [Pl. XVI. 2.]

(*γ*) *Bronze ; round ; type, King on horseback.*

No.	Wt.	Metal. Size.	Obverse.	Reverse.
			ΒΑΣΙΛΕΩΣ ΒΑΣΙΛΕΩΝ ΜΕΓΑ[ΛΟΥ [ΜΑΥΟΥ?] King r. on horseback ; whip over shoulder ; lance couched.	(*Rajadirajasa mahatasa Moasa*). Female figure, facing, diad. ; holds in r. hand, patera, containing offerings ; l. rests on wheel ; on head, turreted crown. (Tyche).
4		Æ 1·2	to r., [monogram].	to l., ΨϚ. [Pl. XVI. 3.]

No.	Wt.	Metal. Size.	Obverse.	Reverse.
			(δ) Bronze; round; other types.	
5		Æ 1·	ΒΑΣΙΛΕΩΣ ΒΑΣΙΛΕΩΝ ΜΕΓΑΛΟΥ ΜΑΥΟΥ Artemis running r., radiate, with veil floating round her head; clad in short chiton and boots.	(*Rajadirajasa mahatasa Moasa*). Indian humped bull l. to l., [monogram]. [Pl. xvi. 4.]
6		Æ 1·		" "
7		Æ 1·		" [monogram].
8		Æ 1·05	Same inscr. Herakles, facing; holds in l., club and lion's skin.	Same inscr. Maneless lion l. to l., [monogram]. [Pl. xvi. 5.]
			(ε) Bronze; square; type, King on horseback.	
9		Æ ·9	ΒΑΣΙΛΕΩΣ ΒΑΣΙΛΕΩΝ ΜΕΓΑΛΟΥ ΜΑΥΟΥ King r. on horseback; whip over shoulder; r. hand advanced.	(*Rajadirajasa mahatasa Moasa*). Pallas r., her garment flying; holds in l. hand, spear and shield; r. extended; before her, altar. to r., ΨϚ. [Pl. xvi. 6.]
10		Æ 1·	Same inscr. King r. on horseback; whip over shoulder; lance couched.	Same inscr. Nike l.; holds wreath and palm. to l., [monogram]. [Pl. xvi. 7.]

No.	Wt.	Metal. Size.	Obverse.	Reverse.
			(ζ) *Bronze; square; other types.*	
11		Æ ·95	ΒΑΣΙΛΕΩΣ ΒΑΣΙΛΕΩΝ ΜΕΓΑΛΟΥ ΜΑΥΟΥ Draped female figure facing, holds sceptre transversely; on her head, crescent; and on either side, star.	(*Rajadirajasa mahātasa Moasa*). Nike l.; holds wreath and palm. to l., $\overset{A}{T}$. [Pl. xvi. 8.]
12		Æ 1·	Same inscr. Zeus, laur., seated l. on throne; holds in l. hand sceptre; r. extended towards small winged female figure, who seems to be an embodiment of the thunderbolt.	Same inscr. Female figure, facing, wearing turreted crown and holding long sceptre; holds out in r. hand her veil. (Tyche). to l., $\overset{A}{T}$. [Pl. xvi. 9.]
13		Æ ·9		" "
14		Æ 1·1	Same inscr. Zeus, seated l. on throne; holds in r. hand Nike, who carries wreath and palm; before him, forepart of elephant r., with trunk raised.	Same inscr. Herakles, facing; holds in l. hand, club and lion's skin; with r., crowns himself?
15		Æ ·95	Same inscr. Poseidon l., clad in himation; r. hand on hip; in l., trident; r. foot placed on shoulder of a river-god.	Same inscr. Female figure, clad in chiton and himation, facing; stands between two vines. (Maenad?). to l., $\overset{A}{T}$. [I. O. C. Pl. xvii. 1.]
16		Æ ·9	(Poseidon raises r. hand); to r., [monogram].	[I. O. C.]

No.	Wt.	Metal. Size.	Obverse.	Reverse.
17		Æ ·9	**ΒΑΣΙΛΕΩΣ ΒΑΣΙΛΕΩΝ ΜΕΓΑΛΟΥ ΜΑΥΟΥ** Poseidon striding l., hurling thunderbolt to r., and holding in left hand aplustre; beside him, river-god, leaping up.	(*Rajadirajasa mahātasa Moasa*). Female figure, clad in chiton and himation, facing; stands between two vines. (Maenad ?). to l., . [I. O. C. Pl. xvii. 2.]
18		Æ 1·1	Same inscr. Male figure l., chlamys flying behind; holds club and trident. to l., .	Same inscr. Female figure r., peplum flying; holds long fillet. to r., ΨϚ. [I. O. C. Pl. xvii. 3.]
19		Æ 1·05		
20		Æ ·9	Same inscr. Female figure l.; r. hand advanced; in l., cornucopiae. (Tyche ?).	Same inscr. Male figure, facing; clad in himation; r. hand on hip; wears petasus. (Hermes ?). to l., A Τ. [Pl. xvii. 4.]
21		Æ ·9	Same inscr. Elephant running r., holds in trunk, wreath: in square of fillet-pattern.	Same inscr. King, facing, seated cross-legged on cushion; sword on his knees: in square of fillet-pattern. to r., . [Pl. xvii. 5.]
22		Æ ·9		" "
23		Æ ·9		" .
24		Æ ·85		" "
25		Æ 1·05	Similar.	Same inscr. Indian humped bull r. to r., . [Pl. xvii. 6.]

No.	Wt.	Metal. Size.	Obverse.	Reverse.
			ΒΑΣΙΛΕΩΣ ΜΑΥΟΥ Apollo l.; holds in r. hand arrow; in l., bow.	𐨨𐨱𐨪𐨗𐨯 𐨨𐨆𐨀𐨯 (*Maharajasa Moasa*). Tripod, in square of dots.
26		Æ ·6	to l., M.	[Pl. xvii. 7.]
27		Æ ·55	„ M.	
			Same inscr. Horse r., trotting.	Same inscr. Bow in case.
28		Æ ·8		to l., M.

No.	Wt.	Metal. Size.	Obverse.	Reverse.
			AZES.	
			(a) *Silver; type, Zeus.*	
			ΒΑΣΙΛΕΩΣ ΒΑΣΙΛΕΩΝ ΜΕΓΑΛΟΥ ΑΖΟΥ The king r., on horseback; holds lance, couched.	(*Maharajasa rajarajasa mahatasa Ayasa*). Zeus l., radiate; r. hand advanced; in l., long sceptre.
1	146·5	Æ 1·1	below, Ƴ.	to l., [monogram]; to r., Ƴ. [Pl. XVII. 8.]
			Similar.	Same inscr. Zeus, facing, laur.; holds winged thunderbolt and long sceptre.
2	145·7	Æ 1·15		to l., [monogram]; to r., Ƶ. [I. O. C. Pl. XVII. 9.]
3	150·3	Æ 1·05		,, ,, ,, ,,
4	140·6	Æ 1·1	below, [monogram].	,, [monogram]; ,, ɂ. [I. O. C.]
5	35·5	Æ ·65		to l., [monogram]; to r., Ƶ. [I. O. C. Pl. XVII. 10.]
			Similar.	Same inscr. Zeus, facing, laur.; hurls with r., thunderbolt; and holds in l., long sceptre.
6	37·9	Æ ·7	below, Ψ.	to l., [monogram]; to r., ɂ. [Pl. XVII. 11.]
7	35·	Æ ·65	,, ,,	,, ,, ,, ,,

No.	Wt.	Metal. Size.	Obverse.	Reverse.
			ΒΑΣΙΛΕΩΣ ΒΑΣΙ-ΛΕΩΝ ΜΕΓΑΛΟΥ ΑΖΟΥ The king r., on horseback; holds whip.	(*Maharajasa rajarajasa mahātasa Ayasa*). Zeus l.; holds in r. hand, wreath-bearing Nike; in l., long sceptre.
8	128·	Æ ·95	below, [monogram].	to l., [monogram]; to r., [monogram].
9	146·7	Æ 1·1	to r., [monogram].	" " " [monogram].
10	140·	Æ 1·1	" [monogram].	" " " [monogram] [monogram].
11	136·8	Æ 1·	" [monogram].	" " " " [I. O. C. Pl. xvii. 12.]
12	142·3	Æ ·95	" [monogram].	" " " "
13	149·	Æ 1·1	" [monogram].	" " " "
14	136·	Æ ·9	" [monogram].	" [monogram]; " [monogram] [monogram].
15	150·4	Æ ·9	" [monogram].	" " " " [I. O. C.]
16	128·7	Æ ·95	" [monogram].	" [monogram]; " [monogram] [monogram]. "
17	148·7	Æ ·95	" [monogram].	" " " [monogram] [monogram].
18	149·	Æ ·9	" [monogram].	" [monogram]; " [monogram] [monogram].
19	147·7	Æ ·95	" [monogram].	" " " " [I. O. C.]
20	147·	Æ ·95	" [monogram].	" [monogram]; " mon. [monogram] "

No.	Wt.	Metal. Size.	Obverse.	Reverse.
			ΒΑΣΙΛΕΩΣ ΒΑΣΙΛΕΩΝ ΜΕΓΑΛΟΥ ΑΖΟΥ The king r., on horseback; holds whip.	𐨨𐨱𐨪𐨗𐨯 𐨪𐨗𐨪𐨗𐨯 𐨨𐨱𐨟𐨯 𐨀𐨩𐨯 (*Maharajaso rajarajasa mahātasa Ayasa*). Zeus l.; holds in r. hand, wreath-bearing Nike; in l., long sceptre.
21	32·9	Æ ·6	to r., Ψ.	to l., [monogram] [letter]; to r., [monogram] [letter].
22	28·5	Æ ·6	" "	" " " "
23	33·3	Æ ·55	" [letter].	" [monogram]; " [letter].
24	34·8	Æ ·6	" [letter].	" " " " [I. O. C. Pl. xvii. 13.]
25	30·	Æ ·6	" [monogram]. (inverted).	" [monogram]; " "
26	36·5	Æ ·6	" [letter].	" " " "
27	37·	Æ ·6	" "	" " " "
28	35·6	Æ ·6	" [letter].	" " " [letter] [letter]. [I. O. C.]
29	36·8	Æ ·6	" [letter].	" " " [letter].
30	33·5	Æ ·55	" [letter].	" [monogram]; " uncertain letter.
31	27·4	Æ ·6	" [letter].	" " " [letter]. [I. O. C.]
32	33·9	Æ ·6	" [letter].	" Σ; " [monogram] [letter].
33	34·	Æ 65	" [letter].	" [monogram]; " mon. [letter].
34	30·5	Æ ·6	" "	" " " " " [I. O. C.]

No.	Wt.	Metal. Size.	Obverse.	Reverse.
			ΒΑΣΙΛΕΩΣ ΒΑΣΙΛΕΩΝ ΜΕΓΑΛΟΥ ΑΖΟΥ The king r., on horseback; holds whip.	[Kharoshthi legend] (*Maharajasa rajarajasa mahātasa Ayasa*). Zeus l.; holds in r. hand, wreath-bearing Nike; in l., long sceptre.
35	31·	Æ ·65	to r., Ψ.	to l., [monogram]; to r., [monogram] [monogram].
36	36·4	Æ ·6	„ [monogram].	„ „ „ „ „
37	36·2	Æ ·6	„ [monogram].	„ „ „ [monogram].
38	37·2	Æ ·6	„ [monogram].	„ „ „ A [monogram].
39	32·9	Æ ·6	„ [monogram].	„ „ „ „ „
40	35·8	Æ ·6	„ [monogram].	„ „ „ O „
41	30·2	Æ ·5	„ [monogram].	„ „ „ „ [monogram]. [I. O. C.]
42	31·	Æ ·55	„ [monogram].	„ „ „ Δ M. [monogram] „
43	33·	Æ ·6	„ [monogram].	„ „ „ [monogram] [monogram].
44	28·7	Æ ·6	„ [monogram].	„ „ „ „ „
45	22·6	Æ ·6	„ [monogram].	„ „ „ „ „
46	35·3	Æ ·6	„ [monogram].	„ „ „ „ [monogram].
47	35·2	Æ ·6	„ [monogram].	„ „ „ „ [monogram].
48	37·2	Æ ·6	„ [monogram].	„ „ „ „ „ [I. O. C.]

No.	Wt.	Metal. Size.	Obverse.	Reverse.
			ΒΑΣΙΛΕΩΣ ΒΑΣΙΛΕΩΝ ΜΕΓΑΛΟΥ ΑΖΟΥ The king r., on horseback; holds whip.	(*Maharajasa rajarajasa mahātasa Ayasa*). Zeus l.; holds in r. hand, wreath-bearing Nike; in l., long sceptre.
49	32·	Æ ·55	to r., h.	to l., ; to r., Ϛ.
50	34·8	Æ ·55	„ Ψ.	„ „ „ .
51	35·5	Æ ·55	„ uncertain letter.	„ „ „ ϵ.
52	34·3	Æ ·55	„ „	„ „ „ „
53	27·5	Æ ·6	„ .	„ „ „ . [I. O. C.]
54	32·	Æ ·6	„ .	„ „ „ „ „
			[Most of the above coins are of base metal and very rude execution. In nos. 16 and 46 the inscr. reads *rajadirajasa*].	
			(*β*) *Silver; type, Poseidon.*	
			ΒΑΣΙΛΕΩΣ ΒΑΣΙΛΕΩΝ ΜΕΓΑΛΟΥ ΑΖΟΥ King r., on horseback; holds whip.	(*Maharajasa rajarajasa mahātasa Ayasa*). Poseidon r.; holds in l. hand, trident.
55	138·	Æ ·95	to r., .	to l., ; to r., . [Pl. XVIII. 1.]

No.	Wt.	Metal. Size.	Obverse.	Reverse.
			(γ) *Silver; type, Pallas.*	
			ΒΑΣΙΛΕΩΣ ΒΑΣΙΛΕΩΝ ΜΕΓΑΛΟΥ ΑΖΟΥ King r., on horseback; holds lance, couched.	(*Maharajasa rajarajasa mahātasa Ayasa*). Pallas l.; in raised r. hand, thunderbolt; l. holds shield.
56	145·8	Æ ·95	to r., .	to l., ; to r., . [Pl. XVIII. 2.]
57	132·6	Æ 1· (plated)	in ex., .	„ „ „ „
58	145·5	Æ 1·05	to r., .	„ „ „ .
59	145·5	Æ ·95		„ „ „ „
60	139·8	Æ 1·	„ .	„ „ „ „
61	147·	Æ 1·	„ .	„ „ „ „ [I. O. C.]
62	32·8	Æ ·65	to r., .	to l., ; to r., .
63	29·6	Æ ·7	„ .	„ „ „ „ [Pl. XVIII. 3.]
64	37·5	Æ ·65	„ .	„ „ „ „
65	35·	Æ ·6	„ .	„ „ „ „
66	36·5	Æ ·7	„ .	„ „ „ „
67	35·	Æ ·7	„ „	„ „ „ „
68	36·7	Æ ·65	„ .	„ „ „ .
69	34·1	Æ ·6	„ „	„ „ „ „ [I. O. C.]

No.	Wt.	Metal. Size.	Obverse.	Reverse.
			ΒΑΣΙΛΕΩΣ ΒΑΣΙΛΕΩΝ ΜΕΓΑΛ Υ ΑΖΟΥ King r., on horseback; holds whip.	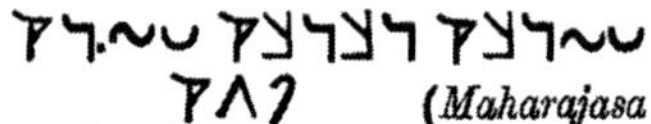 (*Maharajasa rajarajasa mahātasa Ayasa*). Pallas, facing; holds in l. hand, spear and shield; with r., crowns herself.
70	138·5	Æ 1·	to r., .	to l., ; to r., . [Pl. XVIII. 4.]
71	35·	Æ ·6	to r., .	to l., ; to r., .
72	34·5	Æ ·65	" "	" " " " [Pl. XVIII. 5.]
73	38·	Æ ·65	" .	" " " "
74	38·	Æ ·65	" .	" " " "
75	36·4	Æ ·6	" .	" " " "
76	36·	Æ ·65	" .	" " " .
77	39·	Æ ·65	" "	" " " "
78	37·6	Æ ·65	" .	" " " "
79	38·7	Æ ·65	" "	" " " "
80	36·9	Æ ·6	" .	" " " "
81	36·3	Æ ·65	" "	" " " "
82	34·5	Æ ·65	" .	" " " " [I. O. C.]

No.	Wt.	Metal. Size.	Obverse.	Reverse.
			ΒΑΣΙΛΕΩΣ ΒΑΣΙΛΕΩΝ ΜΕΓΑΛΟΥ ΑΖΟΥ King r., on horseback; holds whip.	(*Maharajasa rajarajasa mahātasa Ayasa*). Pallas, facing; holds in l. hand, spear and shield; with r., crowns herself.
83	30·6	Æ ·55	to r., letter.	to l., [monogram]; to r., [monogram].
84	35·3	Æ ·65	" " [monogram].	" [monogram]; " [monogram].
85	33·6	Æ ·65	" "	" " " "
86	36·8	Æ ·65	" [monogram].	" " " "
			Similar.	Same inscr. Pallas, standing l.; r. hand advanced; in l., shield.
87	34·1	Æ ·7	to r., [monogram].	to l., [monogram]; to r., [monogram].
88	36·6	Æ ·6	" [monogram].	" " " [monogram]. [Pl. XVIII. 6.]
			Similar.	Same inscr. Pallas, facing; holds in r. hand, spear; shield slung over back.
89	33·6	Æ ·6	to r., [monogram].	to l., [monogram]; to r., [monogram]. [Pl. XVIII. 7.]

No.	Wt.	Metal. Size.	Obverse.	Reverse.
			ΒΑΣΙΛΕΩΣ ΒΑΣΙΛΕΩΝ ΜΕΓΑΛΟΥ ΑΖΟΥ King r., on horseback; holds whip.	𐨨𐨱𐨪𐨗𐨯 𐨪𐨗𐨪𐨗𐨯 𐨨𐨱𐨟𐨯 𐨀𐨩𐨯 (*Maharajasa rajarajasa mahatasa Ayasa*). Pallas r.; her r. hand advanced; in her l., spear and shield.
90	144·8	Æ ·95	to r., [monogram].	to l., [monogram]; to r., [monogram]. [Pl. XVIII. 8.]
91	146·7	Æ ·95	,, [monogram].	,, [monogram]; ,, [monogram]. (inscr. *rajadirajasa*).
92	140·5	Æ ·95	,, [monogram].	,, [monogram]; ,, [monogram].
93	146·7	Æ ·95	,, ,,	,, ,, ,, [monogram]. (inscr. *rajadirajasa*).
94	130·5	Æ 1·	,, [monogram].	,, Φ [monogram]; ,, [monogram].
95	123·8	Æ 1·05	,, [monogram].	,, [monogram]; ,, [monogram].
96	140·2	Æ 1·	,, [monogram].	,, A [monogram]; ,, [monogram]. [I. O. C.] (inscr. *rajadirajasa*).
97	147·8	Æ ·95	,, [monogram].	,, ,, [letter]; ,, [monogram]. [I. O. C.]
98	143·5	Æ ·95	,, [monogram].	,, ,, ,, ,, ,, ,,
99	142·8	Æ ·95	,, [monogram].	,, ,, ,, ,, ,, ,,
100	147·3	Æ ·95	,, [monogram]; below, uncertain letter.	,, [monogram]; ,, [monogram]. (inscr. *rajadirajasa*).
101	147·	Æ ·95	,, ,,	,, ,, ,, ,, ,,
102	152·9	Æ ·9	,, ,,	,, ,, ,, ,, ,,
103	141·4	Æ ·85	,, [monogram].	,, ,, [monogram]; ,, ,, ,,
104	118·7	Æ ·9	,, [monogram].	,, ,, ,, ,, ,,

No.	Wt.	Metal. Size.	Obverse.	Reverse.
			ΒΑΣΙΛΕΩΣ ΒΑΣΙΛΕΩΝ ΜΕΓΑΛΟΥ ΑΖΟV King r., on horseback; holds whip.	[Kharoshthi] (*Maharajasa rajarajasa mahatasa Ayasa*). Pallas r.; her r. hand advanced; in her l., spear and shield.
105	37·6	Æ ·6	to r., [monogram].	to l., [monogram]; to r., [monogram].
106	36·7	Æ ·65	„ [monogram].	„ „ „ „
107	35·6	Æ ·65		„ „ „ „ [Pl. XVIII. 9.]
108	28·5	Æ ·6	„ uncertain letter.	„ [monogram]; „ [monogram]. [I. O. C.]

(δ) *Silver; type, City?*

No.	Wt.	Metal. Size.	Obverse.	Reverse.
			ΒΑΣΙΛΕΩΣ ΒΑΣΙΛΕΩΝ ΜΕΓΑΛΟΥ ΑΖΟΥ King r., on horseback; holds lance, couched.	[Kharoshthi] (*Maharajasa rajarajasa mahatasa Ayasa*). A City? l.; holds in r. hand, object resembling a brazier; in l., palm bound with fillet.
109	136·5	Æ 1·05	to r., [monogram].	to l., [monogram]; to r., [monogram]. [Pl. XVIII. 10.]
110	143·	Æ 1·	„ [monogram].	„ „ „ „
111	34·3	Æ ·7		to l., [monogram] [monogram]; to r., [monogram]. [Pl. XVIII. 11.]

(ε) *Silver; without figure of King.*

No.	Wt.	Metal. Size.	Obverse.	Reverse.
			ΒΑΣΙΛΕΩΣ ΒΑΣΙΛΕΩΝ ΜΕΓΑΛΟΥ ΑΖΟΥ Zeus l., laur.; r. hand advanced; in l., sceptre held transversely.	𐨨𐨱𐨪𐨗𐨯 𐨪𐨗𐨪𐨗𐨯 𐨨𐨱𐨟𐨯 𐨀𐨩𐨯 (*Maharajasa rajarajasa mahātasa Ayasa*). Nike r., winged; holds wreath and palm bound with fillet.
112	35·5	AR ·7		to r., [monogram]. [Pl. XVIII. 12.]
113	35·1	AR ·7		,, ,,
114	36·7	AR ·7		,, ,, [I. O. C.]

(ζ) *Bronze; type, King, seated.*

No.	Wt.	Metal. Size.	Obverse.	Reverse.
			ΒΑΣΙΛΕΩΣ ΒΑΣΙΛΕΩΝ ΜΕΓΑΛΟΥ ΑΖΟΥ King, facing, seated cross-legged on cushion; holds in r. hand, ankus; in l., sword, which rests on his knees.	𐨨𐨱𐨪𐨗𐨯 𐨪𐨗𐨪𐨗𐨯 𐨨𐨱𐨟𐨯 𐨀𐨩𐨯 (*Maharajasa rajarajasa mahatasa Ayasa*). Hermes l., with chlamys flying; r. hand raised; in l., caduceus.
115		Æ 1·	to l., [monogram].	to l., [monogram]; to r., [monogram].
116		Æ 1·05	,, ,,	,, ,, ,, ,, [I. O. C. Pl. XIX. 1.]
117		Æ ·95	,, [monogram].	,, ,, ,, ,,
118		Æ 1·05	,, ,,	,, [monogram].
119		Æ 1·	,, ,,	,, [monogram]; ,, [monogram].
120		Æ 1·		,, ,, ,, ,,

No.	Wt.	Metal. Size.	Obverse.	Reverse.
			ΒΑΣΙΛΕΩΣ ΒΑΣΙΛΕΩΝ ΜΕΓΑΛΟΥ ΑΖΟΥ King, facing, seated cross-legged on cushion; holds in r. hand, ankus; in l., sword, which rests on his knees.	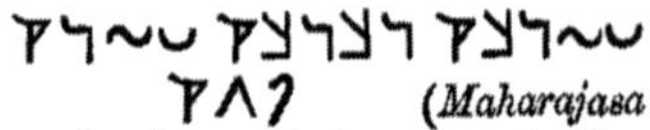 (*Maharajasa rajarajasa mahatasa Ayasa*). Hermes l., with chlamys flying; r. hand raised; in l., caduceus.
121		Æ 1·05	to l., .	to l., ; to r., .
122		Æ ·95	„ uncertain letter.	„ „ „ 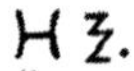. (inscr. *rajadirajasa*).
123		Æ ·95	„ .	„ ; „ 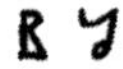.
124		Æ ·7		„ „ „ „
125		Æ 1·	„  (inverted).	„ ; „ . (inscr. *rajadirajasa*).
126		Æ ·9	„ .	„ 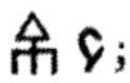; „ 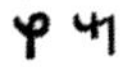.

(η) *Bronze; type, Demeter or City.*

No.	Wt.	Metal. Size.	Obverse.	Reverse.
			ΒΑΣΙΛΕΩΣ ΒΑΣΙΛΕΩΝ ΜΕΓΑΛΟΥ ΑΖΟΥ Demeter? seated l. on throne, modius on head; r. hand raised; in l., cornucopiae.	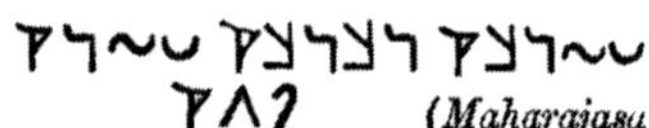 (*Maharajasa rajarajasa mahatasa Ayasa*). Hermes l.; r. hand raised; in l., caduceus.
127		Æ 1·05		to l., ; to r., .
128		Æ 1·05		„ „ „ „
129		Æ 1·05		„ „ „ „ (restruck). [I. O. C. Pl. XIX. 2.]
130		Æ 1·		„ „ „ „ [I. O. C.]
131		Æ 1·		„ „ „ „ „
132		Æ 1·1		„ „

[Restruck on a coin of Azes, cl. κ; types, elephant, humped bull].

No.	Wt.	Metal. Size.	Obverse.	Reverse.
			ΒΑΣΙΛΕΩΣ ΒΑΣΙΛΕΩΝ ΜΕΓΑΛΟΥ ΑΖΟΥ Hermes l., wears chlamys; r. hand advanced; in l., caduceus.	[Kharoshthi legend] (*Maharajasa rajarajasa mahatasa Ayasa*). Demeter? standing l., wears modius; r. hand advanced; in l., cornucopiae.
133		Æ ·75	to l., [monogram].	to l., [monogram]; to r., [Kharoshthi letter]. [Pl. XIX. 3.]
			Same inscr. Lion r.	Similar.
134		Æ ·75		to l., [monogram]; to r., [Kharoshthi letter].
135		Æ ·65	above, [monogram].	" " " ϵ [Kharoshthi letter]. [Pl. XIX. 4.]
136		Æ ·65	" "	" " " o [Kharoshthi letter].

(θ) *Bronze; type, male deity.*

No.	Wt.	Metal. Size.	Obverse.	Reverse.
			ΒΑΣΙΛΕΩΣ ΒΑΣΙΛΕΩΝ ΜΕΓΑΛΟΥ ΑΖΟΥ Female deity, facing, clad in himation; holds in raised r. hand, flower; stands on lotus; beside her, lion? (Lakshmí?).	[Kharoshthi legend] (*Maharajasa rajarajasa mahatasa Ayasa*). Humped bull r.
137		Æ 1·	to l., [monogram].	to r., [Kharoshthi letter]. [Pl. XIX. 5.]

(ι) *Bronze; types, lion and bull.*

No.	Wt.	Metal. Size.	Obverse.	Reverse.
			ΒΑΣΙΛΕΩΣ ΒΑΣΙΛΕΩΝ ΜΕΓΑΛΟΥ ΑΖΟΥ Humped Indian bull r.	[Kharoshthi legend] (*Maharajasa rajadirajasa mahatasa Ayasa*). Lion r.
138		Æ 1·1	above, [monogram].	above, [monogram].
139		Æ 1·1	" "	" "

No.	Wt.	Metal. Size.	Obverse.	Reverse.
			ΒΑΣΙΛΕΩΣ ΒΑΣΙΛΕΩΝ ΜΕΓΑΛΟΥ ΑΖΟΥ Humped Indian bull r.	[Kharoshthi inscription] (*Maharajasa rajadirajasa mahatasa Ayasa*). Lion r.
140		Æ 1·1	above, [monogram].	above, [monogram].
141		Æ 1·	,, [monogram].	,, [monogram].
142		Æ 1·1	,, [monogram]; to r., [monogram].	,, [monogram].
143		Æ 1·05	,, [monogram]; ,, [monogram].	,, [monogram].
144		Æ 1·05	,, ,, ,, [monogram].	,, ,,
145		Æ 1·	,, ,, ,, [monogram].	,, ,,
146		Æ 1·1	,, ,, ,, [monogram].	,, [monogram].
147		Æ ·95	,, ,,	,, [monogram]. [I. O. C.]
148		Æ 1·	,, [monogram].	,, [monogram].
149		Æ 1·1	,, [monogram].	,, [monogram].
150		Æ 1·2	,, ,, ,, [monogram].	,, ,,
151		Æ 1·1	,, [monogram]; ,, ,,	,, [monogram].
152		Æ 1·2	,, [monogram]; ,, [monogram].	,, [monogram]. [Pl. xix. 6.]
153		Æ 1·1	,, ,, ,, [monogram].	,, [monogram].
154		Æ ·85	,, [monogram].	,, [monogram].
155		Æ ·85	,, [monogram]; ,, [monogram]. (inscription barbarous).	to r., [monogram].
156		Æ ·8	,, [monogram].	above, [monogram]. [I. O. C.]

No.	Wt.	Metal. Size.	Obverse.	Reverse.
			(κ) *Bronze ; types, elephant and bull.*	
			ΒΑΣΙΛΕΩΣ ΒΑΣΙΛΕΩΝ ΜΕΓΑΛΟΥ ΑΖΟΥ Elephant r.	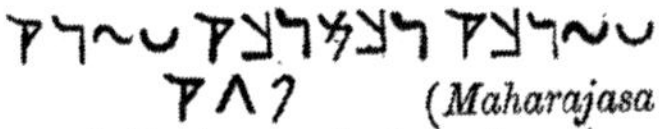 (*Maharajasa rajadirajasa mahatasa Ayasa*). Humped bull r.
157		Æ 1·	above, Α.	above, uncertain letter.
158		Æ ·95	„ „	„ „
159		Æ 1·	„ .	„ 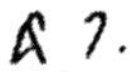. (inscr. *rajarajasa*).
160		Æ 1·05	„ .	„ „ „ [I. O. C." Pl. xix. 7.]
161		Æ 1·	„ .	„ 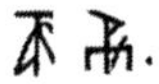. (inscr. *rajarajasa*).
162		Æ 1·	„ .	„ „ „ „ [I. O. C.]
163		Æ ·95	„ „	„ . „
164		Æ 1·1	„ .	„ „ „ „ „
165		Æ 1·05	„ .	„ „ „ „ „
166		Æ 1·05	„ „	„ „ . „
167		Æ 1·05	„ „	„ „ . „
168		Æ 1·05		„ „ .
169		Æ ·75	(inscriptions obscure).	[I. O. C.]
			[In several of the above coins the king's name is misspelt, and appears as ΑΟΖΥ, ΑΟΖΖΥ, ΑΖΟΥ, and so forth.]	

No.	Wt.	Metal. Size.	Obverse.	Reverse.
			(λ) *Bronze; square; type, King on horseback.*	
			ΒΑΣΙΛΕΩΣ ΒΑΣΙΛΕΩΝ ΜΕΓΑΛΟΥ ΑΖΟΥ The king r., on horseback; holds in r. hand, lance, couched.	[Kharoshthi legend] (*Maharajasa rajarajasa mahatasa Ayasa*). Humped bull r.
170		Æ ·95		above, [monogram] [Kharoshthi letter].
171		Æ ·85		" " " (restruck).
172		Æ 1·		" " [monogram]. [I. O. C. Pl. XIX. 8.]
173		Æ ·95		" [monogram]; to r., [monogram].
174		Æ ·1	(inscr. barbarous).	" "
175		Æ ·9	to r., B.	" [monogram] [Kharoshthi letter].
176		Æ ·85	" "	" " [monogram].
177		Æ 1·		" [monogram] [Kharoshthi letter].
			(μ) *Bronze; square; type, King on camel.*	
			ΒΑΣΙΛΕΩΣ ΒΑΣΙΛΕΩΝ ΜΕΓΑΛΟΥ ΑΖΟΥ King r., seated on camel; holds whip.	[Kharoshthi legend] (*Maharajasa rajarajasa mahatasa Ayasa*). Humped bull r.
178		Æ 1·		to r., [monogram].
179		Æ 1·		" " [I. O. C.]
180		Æ ·85		[Pl. XIX. 9.]

No.	Wt.	Metal. Size.	Obverse.	Reverse.
			(ν) *Bronze; square; type, Poseidon.*	
			ΒΑΣΙΛΕΩΣ ΒΑΣΙΛΕΩΝ ΜΕΓΑΛΟΥ ΑΖΟΥ Poseidon l., clad in himation; r. hand on hip; in l., trident; foot placed on shoulder of river-god.	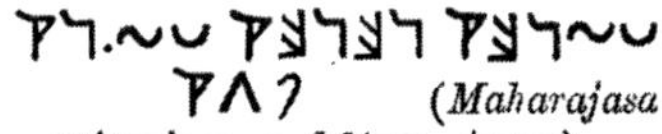 (*Maharajasa rajarajasa mahātasa Ayasa*). Female figure, clad in chiton and himation, facing; holds in each hand, long vine-branch.
181		Æ 1·		to l., . [Pl. XIX. 10.]
182		Æ 1·		" "
183		Æ 1·		" " [I. O. C.]
184*		Æ 1·2		" "
			Same inscr. Male figure l., chlamys flying behind; holds club and trident.	Same inscr. Female figure r., peplum flying; holds long fillet.
185		Æ ·8		to r., .
			(ξ) *Bronze; square; animal types.*	
			ΒΑΣΙΛΕΩΣ ΒΑΣΙΛΕΩΝ ΜΕΓΑΛΟΥ ΑΖΟΥ Herakles, facing; holds in l hand, club and lion's skin; and with r., crowns himself.	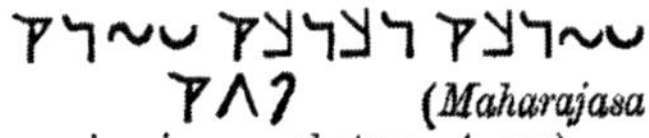 (*Maharajasa rajarajasa mahatasa Ayasa*). Horse r.
186		Æ ·9		above, Ψ.
187		Æ ·95	to l., .	" " [I. O. C. Pl. XIX. 11.]

* Restruck on a coin of Hippostratus; for types see coin of Hippostratus, supra, p. 60, no. 15.

No.	Wt.	Metal. Size.	Obverse.	Reverse.
188		Æ 1·1	ΒΑΣΙΛΕΩΣ ΒΑΣΙΛΕΩΝ ΜΕΓΑΛΟΥ ΑΖΟΥ Elephant r. above, 7.	(*Maharajasa rajarajasa mahatasa Ayasa*). Humped bull r. to r., [monogram].
189		Æ ·45	ΒΑΣΙΛΕΩΣ ΜΕΓΑΛΟΥ ΑΖΟΥ Elephant r.	(*Maharajasa mahatasa Ayasa*). Humped bull r. [Pl. xix. 12.]
190		Æ ·65	ΒΑΣΙΛΕΩΣΒ]ΑΣΙΛΕΩΝΜΕΓΑΛΟΥΑΣ[Lion r. above, [symbol].	(*Maharaja . . . . . Ayasa*). Humped bull l. above, [symbol]. [I. O. C.]

(o) *Billon; semi-barbarous coinage.*

No.	Wt.	Metal. Size.	Obverse.	Reverse.
191	145·4	AR ·85	Corrupt legend. King r., on horseback; holds in r. hand ankus(?); before him, symbol [symbol].*	(*Maharajasa mahatasa dhramikasa rajadirajasa Ayasa*). City l., turreted, and clad in chiton and peplum; r. hand advanced; in l., cornucopiae. to l., [symbol]; to r., [symbol]. [Pl. xx. 1.]
192	141·	AR ·8		" " " "
193	142·2	AR ·8		" " " "

* On most of these coins there is an appearance of various Indian letters in the obverse field which are not here inserted, it being doubtful whether they are not mere blunders.

No.	Wt.	Metal. Size.	Obverse.	Reverse.
			Corrupt legend. King r., on horseback; holds in r. hand ankus(?); before him, symbol .	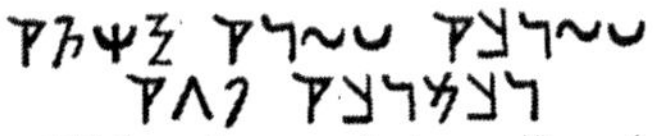 (*Maharajasa mahatasa dhramikasa rajadirajasa Ayasa*). City l., turreted, and clad in chiton and peplum; r. hand advanced; in l., cornucopiae.
194	145·9	Æ ·85		to l., ; to r., .
195	131·5	Æ ·8		„ „ „ „
196	148·2	Æ ·85		„ „ „ . [I. O. C.]
197	144·	Æ ·75		„ „ „ „ „
198	148·5	Æ ·85		„ „ „ „ „
199	142·8	Æ ·8		„ „ „ „ „

(π) *Billon; with name of Aspavarma.*

No.	Wt.	Metal. Size.	Obverse.	Reverse.
			ΒΑΣΙΛΕΩΣ ΒΑΣΙΛΕΩΝ ΜΕΓΑΛΟΥ ΑΖΟΥ King r., on horseback; holds ankus; behind him, bow on saddle; beneath, .	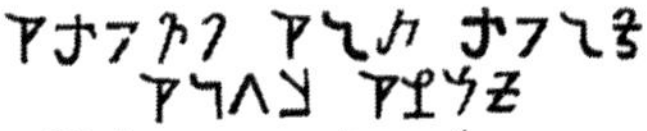 (*Indravarma putrasa Aspavarmasa strategasa jayatasa*). Pallas r., armed; her r. hand advanced; in her l., spear and shield; behind, star and .
200	157·3	Æ ·85	to r., .	to r., ; to l., uncertain letter. [Pl. xx. 2.]
201	140·3	Æ ·8	„ „	„ „ „ .
202	150·9	Æ ·8	„ „	„ „ „ .
203	156·9	Æ ·8	„ „	„ „ „ .
204	146·8	Æ ·8	„ „	„ „ „ .
205	148·3	Æ ·8	„ „	„ „ „ „
206	130·5	Æ ·8	„ „	„ „ „ .

No.	Wt.	Metal. Size.	Obverse.	Reverse.
			ΒΑΣΙΛΕΩΣ ΒΑΣΙΛΕΩΝ ΜΕΓΑΛΟΥ ΑΖΟΥ King r., on horseback; holds ankus; behind him, bow on saddle; beneath, .	(*Indravarma putrasa Aspavarmasa strategasa jayatasa*). Pallas r., armed; her r. hand advanced; in her l., spear and shield; behind, star and .
207	157·2	Æ ·85	to r., .	to r., ; to l., . [I. O. C.]
208	159·4	Æ ·9	„ „	„ „ „ „ „
209	150·	Æ ·85	„ „	„ „ „ ◡. „
210	155·7	Æ ·8	„ „	„ „ „
211	149·	Æ ·8	„ „	„ uncertain letter. „

AZES AND AZILISES.

(a) *Silver.*

No.	Wt.	Metal. Size.	Obverse.	Reverse.
			ΒΑΣΙΛΕΩΣ . . ΗΜΓΑΛΟΥ ΑΖΛΙΣΟΥ The king r., on horseback; holds bow.	(*Maharajasa* [*rajaraja*]*sa mahatasa Ayasa*). Zeus standing l., diad.; holds Nike and long sceptre.
1	31·7	Æ ·6	in front, ◡.	to l., ; to r., . [I. O. C. Pl. xx. 3.]

No.	Wt.	Metal. Size.	Obverse.	Reverse.
			AZILISES.	
			(α) Silver; type, Zeus.	
			ΒΑΣΙΛΕΩΣ ΒΑΣΙΛΕΩΝ ΜΕΓΑΛΟΥ ΑΖΙΛΙΣΟΥ The king r., on horseback; in r. hand, ankus; bow on saddle.	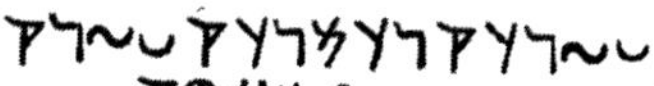 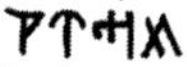 (*Maharajasa rajadirajasa mahatasa Ayilishasa*). Zeus r., diad., wearing himation; holds wreath (?) and long sceptre.
1	148·5	Æ 1·05	to r., .	to l., Λ; to r., . [Pl. xx. 4.]
			(β) Silver; type, Dioscuri.	
			ΒΑΣΙΛΕΩΣ ΒΑΣΙΛΕΩΝ ΜΕΓΑΛΟΥ ΑΖΙΛΙΣΟΥ The king r., on horseback; holds ankus; bow on saddle.	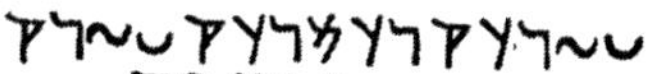 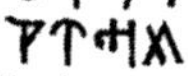 (*Maharajasa rajadirajasa mahatasa Ayilishasa*). The Dioscuri, facing; each wears Phrygian cap and chlamys, and holds spear and sword.
2	146·2	Æ 1·05	to r., .	
3	150·4	Æ 1·05	„ ; below, .	to l., ; to r., . [Pl. xx. 5.]
4	33·3	Æ ·65	„ „	„ „ „ „ [I. O. C. Pl. xx. 6.]
			Similar.	Same inscr. One of the Dioscuri, facing, as above, but bearded and wearing chiton.
5	146·8	Æ 1·1	to r., .	to l., . [Pl. xx. 7.]
6	37·8	Æ ·6	to r., .	to l., . [Pl. xx. 8.]

No.	Wt.	Metal. Size.	Obverse.	Reverse.
			(γ) *Silver; type, City?*	
			ΒΑΣΙΛΕΩΣ ΒΑΣΙΛΕΩΝ ΜΕΓΑΛΟΥ ΑΖΙΛΙΣΟΥ The king r., on horseback; holds lance couched.	𐨨𐨱𐨪𐨗𐨯 𐨪𐨗𐨪𐨗𐨯 𐨨𐨱𐨟𐨯 𐨀𐨩𐨁𐨫𐨁𐨮𐨯 (*Maharajasa rajarajasa mahatasa Ayilishasa*). City (?) l.; holds in r., uncertain object; in l., palm bound with fillet.
7	140·3	Æ 1·05		to l., [monogram] [monogram]; to r., [monogram]. [Pl. xx. 9.]
8	149·8	Æ 1·05	to r., [monogram].	„ „ „ „
9	146·2	Æ 1·	„ [monogram] [monogram].	„ „ „ „ [I. O. C.]
10	139·5	Æ 1·	„ [monogram] „	„ „ „ „ „
11	144·9	Æ 1·1		„ Σ; „ [monogram]. [Pl. xx. 10.]
12	148·5	Æ 1·05		„ [monogram] [monogram]; „ [monogram].
13	35·8	Æ ·7		to l., [monogram] [monogram]; to r., [monogram].
14	35·3	Æ ·7		„ „ „ „
15	32·6	Æ ·65		„ [monogram]; „ [monogram]. [Pl. xx. 11.]
16	32·9	Æ ·7		„ „ „ [monogram].
17	32·2	Æ 7		„ „ „ [monogram].
18	34·7	Æ ·65		„ „ „ [monogram].
19	36·	Æ ·7		„ „ „ [monogram]. [I. O. C.]
20	35·8	Æ ·65		„ [monogram] [monogram]; „ [monogram].
21	35·	Æ ·65	to r., [monogram].	„ „ „ „
22	36·9	Æ ·7	„ [monogram] [monogram].	„ „

No.	Wt.	Metal. Size.	Obverse.	Reverse.
			(δ) *Bronze; square; type, King on horseback.*	
			ΒΑΣΙΛΕΩΣ ΒΑΣΙΛΕΩΝ ΜΕΓΑΛΟΥ ΑΖΙΛΙΣΟΥ King r., on horseback; holds lance couched.	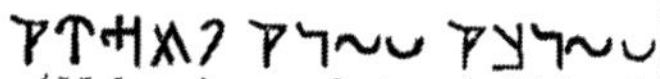 (*Maharajasa mahatasa Ayilishasa*). Herakles, diad., naked, seated l.; holds in r. hand club, which rests on knee.
23		Æ ·9	to r., 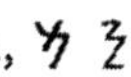.	to l., . [Pl. xxi. 1.]
24		Æ ·95	„ „	„ „ „
			Similar.	Same inscr. Elephant r.
25		Æ ·85		above, 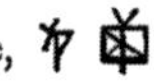.
26		Æ ·75		„ „ „ [I. O. C. Pl. xxi. 2.]
			Similar.	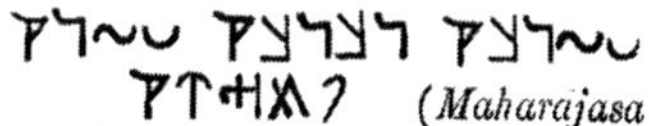 (*Maharajasa rajarajasa mahatasa Ayilishasa*). Humped bull r.
27		Æ ·9		above,  Σ. [Pl. xxi. 3.]
28		Æ 1·05		„ 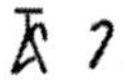.
29		Æ ·95		„ „ „ [I. O. C.]
30		Æ 1·1		„ 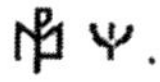.

No.	Wt.	Metal. Size.	Obverse.	Reverse.
			ΒΑΣΙΛΕΩΣ ΒΑΣΙΛΕΩΝ ΜΕΓΑΛΟΥ ΑΖΙΛΙΣΟΥ King r., on horseback; holds lance couched.	(*Maharajasa rajarajasa mahatasa Ayilishasa*). Humped bull l.
31		Æ 1·05		above, Ψ. (restruck coin).
32		Æ ·95	to r.,	„ Σ.
33		Æ ·9	(king to l.)	„ „ „

(ε) *Bronze; square; type, King (?) standing.*

No.	Wt.	Metal. Size.	Obverse.	Reverse.
			ΒΑΣΙΛΕΩΣ ΒΑΣΙΛΕΩΝ ΜΕΓΑΛΟΥ ΑΖΙΛΙΣΟΥ The king (?) standing r., clad in helmet and cloak; holds in l. hand, shield; r. advanced.	(*Maharajasa rajadirajasa mahatasa Ayilishasa*). Nike (?) r., unwinged, clad in short chiton, with inflated veil over her head; holds in r. hand wreath.
34		Æ ·9	to r.,	to r., . [Pl. XXI. 4.]
35		Æ 1·		
36		Æ ·85	„ „	to l., Ψ; to r., uncertain letter. [I. O. C.]
37		Æ ·95	„ „	„ „ „ „ „

(ζ) *Bronze; square; other types.*

No.	Wt.	Metal. Size.	Obverse.	Reverse.
			ΒΑΣΙΛΕΩΣ [ΒΑΣΙΛΕΩΝ ΜΕΓΑ]ΛΥ ΑΖΙΛΙΣΥ Herakles, facing, crowning himself; holds in l. hand club and lion's skin.	(*Maharajasa rajadirajasa mahatasa Ayilishasa*). Horse standing r.
38		Æ ·9	to l.,	above, .
39		Æ ·95	„ „	in field, Ψ . [I. O. C. Pl. XXI. 5.]

No.	Wt.	Metal. Size.	Obverse.	Reverse.
			ΒΑΣΙΛΕΩΣ ΒΑΣΙΛΕΩΝ ΜΕΓΑΛ•Υ ΑΖΙΛΙΣ•Υ Male figure, facing, clad in himation, head turned to r.; holds in r. hand, sceptre; in l., uncertain object.	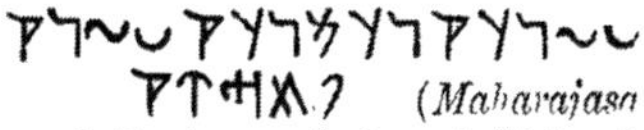 (*Maharajasa rajadirajasa mahatasa Ayilishasa*). Lion r., looking back.
40		Æ 1·05	to l., .	above, . [I. O. C. Pl. xxi. 6.]
			Inscr. obscure. Elephant l.	Inscr. obscure; ends 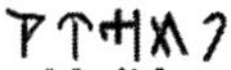 (*Ayilishasa*). Humped bull l.
41		Æ 1·05		to l., mon. [I. O. C.]

No.	Wt.	Metal. Size.	Obverse.	Reverse.
			SPALAHORES, WITH VONONES.	
			(*a*) *Silver.*	
			ΒΑΣΙΛΕΩΣ ΒΑΣΙΛΕΩΝ ΜΕΓΑΛΟΥ ΟΝΩΝΟΥ King r., on horseback; holds lance couched.	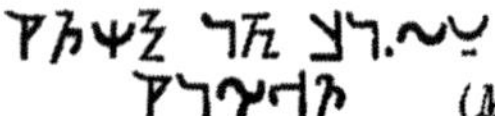 (*Māhāraja bhrata dhramikasa Spalahorasa*). Zeus, laur., facing, clad in himation; holds thunderbolt and long sceptre.
1	144·5	AR 1·05		to r., . [I. O. C. Pl. xxi. 7.]
2	37·5	AR ·6		to r., .
3	37·3	AR ·7		" " [Pl. xxi. 8.]
4	38·	AR ·65		to l., .
5	37·8	AR ·6		" "
			(*β*) *Bronze; square.*	
			ΒΑΣΙΛΕΩΣ ΒΑΣΙΛΕΩΝ ΜΕΓΑΛΟΥ ΟΝΩΝΟΥ Herakles, facing; holds in l. hand, club and lion's skin; and with r., crowns himself.	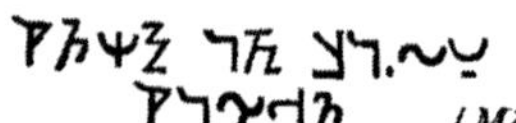 (*Māhāraja bhrata dhramikasa Spalahorasa*). Pallas l., wearing helmet; holds in r. hand, wreath; in l., spear and shield bound with fillet; sword slung round waist.
6		Æ ·85		to l., .
7		Æ ·8		" " [Pl. xxi. 9.]

SPALAGADAMES, WITH VONONES.

(*a*) *Silver.*

No.	Wt.	Metal. Size.	Obverse.	Reverse.
			ΒΑΣΙΛΕΩΣ ΒΑΣΙΛΕΩΝ ΜΕΓΑΛΟΥ ΟΝΩΝΟΥ King r., on horseback; holds lance couched.	*Spalahora putrāsa dhramiasa Spalagadamasa*). Zeus, facing, laur., clad in himation; holds thunderbolt and long sceptre.
1	36·1	AR ·65		to l., [monogram].
2	36·5	AR ·7		" " [Pl. xxi. 10.]
3	36·8	AR ·6		" [monogram].
4	36·2	AR ·65		" " [I. O. C.]

(β) *Bronze; square.*

No.	Wt.	Metal. Size.	Obverse.	Reverse.
			ΒΑΣΙΛΕΩΣ ΒΑΣΙΛΕΩΝ ΜΕΓΑΛΟΥ ΟΝΩΝΟΥ Herakles, facing; holds in l. hand, club and lion's skin; and with r., crowns himself.	*Spalahora putrāsa dhramiasa Spalagadamasa*). Pallas l., wearing helmet; holds in r. hand, wreath (?); in l., spear and shield bound with fillet; sword slung round waist.
5		Æ ·75		to l., [monogram].
6		Æ ·8		" " [Pl. xxi. 11.]

SPALAGADAMES, WITH SPALYRIS.

(a) Bronze; square.

No.	Wt.	Metal. Size.	Obverse.	Reverse.
			ϹΠΑΛΥΡΙΟϹ ΔΙΚΑΙΟΥ ΑΔΕΛΦΟΥ ΤΟΥ ΒΑϹΙΛΕΩϹ King r., on horseback.	(*Spalahora putrāsa dhramiasa Spalagadamasa*). Herakles, diad., seated l. on rocks; holds in r. hand, club, which rests on knee.
1		Æ ·85		to l., [monogram]. [Pl. xxi. 12.]
2		Æ ·8		„ „
3		Æ ·85		„ ⊠.

SPALIRISES; AS KING'S BROTHER.

(a) Silver.

No.	Wt.	Metal. Size.	Obverse.	Reverse.
			ΒΑϹΙΛΕΩϹ ΑΔΕΛΦΟΥ ϹΠΑΛΙΡΙϹΟΥ King r., on horseback; holds lance couched.	* (*Māhāraja bhrahā dhramiasa Spaliriṣasa*). Zeus, facing, wearing himation; holds thunderbolt and long sceptre.
1	36·6	AR ·55		to l., ⊠. [Pl. xxii. 1.]
2	26·7	AR ·6		„ „

* Or *bhratrā*. V. Sallet writes (p. 352), die Form *bhraha* für Bruder wird von sachkundiger Seite für berechtigt erklärt.

SPALIRISES; AS KING.

(*a*) *Bronze; square.*

No.	Wt.	Metal. Size.	Obverse.	Reverse.
			ΒΑCΙΛΕΩΝ ΒΑCΙΛΕΩC ΜΕΓΑΛΟΥ CΠΑΛΙΡΙCΟΥ King, standing l.; holds battle-axe; bow at his side.	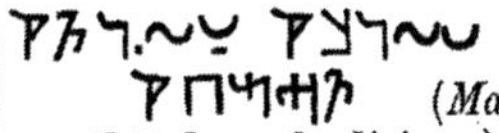 (*Maharajasa māhātakasa Spalirisasa*). Zeus, radiate, seated l. on throne; r. hand extended; in l., sceptre.
1		Æ ·9		to r., .
2		Æ ·9		„ „ *
3		Æ ·95		
4		Æ ·9		„ „ [I. O. C. Pl. XXII. 2.]
5		Æ ·9		„ . [I. O. C.]

* Restruck on copper of Vonones with Spalahores or Spalagadames (?). Club of Herakles seen on obv. (?).

SPALIRISES, WITH AZES.

(a) *Silver.*

No.	Wt.	Metal. Size.	Obverse.	Reverse.
			ΒΑCΙΛΕΩC ΜΕΓΑ-ΛΟΥ ΡΠΑΛΙΡΙCΟΥ King r., on horseback; holds lance couched.	(*Maharajasa mahātakasa Ayasa*). Zeus, facing, laur., clad in himation; holds thunderbolt and long sceptre.
1	37·7	Æ ·6		to l., ; to r., .
2	37·8	Æ ·6		,, ,, ,, ,,
3	34·5	Æ ·65		,, ,, ,, ,, [I. O. C. Pl. XXII. 3.]
4	30·9	Æ ·65		,, ,, ,, ,, [I. O. C.]

(β) *Bronze; round.*

No.	Wt.	Metal. Size.	Obverse.	Reverse.
			ΒΑCΙΛΕΩC ΜΕΓΑ-ΛΟΥ ΙΠΑΛΙΡΙCΟΥ King r., on horseback; holds ankus.	(*Maharajasa mahātakasa Ayasa*). Strung bow and arrow l.
5		Æ ·95		above, ⊗. [Pl. XXII. 4.]

No.	Wt.	Metal. Size.	Obverse.	Reverse.
			GONDOPHARES.	
			(α) *Base silver; type, Zeus.*	
			ΒΑϹΙΛΕШΙϹΙΛΕШΝ ΜΕΓΑΛΙ VИΔΟΦΡΡ The king r., on horseback; arm extended; in front, [illegible].	(*Maharaja rajadiraja tradata devatrata* Gudapharasa*). Zeus, naked to waist, standing r.; r. arm extended; in l., long sceptre.
1	144·2	Æ ·9		to l., [illegible]; to r., [illegible]. [I. O. C. Pl. xxii. 5.]
2	136·5	Æ ·95	inscr. ΒΑϹΙΛΕШϹ ΒΑϹΙΛΕШΝ &c.	„ „ B; „ [illegible]. [I. O. C.]
			(β) *Base silver; type, Pallas.*	
			ΒΑϹΙΛЄ. ΒΑϹΙΛЄѠΝ ΜЄΓΑΛ· ΥΝΔΟΦΕΡΡΟ The king, diad., r., on horseback; to r., [illegible].	(*Maharaja rajadiraja tradata devatrata Gudapharasa*). Pallas r., armed; in her l. hand, spear and shield; her r. advanced.
3	142·	Æ ·95		to l., [illegible]; to r., [illegible]. [Pl. xxii. 6.]
4	143·	Æ ·9	inscr. ΒΑϹΙΛΕѠϹ □V □Ε□V VИΔ□ □ΕΡΡ	„ „ „ „ „
			Inscr. barbarous. Head of the king r., diad.	(or Λ) (*Maharajasa mahatasa Gudapharasa*). Pallas r., fighting; holds thunderbolt and shield.
5	37·6	Æ ·45		in field, [illegible]. [Pl. xxii. 7.]
6	38·5	Æ ·45		„ „ „
7	40·6	Æ ·5		„ „ „

* *Devatrâta*, protected by the Gods. This word has been read by Gen. Cunningham *Devahada*, as a rendering of *θεότροπος*.

No.	Wt.	Metal. Size.	Obverse.	Reverse.
			(γ) *Base silver; type, Siva.*	
			ΒΑCΙΛΕωC ΒΑCΙΛΕωΝ ΜΕΓΑΛΟΥ VΝΔΟΦΕΡΡΟΥ The king l., on horseback; r. hand raised; behind him, Nike flying l., holding wreath and palm; to l., .	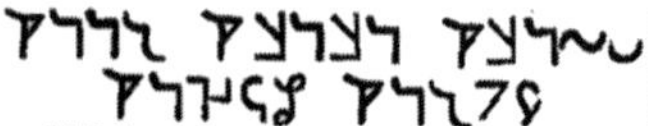 (*Maharajasa rajarajasa tradatasa devatratasa Gudapharasa*). Siva, facing; holds in r. hand, trident; in l., palm.
8	146·2	Æ ·95		to l., ; to r., . [Pl. xxii. 8.] 
9	137·4	Æ ·95	below, .	" " " " [I. O. C.] (Λ for  in inscr.)
			ΒΑCΙΛΕШΝ ΒΑCΙΛΕШΙΙ ΓΟΝΔΟΦΑΓΟΥ The king r., on horseback; holds ankus in extended r. hand; to r., .	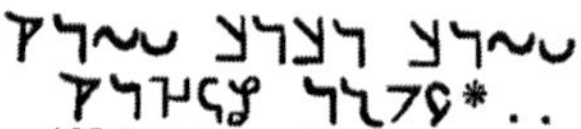 (*Maharaja rajaraja mahatasa . . devatrata Gudapharasa*). Siva, facing; r. extended; in l., trident.
10	145·8	Æ ·95	below, .	to l., ; to r., mon. [I. O. C. Pl. xxii. 9.]
11	146·7	Æ ·9	" "	" " " "
			(δ) *Base silver; type, Nike.*	
			ΒΑ CΙΛΕ The king, diad., seated l. on throne with back; on the top of which ; r. hand raised.	ΑΛΟVVΝΔΟΦ Nike r.; holds wreath and palm.
† 12	108·5	Æ ·85		to l., ; to r., Φ. [Pl. xxii. 10.]

* The missing letters look like 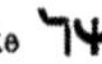 *mita* (for *mitra* ?).

† This coin, as well as some of those which precede it, is apparently wholly or almost wholly made of copper; but the nature of the types indicates that it was intended to pass among the debased silver coins of the period.

No.	Wt.	Metal. Size.	Obverse.	Reverse.
			(ϵ) *Copper; type, Nike.*	
			BACIΛEΩC CΩTHPOC YNΔOΦEPPOV Bust of the king r., diad.	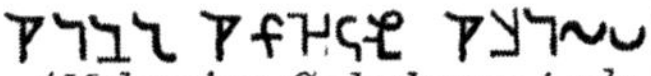 (*Maharajasa Gudaphanasa tradatasa*). Nike r.; holds wreath and palm.
13		Æ ·9		
14		Æ 1·		
15		Æ ·95		
16		Æ ·95		
17		Æ ·85	(ω for Ω in inscr.).	
18		Æ ·95		
19		Æ ·9		
20		Æ ·9		
21		Æ ·9	(inscr. begins BACIΛEON).	[I. O. C. Pl. xxii. 11.]
			(ζ) *Bronze; square.*	
			ΦAΓOV EΓAΛOV ΓONΔA *sic.* King l., on horseback; received by Nike, who holds wreath.	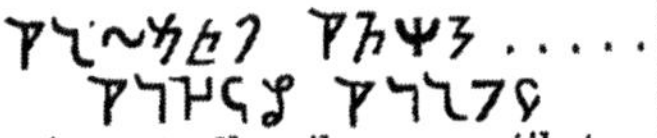 (. . . . . *dhamikasa apratihatasa devatratasa* (*devahadasa*) *Gadapharasa*). .
22		Æ ·85		to l., ; to r., . [I. O. C. Pl. xxii. 12.]

No.	Wt.	Metal. Size.	Obverse.	Reverse.
			(η) *Base silver; with inscr. Sasasa.*	
			Inscr. corrupt. The king, diad., r., on horseback; r. hand raised; to r., .	(*Maharajasa mahatasa devatratasa* (*devahadasa*) *Gadapharasa*); in ex., (*Sasasa*). Zeus, diad., standing r.; r. hand advanced; in l., long sceptre; to l., .
23	149·8	Æ ·9	below, ; to r., .	to l., uncertain letter; to r., .
24	153·4	Æ ·85	,, .	below, A; to r., .
25	138·	Æ ·8	,, uncertain letters.	,, B; ,, ,, ,,
26	148·	Æ ·8	,, .	,, N; ,, ,, ,,
27	129·5	Æ ·8	,, ,, ,,	,, ,, ,, ,, ,,
28	154·3	Æ ·85	,, ,,	,, ; ,, ,, ,,
29	134·9	Æ ·8	(obscure).	(obscure).
			Similar.	.... (*Maharajasa rajadirajasa .... Gadapharasa*); in ex., (*Sasasa*). Zeus l.; Nike in extended r. hand.
30	152·5	Æ ·8	to r., 7.	to l., ; to r., . [I. O. C. Pl. XXII. 13.]
31	151·8	Æ ·85	,, ,,	,, ,, ,, ,, [I. O. C.]
32	150·7	Æ ·8	,, .	,, ,, ,, ,, ,,

ABDAGASES.

(a) Copper; as King.

No.	Wt.	Metal. Size.	Obverse.	Reverse.
			ΒΑCΙΛΕωC CωΤΗ-ΡΟC Α[ΒΔΑΓ]ΑCΟV Bust of the king r., diad.	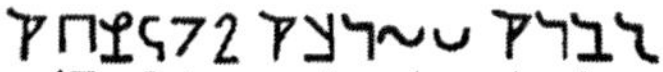 (*Tradatasa maharajasa Avadagaṣasa*). Nike r., holding wreath and palm.
1		Æ ·85		[Pl. XXIII. 1.]
2		Æ ·85		to l., uncertain letters.
3		Æ ·9		
4		Æ ·9	(inscr. ΒΑCΙΛΕΥC CωΤΗΡ . . . .).	

(β) Base silver; as King's nephew.

No.	Wt.	Metal. Size.	Obverse.	Reverse.
			ΒΑΣΙΛΕΥΟΝΤΟΣ ΒΑΣΙΛΕωΝΙ ΑΒ-ΔΑΓΑΣΟΥ (The ΒΑ of Abdagases' name read sometimes as the first letters of ΒΑΣΙΛ-ΕΥΟΝΤΟΣ; the letter which follows ΒΑ-ΣΙΛΕΩΝ is uncertain [Ι or Σ?]). The king l., on horseback; in front, .	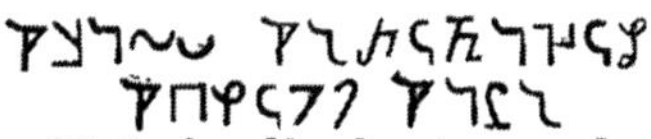 (*Gadapharabhradaputrasa maharajasa tradatasa Avadagaṣasa*). Zeus, standing r.; holds sceptre; r. hand advanced.
5	150·	AR ·85	to l., .	to l., ; to r., 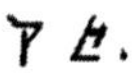.
6	155·5	AR ·9	„ „	„ 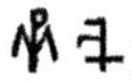; „ 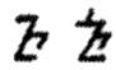. [Pl. XXIII. 2.]
7	150·1	AR ·85	„ „	„ „ „ „ „ „

No.	Wt.	Metal. Size.	Obverse.	Reverse.
			ΒΑΣΙΛΕΥΟΝΤΟΣ ΒΑΣΙΛΕΩΝΙ ΑΒ-ΔΑΓΑΣΟΥ (The ΒΑ of Abdagases' name read sometimes as the first letters of ΒΑΣΙΛ-ΕΥΟΝΤΟΣ; the letter which follows ΒΑ-ΣΙΛΕΩΝ is uncertain [Ι or Σ?]). The king l., on horseback; in front, ☿.	(*Gadapharabhradaputrasa maharajasa tradatasa Avadagaṣasa*). Zeus, standing r.; holds sceptre; r. hand advanced.
8	149·5	Æ ·85		to l., ; to r., . [I. O. C.]
9	149·2	Æ ·85	to l., .	,, ,, ,, Β; ,, ,, ,,
10	146·4	Æ ·8	,, .	,, ,, ,, ,, ,,
11	142·5	Æ ·9	,, .	,, ,, ,, ,, ,, ,,
12	158·5	Æ ·85	,, .	,, ,, ,, ,, ,, ,,
13	142·4	Æ ·95	type r.	,, ,, ,, .
14	150·2	Æ ·95	,,	,, ,, ,, ,, . [I. O. C.]
15	124·4	Æ ·85	,,	,, ,, ,, .
16	121·5	Æ ·85	inscr. ΓΥ]ΝΔΙΦΕΡΟΑ-ΔΕΛΦΙ[ΔΕΩϹ	,, ; ,, . [Pl. XXIII. 3.]

ORTHAGNES.

(a) *Bronze.*

No.	Wt.	Metal. Size.	Obverse.	Reverse.
			ΒΑCIΛЄVC ΒΑCIΛЄΩΝ ΜЄΓΑC ΟΡΘΑΓΝΗC Bust of the king l., diad.; wears torquis.	[Kharoshthi] (*Maharajasa rajadirajasa mahatasa Gudaphara sagaba. ?*).* Nike r.; holds wreath and palm.
1		Æ ·9		to l., [Kharoshthi]; to r., [Kharoshthi]. [Pl. XXIII. 9.]
2		Æ 1·05		„ „ „ „ [Kharoshthi].
3		Æ ·95		„ [Kharoshthi]; „ „
4		Æ ·9		„ [Kharoshthi]; „ „ (last letter of inscr. absent).
5		Æ ·9		„ „ „ „ „ „
6		Æ 1·05	inscr. ends ΟΡΘΑΓΝ.	to l., uncertain letter; to r., [Kharoshthi].
			Β ΜЄΓΑΛΟΥ ΟΡΘΑΓΝΟΥ Similar.	Illegible inscr. Similar type.
7		Æ ·95		to l., Ψ; to r., [Kharoshthi].

* This is Gen. Cunningham's reading: *sagaba* he supposes to stand for *sagarbha*, 'brother.' On no. 2 of the British Museum coins there is another letter at the end, which looks like [Kharoshthi] (*na* or *da*), but which may be a badly formed [Kharoshthi].

No.	Wt.	Metal. Size.	Obverse.	Reverse.
			PACORES.	
			(a) Bronze.	
			ΒΑCΙΛΕΥC ΒΑCΙΛΕΩΝ ΜΕΓΑC ΠΑΚΟΡΗC Bust of the king l., wears torquis; behind, star.	[Kharoshthi] (*Maharajasa rajadirajasa mahatasa Pakurasa*). Nike l.; holding wreath and palm.
1		Æ ·95		to l., uncertain letter; to r., [Kharoshthi]. [Pl. xxiii. 8.]
2		Æ ·85		„ [Kharoshthi]; „ „
3		Æ 1·		„ uncertain letter; „ „
4		Æ 1·		„ [Kharoshthi]; „ „
5		Æ 1·		„ „ „ „
6		Æ ·9		„ uncertain letter; „ „
			ZEIONISES.	
			(a) Silver; type, King on horseback.	
			CΑΤΡΑΠΥ ΖΕ . . ΝΙCΟΥ The king r., on horseback; in r. hand whip; bow tied to saddle; to r., [Kharoshthi].	[Kharoshthi] ([*Mani?*]*gulasa chhatrapasa putrasa chhatrapasa Jihuniasa*). King r., facing a City who wears mural crown, and holds wreath and cornucopiae.
1	157·6	AR 1·05	beneath, [Kharoshthi].	to l., [Kharoshthi]; to r., [Kharoshthi]. [Pl. xxiii. 4.]
2	139·4	AR 1·05	„ [Kharoshthi] and other letters.	„ „ „ „ [I. O. C.]

No.	Wt.	Metal. Size.	Obverse.	Reverse.
			(β) *Bronze; types, lion and bull.*	
			]ΛOYYIYCATPAΠ[Humped bull r.; above, [illegible].	[illegible][([*Mani?*]* *gulaputrasa chhatrapasa Jihuniasa*). Lion r.
3		Æ 1·	to r., [illegible].	to l., [illegible]; to r., [illegible]; below, [illegible]. [Pl. XXIII. 5.]
4		Æ 1·	„ [illegible].	„ „ „ [illegible].

UNCERTAIN KINGS.

(α) *Bronze; square.*

No.	Wt.	Metal. Size.	Obverse.	Reverse.
			Illegible Greek inscription; in which sometimes the word CATPAΠ and sometimes XAPANШ is visible. King r., on horseback; lance couched.	Illegible Indian inscription; the words [illegible] (*chhatrapasa*) and [illegible] (*putrasa*) sometimes visible. Lion r.
1		Æ 1·	to r., [illegible].	above, [illegible]; to r., X.
2		Æ 1·	„ „	„ „ „ „
3		Æ 1·	„ „	„ „ „ „ [Pl. XXIII. 6.]
4		Æ ·85	„ „	„ „ „ „ [I. O. C.]
5		Æ ·8	„ [illegible].	„ „ „ „ „
6		Æ ·8	„ [illegible].	„ [illegible] „ „ „

* Or *mahigulasa*. This is supposed to give us the name of the father of Zeionises. The word *Jihuniasa* is not clear on any British Museum specimens in bronze.

No.	Wt.	Metal. Size.	Obverse.	Reverse.
			(β) Bronze; round.	
			Debased Greek legend. Humped bull r.; above, [symbol].	Undetermined Indian legend. Bactrian camel r.
7		Æ ·9	to r., uncertain letter.	to r., [symbol]; above, [symbol].
8		Æ ·85	„ „	„ „
9		Æ ·9	„ „	„ uncertain letter.
10		Æ ·95	„ [symbol].	„ [symbol]. [Pl. XXIII. 7.]
11		Æ ·9	„ [symbol].	„ [symbol].
12		Æ ·95	„ „	„ uncertain letter. (inscr. [symbol] &c.)
13		Æ ·9		to r., uncertain letter.
14		Æ ·9	„ [symbol].	above, uncertain letter; to r., [symbol].
15		Æ ·75	above, BA [symbol]; to r., uncertain letter.	to r., uncertain letter. (inscr. [symbol] &c.)
16		Æ ·65	„ „	to r., uncertain letter.

[Various readings of these two classes of coins have been published by Gen. Cunningham, *J. A. S. B.* 1854, pp. 695, 698; and by von Sallet, *Zeitsch. f. Num.* 1879, 369, 370. The British Museum specimens are not sufficiently well-preserved to enable us to give any certain readings].

SANABARES.

(α) *Silver.*

No.	Wt.	Metal. Size.	Obverse.	Reverse.
1	58·5	AR ·75	Bust of the king l., wearing tiara of late Parthian form, and torquis; behind, 𐨀𐨠 (*ath*).	ΒΑϹΙΛΕΥϹ ΜΕΓΑϹ ϹΑΝΑΒΑ King dressed in Parthian style, seated r. on throne with back; holds bow. in front, [monogram]; above, ΓΙΤ. [Pl. XXIII. 10.]

(β) *Bronze; Parthian class.*

No.	Wt.	Metal. Size.	Obverse.	Reverse.
2		Æ ·65	Head of the king l., diad. Inscr. (?)	ΒΑϹΙΛΕ ϹΑΝΑΒΑΡΗϹ King seated r. on stool; holds bow. in front, Π. [Pl. XXIII. 11.]
3		Æ ·65		„ „
4		Æ ·6		„ Α Π. (barbarous).

(γ) *Bronze; Bactrian class.*

No.	Wt.	Metal. Size.	Obverse.	Reverse.
5		Æ ·85	ΒΑΣΙΛЄΥΣ . . . ? (corrupt). Bust of the king l., wearing tiara.	. . . . ϹΑΝΑ[illegible]ΑΡΟΥ Nike r., holds wreath. [Pl. XXIII. 12.]

BASILEUS SOTER MEGAS.

(α) Base silver; with Greek and Indian legends.

No.	Wt.	Metal. Size.	Obverse.	Reverse.
1	146·4	AR ·9	ΒΑCΙΛΕΥC ΒΑ]CΙ-ΛΕΥΩΝ CΩΤΗΡ ΜΕΓΑC The king r., on horseback; r. hand advanced; to r.,	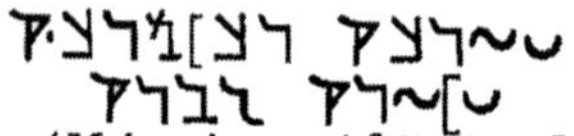 (*Maharajasa raja*]*dirajasa* [*ma*]-*hatasa tradatasa*). Zeus, standing r., clad in himation; r. hand raised; in l., sceptre. to l, ; to r., uncertain object. [Pl. XXIV. 1.]

(β) Copper; with Greek legends.

No.	Wt.	Metal. Size.	Obverse.	Reverse.
			Bust of the king r., diad. and radiate; hand holds lance, bound with fillet; behind, .	ΒΑCΙΛΕVC ΒΑCΙΛΕVΩΝ CΩΤΗΡ ΜΕΓΑC (frequently blundered). The king r., on horseback, diad.; holds ankus? to r., .
2		Æ ·8		
3		Æ ·8		[Pl. XXIV. 2.]
4		Æ ·8		
5		Æ ·8		[I. O. C. Pl. XXIV. 3.]
6		Æ ·8		[I. O. C.]
7		Æ ·8		
8		Æ ·9		
9		Æ ·8		

No.	Wt.	Metal. Size.	Obverse.	Reverse.
10		Æ ·85	Bust of the king r., diad. and radiate; hand holds lance, bound with fillet; behind, [symbol].	**ΒΑϹΙΛΕVϹ ΒΑϹΙΛΕVШΝ ϹШΤΗΡ ΜΕΓΑϹ** (frequently blundered). The king r., on horseback, diad.; holds ankus? to r., [symbol].
11		Æ ·75		(inscr. ends **ΒΑϹΙΛΕШΝϹШΤΗ**).
12		Æ ·8		(inscr. barbarous). [I. O. C.]
13		Æ ·55	Similar.	**ΒΑϹΙΛΕVϹ ΒΑϹΙΛΕVШΝ ϹШΤΗΡ Μ** Similar.
14		Æ ·55		
15		Æ ·6		
16		Æ ·5		
17		Æ ·5		
18		Æ ·55		
19		Æ ·6		[I. O. C. Pl. xxiv. 4.]
20		Æ ·5		
21		Æ ·5		[I. O. C.]
22		Æ ·55		(inscr. barbarous).

No.	Wt.	Metal. Size.	Obverse.	Reverse.
			Bust of the king r., diad.; to r., [monogram].	]BACIΛ[ЄωN]CωTHPM[Zeus, standing l.; holds in r. hand, thunderbolt over altar; in l., sceptre.
23		Æ ·7		
24		Æ ·7		
25		Æ ·7		(inscr. . . BACIΛEYωИ . . . . .). [Pl. xxiv. 5.]
			Bust of the king l., wearing crested helmet; in r. hand, lance: fillet border.	BACIΛЄV BACIΛЄVω[N C]ωTHP MЄΓAC King on horseback r., holding ankus; to r., [monogram].
26		Æ ·95	to l., [monogram]; to r., [monogram].	
27		Æ ·95	” ” ” ”	[I. O. C. Pl. xxiv. 6.]

HERAÜS (ERAÜS).

(a) *Silver.*

No.	Wt.	Metal. Size.	Obverse.	Reverse.
			Bust of the king r., diad.: fillet-border.	TY/ANNOYNTOC H/AOY ΣAИ A ИO//ANOY* The king r., on horseback; bow and quiver tied to saddle; behind, Nike r., crowning him.
1	184·4	AR 1·2		in field r., B. [Pl. xxiv. 7.]

* As to this legend, *see* Introduction.

No.	Wt.	Metal. Size.	Obverse.	Reverse.
			HYRCODES.	
			(a) Silver; type, a Deity standing.	
			ΥΡΚΩΔΟΥ Bust of the king with peaked beard r., diad.	ΜΑΚΑΡΟΥ ΑΡΔΗΘΡΟΥ Figure of a Deity (?), facing; holds spear in r. hand; flames on shoulders.
1	44·9	Æ ·65		[Pl. xxiv. 8.]
2	43·5	Æ ·7		
3	45·2	Æ ·65		[I. O. C.]
4	27·5	Æ ·7		
			VᒐΚΩΔΟΥ Similar.	ΟΔΚΑΡΟ ΟⱯΗΟΡ Similar.
5	44·	Æ ·7		
6	42·5	Æ ·65		[I. O. C.]
7	39·7	Æ ·65		[Pl. xxiv. 9.]
8	51·5	Æ ·7		
			Barbarous imitation of the above.	Barbarous imitation.
9	30·	Æ ·55		[I. O. C.]
10	20·2	Æ ·55		
11	23·2	Æ ·6		
12	26·	Æ ·6		[Pl. xxiv. 10.]
13	17·5	Æ ·55		

No.	Wt.	Metal. Size.	Obverse.	Reverse.
			Barbarous imitation further degraded.	Barbarous imitation.
14	34·4	Æ ·55		[I. O. C.]
15	19·	Æ ·5		
16	17·6	Æ ·55		
17	12·3	Æ ·5		
18	10·	Æ ·55		
19	13·8	Æ ·45		
20	10·1	Æ ·4		[Pl. xxiv. 11.]
			(β) Silver; type, horse.	
			VPKωΔ Bust of the king r., diad.	VPKωΔ Forepart of bridled horse r.
21	23·3	Æ ·55		
22	23·8	Æ ·5		[Pl. xxiv. 12.]
23	22·5	Æ ·5		
24	14·	Æ ·45		[I. O. C.]
25	10·8	Æ ·5		
26	14·2	Æ ·45		
27	14·	Æ ·5	(barbarous legend).	(barbarous legend). [Pl. xxiv. 13.]
28	11·6	Æ ·5	"	"

No.	Wt.	Metal. Size.	Obverse.	Reverse.

KINGS OF UNCERTAIN NAME.

SAPADBIZES (?).

(*a*) *Silver.*

No.	Wt.	Metal. Size.	Obverse.	Reverse.
			Bust of a king r., in helmet like that of Eucratides.	NANAIA NANAIA Lion r.
1	25·3	Æ ·65	behind, ΑΓΕЄΙ ΗΛ	above, ̆Λ.
2	26·2	Æ ·6	„ ϹΑΠΑΔΒΙΖ	„ „ [I. O. C. Pl. XXIV. 14.]
3	31·5	Æ ·6	„ ϹΑΠΑΔ?ΒΙΖΗϹ	„ „ [I. O. C. Pl. XXIV. 15.]

PHSEIGACHARIS (?).

(*a*) *Silver.*

No.	Wt.	Metal. Size.	Obverse.	Reverse.
			Bust of Scythian king r., diad.	ΦϹΕΙΓΑ ΧΑΡΙϹ Herakles, facing; holds in r. hand, club; in l., lion's skin.
1	37·6	Æ ·6		[I. O. C. Pl. XXIV. 16.]
2	36·8	Æ ·6		

No.	Wt.	Metal. Size.	Obverse.	Reverse.
			HERMAEUS AND KADPHISES I.	
			(a) Copper; type of rev., Herakles.	
			ΒΑΣΙΛΕΩΣ ΣΤΗ-ΡΟΣ ΣV ΕΡΜΑΙΟV (often corrupted). Bust of Hermaeus r., diad.	[Kharoshthi legend]* (*Kujula kasasa kushana yavu(?)gasa dhramaṭhidasa*). Herakles, facing, diad.; holds in r. hand, club; in l., lion's skin.
1		Æ ·9		
2		Æ ·85		
3		Æ ·9		
4		Æ ·9		[I. O. C. Pl. xxv. 1.]
5		Æ ·9		
6		Æ ·9		[I. O. C.]
7		Æ ·9		
8		Æ ·9		
9		Æ ·85		
10		Æ ·85		

* This reading is made up from several specimens. General Cunningham transliterates the last two words *yathagasa dharmapidasa* (*J. A. S. B.*, 1854). The reading of the last word adopted in the text is Lassen's.

No.	Wt.	Metal. Size.	Obverse.	Reverse.
			ΒΑΣΙΛΕΩΣ ΣΤΗ-ΡΟΣ ΣΥ ΕΡΜΑΙΟΥ (often corrupted). Bust of Hermaeus r., diad.	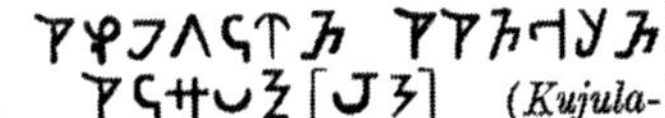 (*Kujula-kasasa kushaṇa yavu*(?)*gasa dhra-*(*dha*)*maṭhidasa*). Herakles, facing, diad.; holds in r. hand, club; in l., lion's skin.
11		Æ ·9	lower line of inscr. ΖΑΕΟΥ	
12		Æ ·9	inscr. retrograde.	inscr. varied. [Pl. xxv. 2.]
13		Æ ·9	inscr. retrograde and barbarous.	,, ,,
14		Æ 1·	twice struck.	inscr. varied; in field, .
15		Æ ·8	degraded copy.	degraded copy.
16		Æ ·75	,,	
17		Æ ·85	,,	
18		Æ ·7	,,	
19		Æ ·7	,,	
20		Æ ·6	,,	
21		Æ ·6	,,	

KADPHISES I.

(*a*) *Copper; type, Herakles.*

No.	Wt.	Metal. Size.	Obverse.	Reverse.
			Inscr. as below. Bust of Hermaeus r., diad.	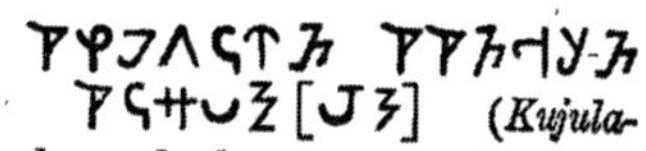 (*Kujula-kasasa kushaṇayavugasa dhra(dha)-maṭhidasa*). Herakles, facing, diad.; holds in r. hand, club; in l., lion's skin.
1		Æ ·95	KOPCNAKOZOVAO-KAΔΦIZOV	in field, 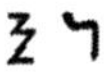. [I. O. C. Pl. xxv. 3.]
2		Æ ·95	KOZOVAOKAΔΦI-ZOV	[I. O. C.] (inscr. varied).
3		Æ ·9	KOPOИAKOZOVAO	„ 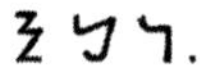. [Pl. xxv. 4.]
4		Æ ·85	ИOKAΔΦICHOH	„ . (inscr. varied).
5		Æ ·9	AΔΦIΣ	„ uncertain letter. „ „
6		Æ ·9	ΦIZOVKOΛC	„ 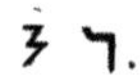.
7		Æ ·9	K..ZOYΛOKAΔ ZV	„ 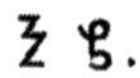. [I. O. C.]
8		Æ ·85	inscr. blundered.	„ . [I. O. C.]

KADAPHES.

(a) Bronze; type of rev., king seated.

No.	Wt.	Metal. Size.	Obverse.	Reverse.
			ΧΟΡΑΝCΥ ΖΑΟΟΥ* ΚΟΖΟΛΑ ΚΑΔΑΦΕϹ Head of the king r., diad. (closely resembling that of Augustus).	[illegible] (*Khushanasa yauasa kuyula kaphsasa sachadhramathidasa*). The king seated r. on seat like curule chair; his r. hand extended; in field l., [symbol].
1		Æ ·8		[Pl. xxv. 5.]
2		Æ ·7		
3		Æ ·7		
4		Æ ·7		[I. O. C.]
5		Æ ·7		[I. O. C.]
6		Æ ·7		[I. O. C.]
7		Æ ·75		
8		Æ ·7		to r., [symbol]. [I. O. C.]
9		Æ ·7		„ „
10		Æ ·7		„ „
11		Æ ·65	barbarous inscr.; head l.	barbarous. [I. O. C.]

* The first Ο in ΖΑΟΟΥ has been read as a Θ; but wrongly, as is shewn by the corresponding Sanskrit form *yauasa*.

KADPHISES II.

(a) *Gold ; type, figure or head of king.*

No.	Wt.	Metal. Size.	Obverse.	Reverse.
			BACIΛEYCOOH MO-KAΔΦICHC The king, wearing helmet and diadem, seated facing on throne; head turned to l.; flames ascend from his shoulders;* in his right a branch; beneath his feet a footstool; to r., .	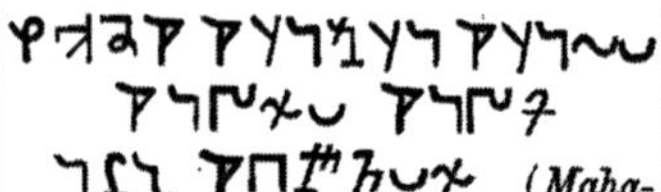 (*Maharajasa rajadirajasa, sarvaloga iṣvarasa mahiṣvarasa hi*(†)*makapiṣasa tradata*). Siva facing, head l.; holds trident in r. hand; drapery over l. arm and hanging at back; flames rising from head; behind him, humped bull r.; to l., .
1	244·2	AV ·95	to l., club.	[I. O. C. Pl. xxv. 6.]
			Same inscr. The king, wearing helmet and diadem, seated facing, cross-legged, on clouds; head turned to r.; in his r. is a club; his head is surmounted by a trident; to l., .	Similar.
2	245·	AV 1·		[Pl. xxv. 7.]
			Same inscr. Upper part of the king r., emerging from clouds; wears helmet and diadem, and Greek chlamys; club in r. hand; to l., .	Same inscr. (*i* of *iṣvarasa* wanting). Siva facing, wears headdress and drapery over shoulder; holds trident in r. hand; behind him bull r.; to l., .
3	122·4	AV ·75		

* This is so usual on the gold coins of this king, that it will be omitted in subsequent descriptions.

† This letter looks on the coins rather like *tri* or *dri* than *hi*.

No.	Wt.	Metal. Size.	Obverse.	Reverse.
4	123·2	AV ·75	BACIΛEYCOOH MO-KAΔΦICHC Similar, king wears diadem, but not helmet.	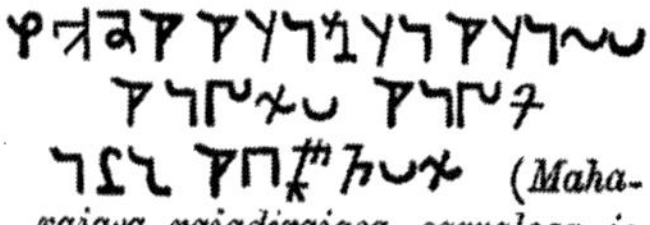 (*Maharajasa rajadirajasa, sarvaloga iṣvarasa mahiṣvarasa himakapiṣasa tradata*), last letters obscure. Siva facing, wears headdress and drapery over shoulder; holds trident in r. hand; behind him bull r.; to l., . [I. O. C. Pl. xxv. 8.]
5	120·	AV ·7	Similar.	Same inscr. (last letters obscure). Siva facing, head l.; holds in r. hand, trident and battle-axe combined; in l., gourd; tiger-skin on l. arm; hair arranged in spiral form; to l., ; to r., . [I. O. C.]
6	122·	AV ·75	Same inscr. Upper part of the king l., emerging from clouds, wears diadem and helmet surmounted by trident; holds in r. hand, club; in l., elephant-goad; to r., .	Similar. [I. O. C. Pl. xxv. 9.]
7	121·2	AV ·7		
8	121·2	AV ·85	Same inscr. Upper part of the king r., emerging from clouds, wears diadem and helmet surmounted by trident; holds in r. hand, club; to l., .	Similar. [I. O. C.]
9	122·4	AV ·8		

No.	Wt.	Metal. Size.	Obverse.	Reverse.
10	30·5	AV ·45	BACIΛEYCOOH[.MO-KAΔΦICHC Head of king r., wearing helmet and diadem; within square frame.	(*Maharaja rajadiraja hima kapiṣasa*). Trident and battle-axe combined; to l., ; to r., . [Pl. xxv. 10.]

(β) *Silver; type, king standing.*

No.	Wt.	Metal. Size.	Obverse.	Reverse.
11	56·5	AR ·7	BACIΛEVC BACIΛEWN MEΓAC OOHMO KAΔΦICHC The king standing l., wearing diadem and helmet, sacrificing at altar; to l., trident and axe combined; to r., club and .	(*Maharajasa rajadirajasa sarvaloga iṣvara mahiṣvara himakapisasa tradata*). Siva facing; wears headdress and drapery over shoulder; holds trident in r. hand; behind him, bull r. [I. O. C. Pl. xxv. 11.]

[This coin, which is quite genuine, is the only known specimen of the class in silver.]

(γ) *Copper; type, king standing.*

[Inscription on both sides varied and incomplete in various specimens.]

No.	Wt.	Metal. Size.	Obverse.	Reverse.
12		Æ 1·1	BACIΛEVC BACIΛEWN CWTHP MEΓAC OOHMO KAΔΦICHC The king l., sacrificing at altar; to l., trident and axe combined; to r., club and .	(*Maharajasa rajadirajasa, sarvaloga iṣvarasa mahiṣvarasa himakapiṣasa tradata*). Siva facing, holding trident; drapery hanging at his back; behind him, bull; to l., . [I. O. C. Pl. xxv. 12.]
13		Æ 1·1		,,

No.	Wt.	Metal. Size.	Obverse.	Reverse.
			ΒΑCΙΛΕVC ΒΑCΙ-ΛΕωΝ CωΤΗΡ ΜΕΓΑC ΟΟΗΜΟ ΚΑΔΦΙCΗC The king l., sacrificing at altar; to l., trident and axe combined; to r., club and .	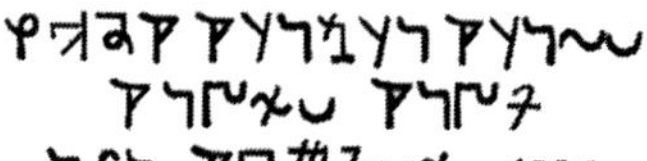 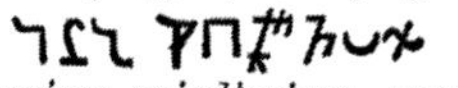 (*Maharajasa rajadirajasa, sarvaloga iṣvarasa mahiṣvarasa himakapiṣasa tradata*). Siva facing, holding trident; drapery hanging at his back; behind him, bull; to l., .
14		Æ 1·05		[I. O. C]
15		Æ 1·1		”
16		Æ 1·1		”
17		Æ 1·05		
18		Æ 1·25	(twice struck).	
19		Æ 1·		
20		Æ 1·05		
21		Æ 1·1		
22		Æ 1·05		
23		Æ 1·15		
24		Æ 1·15		
25		Æ 1·1		
26		Æ 1·		in inscr. 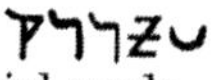 between second and third words.

No.	Wt.	Metal. Size.	Obverse.	Reverse.
27		Æ ·85	ΒΑCΙΛΕVC ΒΑCΙΛΕΩΝ CΩΤΗΡ ΜΕΓΑC ΟΟΗΜΟ ΚΑΔΦΙCΗC The king l., sacrificing at altar; to l., trident and axe combined; to r., club and .	(*Maharajasa rajadirajasa, sarvaloga iṣvarasa mahiṣvarasa himakapiṣasa tradata*). Siva facing, holding trident; drapery hanging at his back; behind him, bull; to l., . [Pl. xxv. 13.]
28		Æ ·65		[I. O. C. Pl. xxv. 14.]
29		Æ ·75		[I. O. C.]
30		Æ ·7		„
31		Æ ·75		
32		Æ ·7		
33		Æ ·7		
34		Æ ·7		
35		Æ ·7		in place of inscr., fillet-border.

No.	Wt.	Metal. Size.	Obverse.	Reverse.
			KANERKES.	
			(*a*) *Gold; inscription, βασιλεὺς βασιλέων.*	
1	121·8	AV ·8	ΒΑCΙΛΕΥC ΒΑCΙ ΛΕωΝ ΚΑΝΗΡ-ΚΟΥ The king l., wearing helmet and diadem, clad in coat and trousers, and cloak, sacrificing at altar; flames rise from shoulders; holds in l. hand, spear.	CΑΛΗΝΗ Selene * (male) l., diad., clad in chiton and himation; crescent behind shoulders; r. hand advanced; holds in l. long sceptre, bound with fillet; sword girt round waist; to l., . [I. O. C. Pl. xxvi. 1.]
			(*β*) *Bronze; inscription, βασιλεὺς βασιλέων.*	
2		Æ ·9	ΒΑCΙΛΕΥC ΒΑCΙ ΛΕωΝ ΚΑΝΗΡ-ΚΟΥ The king as above.	ΗΛΙΟC Helios l., diad., clad in chiton and himation; radiate disk behind head; r. hand advanced; l. on hip; to l., . [I. O. C. Pl. xxvi. 2.]
3		Æ ·9		
4		Æ ·9		
5		Æ ·9	Similar.	ΝΑΝΑΙΑ Nanaia r., nimbate and diad.; holds in r. hand sceptre ending in forepart of horse; to r., . [I. O. C. Pl. xxvi. 3.]
6		Æ ·9		"
7		Æ ·9		"
8		Æ ·85		
9		Æ ·9		

* The figure of Selene is identical with that which appears on the coin inscribed ΜΑΟ; it is that of a male moon-deity.

(γ) *Gold; inscription,* PAONANO &c.

No.	Wt.	Metal. Size.	Obverse.	Reverse.
			PAONANOPAOKA NHPKIKOPANO The king standing l., wearing helmet and diadem, clad in coat and trousers, and cloak; flames rise from his shoulders; he holds in r. hand elephant-goad over altar; in his l., spear; sword at his waist.	AΘPO Bearded deity, fire-god, l., diad., clad in chiton and himation; holds in r. hand, wreath; in l., which rests on hip, tongs; to l., [monogram].
10	122·8	AV ·8		[Pl. XXVI. 4.]
11	121·9	AV ·75		
12	27·7	AV ·5		[I. O. C. Pl. XXVI. 5.]
			Similar.	APΔOXPO Female figure r., wearing modius and nimbate, clad in chiton and himation; holds cornucopiae; to r., [monogram].
13	122·8	AV ·8		[Pl. XXVI. 6.]
			Similar.	ΛPOOACΠO Bearded deity r., diad., clad in sleeved tunic; holds in r. hand, wreath; beside him, horse r., saddled, trotting; to l., [monogram].
14	120·2	AV ·75		[Pl. XXVI. 7.]
15	122·	AV ·75	(same die).	(same die). [I. O. C.]
			Similar.	BOΔΔO Buddha, facing, nimbate, clad in chiton and himation; r. hand advanced; in l., wallet; to r., [monogram].
16	109·2	AV ·8		[I. O. C. Pl. XXVI. 8.]

No.	Wt.	Metal. Size.	Obverse.	Reverse.
			ΡΑΟΝΑΝΟΡΑΟΚΑ ΝΗΡΚΙΚΟΡΑΝΟ The king standing l., wearing helmet and diadem, clad in coat and trousers, and cloak; flames rise from his shoulders; he holds in r. hand elephant-goad over altar; in his l., spear; sword at his waist.	ΜΑΟ Male deity (moon-god) l., diad., clad in chiton and himation; crescent behind shoulders; r. hand advanced; holds in l., long sceptre, bound with fillet; sword girt round waist; to l., .
17	121·9	AV ·75		[Pl. xxvi. 9.]
18	122·3	AV ·8		(no sword).
			Similar.	ΜЄΙΡΟ Mithras, diad. and with radiate disk, to l.; r. hand advanced; in l., sceptre bound with fillet; sword girt round waist; to l., .
19	118·	AV ·8		
			Similar.	ΜΙΙΡΟ Mithras, to l.; r. hand advanced; l. rests on hip; sword at waist; to l. .
20	122·3	AV ·8		[Pl. xxvi. 10.]
			Similar.	ΝΑΝΑ Nanaia r., nimbate and diad., head surmounted by crescent; holds sceptre ending in forepart of horse, and patera; to r., .
21	123·2	AV ·8		
			Similar.	ΝΑΝΑΡΑΟ Similar figure of Nanaia; to r., .
22	120·3	AV ·75		
23	122·2	AV ·75		(sword at waist). [Pl. xxvi. 11.]
24	30·2	AV ·5		" " [I. O. C. Pl. xxvi. 12.]

No.	Wt.	Metal. Size.	Obverse.	Reverse.
			ΡΑΟΝΑΝΟΡΑΟΚΑ ΝϷΡΚΙΚΟΡΑΝΟ The king standing l., wearing helmet and diadem, clad in coat and trousers, and cloak; flames rise from his shoulders; he holds in r. hand elephant-goad over altar; in his l., spear; sword at his waist.	ΟΚΡΟ Siva l., nimbate; hair in horn on top of head; has four arms and hands, in which he holds respectively a vase, a drum, a trident, and a goat, the last by the horns; to l., .
25	123·	*AV* ·8		[Pl. xxvi. 13.]
26	123·4	*AV* ·75		[I. O. C.]
27	122·	*AV* ·75		"
28	29·	*AV* ·5		[I. O. C. Pl. xxvi. 14.]
			Similar.	ΟΡΛΑΓΝΟ War-god (Bahram ?) r., wearing diadem, helmet surmounted by eagle, and clad like the king; holds in r. hand, spear; in l., sword; to r., .
29	121·3	*AV* ·85		[Pl. xxvi. 15.]
			Similar.	ΦΑΡΡΟ Male figure to r., diad. and nimbate, clad in chiton and himation; holds spear in l. hand, and mountain or fire in r.; to r., .
30	122·8	*AV* ·8		[Pl. xxvi. 16.]
			ΡΑΟΝΑΝΟΚΑΝΗΡ ΚΙ ΚΟΡΑΝΟ Bust of the king l., diad. and wearing helmet; l. hand raised, holds spear; body emerges from clouds.	ΑΘΡΟ Bearded deity l., clad in chiton and himation; holds in r. hand wreath; in l., which rests on hip, tongs; to l., .
31	30·8	*AV* ·5		[I. O. C. Pl. xxvi. 17.]
			Similar.	ΟΚΡΟ Siva, as above, not nimbate; to l. .
32	30·1	*AV* ·5		[Pl. xxvi. 18.]

No.	Wt.	Metal. Size.	Obverse.	Reverse.
			Later period.	
33	30·6	AV ·5	PAO NANOPA[O [KA]NHPKOKOPANO The king standing l. at altar, nimbate; holds r. hand over altar; in l., spear bound with fillet; to l., trident bound with fillet.	A]PΔOKPO Goddess, seated facing on throne, nimbate; under feet, footstool; holds wreath and cornucopiae to l., [monogram]. [I. O. C. Pl. XXVI. 19.]
			(δ) *Bronze; inscr.* PAO *&c.*	
34		Æ 1 05	PAOKA NHPKI The king, clad as in last class, standing l. by altar; holds in l. hand spear; r. extended over altar.	AΘPO Bearded deity l.; holds in r. hand, wreath; in l., which rests on hip, tongs (?); to l., [monogram]. [Pl. XXVII. 1.]
35		Æ 1·		
36		Æ 1·05	inscr. barbarous.	
37		Æ ·85	Similar.	OΔYOBOY CAKAMA Buddha facing, nimbate; his r. hand raised as in teaching; in l., wallet; to l., [monogram]. [Pl. XXVII. 2.]
38		Æ ·9		[I. O. C.]
39		Æ 1·05	Similar. king nimbate; to l., [monogram].	MAO Male deity l., clad as king; crescent behind shoulders; r. hand advanced; in l., long sceptre bound with fillet; sword at waist; to l., [monogram]. [Pl. XXVII. 3.]
40		Æ 1·05		deity does not hold sceptre.
41		Æ ·85		

No.	Wt.	Metal. Size.	Obverse.	Reverse.
			PAOKA NHPKI The king standing l. as before; holds in l. hand spear; r. extended over altar.	MAO Male deity l., clad as king; crescent behind shoulders; r. hand advanced; in l., long sceptre bound with fillet; sword at waist; to l., .
42		Æ ·75	to l., . (inscr. retrogr.)	(inscr. retrogr.)
43		Æ ·75	„ „	deity does not hold sceptre.
44		Æ ·75	„ „	„ „ „
45		Æ ·5	„ „	„ „ „
			Similar.	MIOPO Sun-god, Mithras, l., diad. with radiate disk, clad as king; r. hand advanced; in l., sword; to l., .
46		Æ 1·05		[Pl. xxvii. 4.]
47		Æ 1·05		
48		Æ 1·		inscr. MIIPO.
49		Æ 1·1		„ „
50		Æ ·8		„ „
51		Æ ·85		
52		Æ ·65		
53		Æ ·7		inscr. MIYPO.
			Similar.	NANA Nanaia r., nimbate and diad.; holds sceptre, ending in forepart of horse, and patera; to r., .
54		Æ 1·05		[I. O. C. Pl. xxvii. 5.]
55		Æ ·95		
56		Æ 1·		

No.	Wt.	Metal. Size.	Obverse.	Reverse.
			PAOKA NҺPKI The king standing l. by altar; holds in l. hand spear; r. extended over altar.	NANA Nanaia r., nimbate and diad.; holds sceptre, ending in forepart of horse, and patera; to r., .
57		Æ ·7	to l., .	
58		Æ ·7	" "	
59		Æ ·7	" "	
60		Æ ·55		
61		Æ ·6		
			Similar.	OAΔO Wind-god running l., his hair loose; holds in both hands ends of his garment which floats about him; to l., .
62		Æ 1·05		[I. O. C. Pl. XXVII. 6.]
63		Æ 1·05		[I. O. C.]
64		Æ 1·05		
65		Æ ·65		
			Similar.	OKPO Siva l., nimbate; has four arms and hands, in which he holds a wreath, a drum, a trident, and a vase; to l., .
66		Æ 1·		[I. O. C.]
67		Æ 1·		
68		Æ ·8		
69		Æ ·8		[I. O. C. Pl. XXVII. 7.]
			Similar.	OKPO Siva l., nimbate; holds in r. hand, trident; to l., .
70		Æ ·75	to l., .	
71		Æ ·75	" "	(not nimbate).

HOOERKES.

(a) *Gold.*

No.	Wt.	Metal. Size.	Obverse.	Reverse.
1	121·5	AV ·8	PAONANOPAOO Upper part of king l., emerging from clouds; is diad. and nimbate; wears conical helmet and coat of mail; holds ear of corn and spear.*	AΘOPO Hephaestus standing r., flames rising from shoulders; holds hammer and tongs; to r., . [Pl. XXVII. 8.]
2	123·5	AV ·85	PAONANOP AOOOH-PKIKO Similar.	AΘPO Similar.
3	120·9	AV ·85	PAONANOPAOOO HPKIKOPANO Similar.	Similar; symbol to l.
4	123·5	AV ·85	Similar.	APAЄIXPO Sun-god l., diad. and with radiate disk; r. hand advanced, and two fingers raised; l. rests on hip; to l., . [Pl. XXVII. 9.]
5	122·8	AV ·9		[I. O. C.]

* It has been judged unnecessary to describe at length the details of the king's costume in this and other coins.

No.	Wt.	Metal. Size.	Obverse.	Reverse.
			ΡΑΟΝΑΝΟΡΑΟ ΟΟ ÞΡΚΙΚΟΡΑΝΟ Upper part of king l., emerging from clouds; diad. and nimbate; wears conical helmet and coat of mail; holds ear of corn and spear.	ΑΡΔΟΧΡΟ Female deity r., in Greek attire; holds in both hands cornucopiae; to r., [symbol].
6	124·5	AV ·8		[Pl. xxvii. 10.]
7	122·	AV ·85		
8	122·5	AV ·8		
9	122·4	AV ·8		to r., fire (?).
10	58·3 (plated)	AV ·8		
11	122·	AV ·85		inscr. ΑΡΔΟΧΡΑ. [I. O. C.]
12	123·5	AV ·85		type l., and symbol to l. [I. O. C.]
13	30·6	AV ·55	inscr. ΡΑΟΝΑΝΟ ΟΟÞ	[I. O. C.]
			ΡΑΟΝΑΝΟ ΡΑΟΟ ΟÞΡΚΙΚΟΡΑΝΟ Upper part of king l., emerging from clouds, diad.; wears rounded helmet; holds ear of corn and elephant-goad.	Similar.
14	122·5	AV ·85		deity with modius and nimbus.
15	120·7	AV ·8	inscr. ΟΥΟÞΡΚΙ for ΟΟÞΡΚΙ.	inscr. ΟϘΟΔϘΑ.
16	120·6	AV ·8		type l., and symbol to l.
17	30·6	AV ·5		deity with modius and nimbus. [Pl. xxvii. 11.]
			ΡΑΟΝΑΝΟΡΑΟ ΟΟÞΡΚΟΚΟΡΑΝΟ The king r., riding on elephant; holds sceptre and elephant-goad.	Similar. Deity with modius and nimbus.
18	120·9	AV ·8		[Pl. xxvii. 12.]

No.	Wt.	Metal. Size.	Obverse.	Reverse.
			Inscr. obscure. Upper part of king l., emerging from clouds, diad.; wears rounded helmet; holds ear of corn and elephant-goad.	ΔOXPO Female figure l., nimbate; holds wreath and cornucopiae; to l., .
19	122·5	AV ·8		[Pl. xxvii. 13.]
20	123·3	AV ·8		
			PAONANOPAOOO ÞPKIKOPANO Upper part of the king l., emerging from clouds, diad. and nimbate; wears conical helmet and chlamys over armour; holds ear of corn and spear.	MIOPO Female deity r., diad. and nimbate, in Greek attire; holds cornucopiae in both hands; to r., .
21	123·	AV ·8		[Pl. xxvii. 14.]
			PAONANOPA OOOÞPKI The king seated cross-legged to l., diad. and nimbate; flames rising from shoulders; wears conical helmet, and holds ear of corn and spear.	ÞPAΓIΛO Bearded Heracles l., naked; holds in r. hand, club; over l. arm, lion's skin; in l. hand, apple; to l., .
22	123·3	AV ·8		[Pl. xxvii. 15.]
			PAONANOPAOO OÞPKIKOPANO Upper part of the king l., emerging from clouds, diad.; wears rounded helmet; holds ear of corn and elephant-goad.	MAACÞNO Male deity (Mahásená) facing, nimbate and diad., clad in coat and chlamys; holds in r. hand, standard surmounted by bird; in l., sword; to l., .
23	125·5	AV ·8		[I. O. C. Pl. xxvii. 16.]
24	112·7	AV ·75		

No.	Wt.	Metal. Size.	Obverse.	Reverse.
			ΡΑΟΝΑΝΟΡΑΟΟ ΟÞΡΚΙΚΟΡΑΝΟ Upper part of the king l., emerging from clouds, diad.; wears rounded helmet; holds ear of corn and elephant-goad.	ΜΑΝΑΟΒΑΓΟ Moon-god facing, seated on throne; feet resting on footstool; wears helmet; crescent behind shoulders; has four arms and hands, in three of which he grasps sceptre, wreath? and fire?, fourth hand rests on hip; to r., .
25	122·	AV ·75		[Pl. xxvii. 17.]
26	122·5	AV ·8		
			ΡΑΟΝΑΝΟΡΑΟΟ ΟÞΡΚΙΚΟΡΑΝΟ Upper part of the king l., emerging from clouds, diad. and nimbate; wears conical helmet and coat of mail; holds ear of corn and spear.	ΜΑΟ Moon-god l., crescent behind shoulders; clad in coat; holds wreath and sceptre; sword at waist; to l., .
27	122·3	AV ·85		[Pl. xxvii. 18.]
			Similar.	ΜΑΟ Moon-god l., crescent behind shoulders; clad in chiton and chlamys; sword in l.; holds wreath in r. hand; to l., .
28	122·2	AV ·85		
29	123·2	AV ·8		[I. O. C.]
			Similar.	ΜΑΟ Moon-god l.; holds sceptre in l.; r. hand advanced; to l., .
30	122·6	AV ·85		[I. O. C. Pl. xxvii. 19.]
			ΡΑΟΝΑΝΟΡ ΑΟΟΟÞΡΚΟ Similar type.	ΜΑΟ Moon-god l.; r. hand extended; in l., sword; to l., .
31	30·2	AV ·5		[I. O. C. Pl. xxvii. 20.]

No.	Wt.	Metal. Size.	Obverse.	Reverse.
			PAONANOPAOO OhPKIKOPANO Upper part of the king l., emerging from clouds, diad.; wears rounded helmet, and chlamys over armour; holds ear of corn and elephant-goad.	MAO Moon-god l.; holds sceptre in l. hand; to l., .
32	120·4	AV ·9		
			Similar.	MAO Moon-god l.; holds sceptre in r. hand; to l., .
33	121·2	AV ·8		[Pl. XXVII. 21.]
34	122·5	AV ·8		[I. O. C.]
			Similar.	MAO Moon-god l.; r. hand extended; in l., sceptre, held transversely; to l., 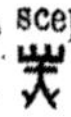.
35	122·4	AV ·75		
36	121·2	AV ·8		sceptre bound with fillet.
37	121·2	AV ·8		" " [Pl. XXVII. 22.]
38	123·	AV ·85		(inscr. MAOO).
			Similar.	MAO Moon-god l.; r. hand extended; sword in l.; to l., .
39	122·8	AV ·85		
40	121·4	AV ·8		(inscr. MAOO).
			Similar.	MAO Moon-god r., diad.; holds in r. hand, wreath; in l., sceptre; to r., 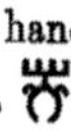.
41	122·	AV ·8		[Pl. XXVII. 23.]

No.	Wt.	Metal. Size.	Obverse.	Reverse.
42	121·1	AV ·8	ΡΑΟΝΑΝΟΡΑΟΟ ΟϸΡΚΙΚΟΡΑΝΟ Upper part of the king l., emerging from clouds, diad.; wears rounded helmet, and chlamys over armour; holds ear of corn and elephant-goad.	Bearded moon-god r., diad.; crescent behind shoulders; holds in r. hand, sceptre, bound with fillet; in l., elephant-goad: and sun-god l., radiate; r. hand advanced; in l., sceptre, bound with fillet; behind the two, the names ΜΑΟ and ΜΙΙΡΟ respectively; between them, . [Pl. xxvii. 24.]
43	123·	AV ·85	ΡΑΟΝΑΝΟΡΑΟΟΟ ϸΡΚΕΚΟΡΑΝΟ Upper part of the king l., emerging from clouds, diad. and nimbate; flames rising from shoulders; wears conical helmet; holds ear of corn and spear.	ΜΙΙΡΟ Sun-god l., nimbate; holds wreath and sceptre; sword at waist; to l., .
44	122·3	AV ·85		
45	123·	AV ·8	Similar; no flames.	ΜΟΡΟ Sun-god l., radiate; holds wreath and sceptre; sword at waist; to l., . [Pl. xxviii. 1.]
46	121·7	AV ·8	Similar.	ΜΙΟΡΟ Sun-god l., radiate; holds wreath and sceptre, bound with fillet; to l., . [I. O. C.]
47	122·8	AV ·8	Similar; king holds standard instead of spear.	ΜΙΟΡΟ Sun-god l., diad. and nimbate; holds wreath and sword; to l., 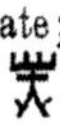.

No.	Wt.	Metal. Size.	Obverse.	Reverse.
48	122·2	AV ·9	PAONANOPAOOO ҺPKIKOPANO Upper part of the king l., emerging from clouds, diad. and nimbate; wears conical helmet; holds ear of corn and spear.	MIYPO Sun-god l., diad. and radiate; holds wreath and sword; to l., .
49	121·3	AV ·85	Similar.	MIIPO Sun-god r., radiate; holds spear and sword; to r., . [I. O. C. Pl. XXVIII. 2.]
50	30·2	AV ·5	PAOOOҺ Similar.	MYPO Sun-god l., nimbate; r. hand advanced; in l., sceptre; to l., . [I. O. C. Pl. XXVIII. 3.]
51	30·7	AV ·55	PAONANOPA OOOҺPKI Upper part of the king l., emerging from clouds, diad.; wears rounded helmet; holds ear of corn and elephant-goad.	MIOPO Sun-god l., radiate; holds wreath and sceptre; to l., . [I. O. C.]
52	120·8	AV ·8	PAONANOPAOOY OҺPKIKOPANO Similar.	MIOPO Sun-god l., radiate; r. hand holds spear; l. grasps sword; to l., .
53	122·8	AV ·8		[I. O. C.]
54	122·2	AV ·85	PAONANOPAO OOҺPKIKOPANO Similar.	MIOPO Sun-god l., radiate; l. hand holds spear; r. rests on hip; sword at waist; to l., . [Pl. XXVIII. 4.]

No.	Wt.	Metal. Size.	Obverse.	Reverse.
55	123·	AV ·8	**PAONANOPAO OOÞPKIKOPANO** Upper part of the king l., emerging from clouds, diad.; wears rounded helmet; holds ear of corn and elephant-goad.	**MIIPO** Sun-god l., radiate; r. hand extended; in l., sceptre, held transversely, bound with fillet; to l., .
56	121·4	AV ·75		inscr. **MIOPO**.
57	120·8	AV ·8	(bust only of king).	
58	120·	AV ·8	,, ,,	[I. O. C.]
59	122·7	AV ·8		inscr. **MYPO**. [I. O. C.]
60	30·2	AV ·5		
61	29·5	AV ·5		
62	120·6	AV ·75	Similar.	**MIPPO** Sun-god l., radiate; r. hand advanced; l. holds sword; to l., .
63	122·3	AV ·8		inscr. **MIIPO**. [I. O. C.]
64	119·5	AV ·8		,, **MIPO**. ,,
65	118·	AV ·8	Same inscr. Upper part of king as above, to r.	**MIIPO** Similar. [I. O. C.]
66	122·3	AV ·85	Same inscr. Upper part of king as above, to l.	**MIIPO** Sun-god r., diad. and radiate; holds wreath and sword; to r., .
67	122·4	AV ·8		[Pl. XXVIII. 5.]

No.	Wt.	Metal. Size.	Obverse.	Reverse.
			PAONANOPAO OOҺPKIKOPANO Upper part of king l., emerging from clouds, diad. and nimbate; wears conical helmet; holds ear of corn and spear.	OИIA Sun-god advancing l., radiate; r. hand advanced; l. holds sword; to l., .
68	26·	AV ·5		
69	28·8	AV ·5		[I. O. C.]
70	30·2	AV ·55		[I. O. C. Pl. xxviii. 6.]
			PAONANOPAOOO ҺPKEKOPANO Upper part of king l., emerging from clouds, diad. and nimbate; flames rise from shoulders; wears conical helmet; holds ear of corn and spear.	ҺPO (MEIPO ?) Artemis standing r., clad in long chiton and himation; holds in l. hand, bow; and with r., draws arrow from quiver; to r., .
71	122·3	AV ·85		[Pl. xxviii. 7.]
			PAONANOPAOOO ҺPKIKOPANO Upper part of king l., emerging from clouds, diad. and nimbate; wears conical helmet; holds ear of corn and spear.	NANA Nanaia l., wears stephane; holds sceptre, ending in forepart of horse, and patera; to l., 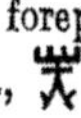.
72	121·7	AV ·8		[Pl. xxviii. 8.]
			Similar.	NANO Nanaia r., diad. and nimbate; crescent on head; holds sceptre and patera; to r., 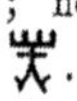.
73	124·	AV ·85		[I. O. C.]
74	123·	AV ·85	king's name OOҺPKO.	inscr. NANA. [I. O. C.]
75	121·3	AV ·85	" OҺPKO.	" "

No.	Wt.	Metal. Size.	Obverse.	Reverse.
			PAONANOPAOOO ĥPKIKOPANO Upper part of king l., emerging from clouds, diad. and nimbate; wears conical helmet; holds ear of corn and spear.	NANO Nanaia r., diad. and nimbate; crescent on head; holds sceptre and patera; to r., .
76	122·9	AV ·8	king holds double ear of corn.*	[Pl. XXVIII. 9.]
77	122·5	AV ·85	king's name OOĥPKO.	[I. O. C.]
78	121·2	AV ·85	„ OOĥPKE.	inscr. barbarous.
79	122·5	AV ·8	„ „	„ „
80	122·6	AV ·85	„ „	„ „ [I. O. C.]
			PAONANOPAOO OĥPKOKOPANOPAO King seated cross-legged on clouds, head r., diad. and helmeted; holds in l., standard, surmounted by bird.	NANA Nanaia r., diad. and nimbate; crescent on head; sword at waist; holds sceptre and patera; to r., .
81	120·8	AV ·85		
82	119·5	AV ·8		[I. O. C. Pl. XXVIII. 10.]
			PAONANOPAOO OĥPKIKOPANO Upper part of the king l., emerging from clouds, diad.; wears rounded helmet; holds ear of corn and elephant-goad.	NANAPAO Nanaia r., diad. and nimbate; crescent on head; sword at waist; holds sceptre and patera; to r., 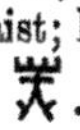.
83	118·8	AV ·8		
84	121·3	AV ·8		[I. O. C.]

* This specimen proves that the object in the king's r. hand is an ear of corn, and not a club as it has usually been supposed to be.

U

No.	Wt.	Metal. Size.	Obverse.	Reverse.
			ΡΑΟΝΑΝΟΡΑΟΟ ΟϸΡΚΙΚΟΡΑΝΟ Upper part of the king l., emerging from clouds, diad.: wears rounded helmet; holds ear of corn and elephant-goad.	ΝΑΝΑ Nanaia r., diad. and nimbate; crescent on head; sword at waist; holds sceptre and patera; to r., .
85	122·4	AV ·8		[I. O. C.]
86	122·	AV ·8		
87	119·7	AV ·8		
88	121·4	AV ·8		inscr. ΝΑΝΟ.
			Similar.	ΝΑΝΑ Nanaia l., diad. and nimbate; crescent on head; holds sceptre in outstretched r. hand; in l., patera; to l., .
89	121·6	AV ·85		[I. O. C.]
90	120·	AV ·8		inscr. ΝΑΝΟ. [I. O. C. Pl. xxviii. 11.]
91	122·4	AV ·8		" "
92	121·2	AV ·8		" "
93	121·1	AV ·85	inscr. barbarous.	inscr. barbarous.
			Similar.	ΟΔΙΙΟ Nanaia r., diad. and nimbate; holds sceptre, bound with fillet, and patera; to r., .
94	119·6	AV ·85		[Pl. xxviii. 12.]

No.	Wt.	Metal. Size.	Obverse.	Reverse.
95	122·	AV ·85	ΡΑΟΝΑΝΟΡΑΟΟΟ ϷΡΚƐΚΟΡΑΝΟ Upper part of king l., emerging from clouds, diad. and nimbate; wears conical helmet; flames rising from shoulders; holds ear of corn and spear.	ΟΑΝΙΝΔΑ Nike standing l.; holds wreath and trophy-stand, as on coins of Alexander; to r., . [Pl. XXVIII. 13.]
96	121·7	AV ·8		inscr. ΟΑΝΙΝΔΟ.
97	122·7	AV ·8	ΡΑΟΝΑΝΟΡΑΟΟ ΟϷΡΚΙΚΟΡΑΝΟ Upper part of king l., emerging from clouds, diad.; flames rising from shoulders; wears rounded helmet; holds ear of corn and elephant-goad.	ΟΚΡΟ Siva l., nimbate; wears necklace, and has four arms and hands, in which are (1) vase and elephant-goad, (2) thunderbolt, (3) trident, (4) goat; to l., . [Pl. XXVIII. 14.]
98	121·5	AV ·8		[I. O. C.]
99	120·1	AV ·8		
100	123·	AV ·85	Inscr. barbarous. Similar	ΟΚΡΟ Siva l., with four arms and hands, in which are (1) wreath, (2) ?, (3) trident, (4) goat; to l., .
101	122·2	AV ·85	ΡΑΟΝΑΝΟΡΑ ΟΟϷΡΚ Upper part of king l., emerging from clouds, diad. and nimbate; wears rounded helmet; holds ear of corn and standard surmounted by bird.	ΟΚΡΑ Siva facing, three-headed; has four arms and hands, in which are vase, thunderbolt, trident, and club; to l., . [Pl. XXVIII. 15.]

No.	Wt.	Metal. Size.	Obverse.	Reverse.
102	123·5	AV ·85	PAONANOPA OOOhPKIKOPANO Upper part of the king l., emerging from clouds, diad. and nimbate; wears conical helmet; holds ear of corn and spear.	OKPO Siva facing, three-headed, nimbate; clad only in waistband, ithyphallic; has four arms and hands, in which are goat, wheel, trident, and thunderbolt; to r., . [Pl. xxviii. 16.]
103	123·	AV ·8	Similar.	PAOPhOPO Ares standing r., in Greek helmet and armour; holds spear, and shield which rests on ground; to r., . [Pl. xxviii. 17.]
104	121·7	AV ·8	inscr. barbarous.	inscr. VAOPHOO. [I. O. C.]
105	122·5	AV ·85	(last letters of inscr. wanting).	
106	122·8	AV ·85	PAONANOPAOO OhPKOK Similar type.	PAOPHOAP Similar.
107	122·5	AV ·85	PAONANOPAOOO hPKЄKOPANO Similar type.	PAOPHOPO Ares l., in Greek helmet and armour; holds shield in r. hand, spear in l.; to l, . [Pl. xxviii. 18.]
108	123·	AV ·8	Same inscr. Upper part of king, as above; holds ear of corn and sceptre.	PAOPHOPO Ares r., in Greek helmet and armour, nimbate; holds spear and sword; to l., . [Pl. xxviii. 19.]

No.	Wt.	Metal. Size.	Obverse.	Reverse.
109	123·5	AV ·85	Inscr. obscure. Upper part of king l., emerging from clouds, diad.; wears rounded helmet; holds ear of corn and elephant-goad.	PIDM Roma or Pallas standing r., wearing helmet and long chiton; holds spear and shield; to r., [symbol]. [Pl. xxviii. 20.]
110	123·1	AV ·85	PAONANOPA OOYOϷPKIKOP Similar.	CAPAΠO Sarapis standing l., diad. and clad in himation; r. hand advanced; in l., sceptre; to l., [symbol]. [Pl. xxviii. 21.]
111	121·6	AV ·85		[I. O. C.]
112	123·	AV ·8	PAONANOPAOO OϷPKIKOPANO Upper part of king l., emerging from clouds, diad.; wears rounded helmet; holds ear of corn and elephant-goad.	CKANΔOKO M BIZAΓO APO Skanda and Viṣākha* standing face to face, nimbate; each wearing chlamys and necklace, and sword at waist; but Skanda holds in r. hand, standard surmounted by bird; Viṣākha holds in l. hand, spear; between them, [symbol]. [Pl. xxviii. 22.]
113	121·3	AV ·8		
114	31·	AV ·5	Similar; last letter of inscr. wanting.	CKANΔOKOMAPO B IZAΓO Skanda and Viṣākha standing face to face, nimbate; Skanda holds in r. hand, standard; Viṣākha holds in l. hand, spear; between them, [symbol]. [I. O. C. Pl. xxviii. 23.]

* A son and impersonation of Skanda. *See* Introduction.

No.	Wt.	Metal. Size.	Obverse.	Reverse.
115	121·	AV ·8	PAONANOPAOO OҺPKIKOPANO Upper part of king l., emerging from clouds, diad.; wears rounded helmet; holds ear of corn and elephant-goad.	CKANΔOK OMAPOMA ACҺ NOBIZAΓO Niche on basis, within which, Skanda and Viṣā-kha standing as above; between them, Mahāsena, horned (?), facing, nimbate, clad in chlamys; sword at waist; to l., . [Pl. XXVIII. 24.]
116	123·2	AV ·8	PAONANPAOO OҺKIKOPANO Upper part of king l., emerging from clouds, diad. and nimbate; wears conical helmet; holds ear of corn and spear.	ΦAPPO Male deity l., head winged; clad in coat; holds in r. hand, fire; l. grasps sword at waist; to l., . [I. O. C. Pl. XXVIII. 25.]
117	122·4	AV ·85	ҺPKIKOPANO Upper part of king l., emerging from clouds, diad. and nimbate; flames rise from shoulders; wears conical helmet; holds ear of corn and standard.	ΦAPPO Male deity l., head winged, diad.; flames rising from shoulders; wears coat and chlamys; holds in r. hand, fire; l. grasps sword at waist; to l., .
118	121·6	AV ·8	PAONANOPAO OOҺPKIKOPANO Upper part of king l., emerging from clouds, diad. and nimbate; wears conical helmet; holds ear of corn and standard surmounted by bird.	ΦAPPO Similar; deity nimbate.

No.	Wt.	Metal. Size.	Obverse.	Reverse
119	123·4	AV ·8	PAONANOPAOOO ҺPKIKOPANO King as last; holding ear of corn and spear.	ΦAPO Male deity l., head winged, nimbate; wears coat and chlamys; r. hand advanced; in l., long sceptre; sword at waist; to l., . [I. O. C.]
120	121·2	AV ·8	Same inscr. King as last; holding ear of corn and sceptre.	ΦAPPO Male deity l., nimbate; flames rising from shoulders; holds in extended r. hand, fire; in l., sceptre; to l., . [Pl. XXVIII. 26.]
121	123·3	AV ·8	Same inscr. King as before; holding ear of corn and spear.	ΦAPPO Male deity r., head winged, nimbate; clad in coat; holds sceptre and fire; to r., . [Pl. XXVIII. 27.]
122	122·4	AV ·8	Same inscr.? King as before; holding double ear of corn and spear.	ΦAPPO Male deity l., head winged, nimbate; clad in coat and chlamys; holds purse and caduceus; to l., . [I. O. C.]
123	123·5	AV ·8	PAONANOPA OOOҺPKЄKOPA King as before; holding ear of corn and spear.	ΦAPO Similar figure; holds purse? and long sceptre; to l., . [Pl. XXVIII. 28.]
124	121·5	AV ·8	PAONANOPAOOO ҺPKIKOPANO Similar.	ΦAPPO Male deity r., head winged, diad. and nimbate; clad in coat; holds sceptre and elephant-goad; to l., . [Pl. XXVIII. 29.]

No.	Wt.	Metal. Size.	Obverse.	Reverse.
125	124·1	AV ·85	PAONANOPAO OOHPKOKOP Upper part of king l., emerging from clouds, diad. and nimbate; wears rounded helmet; holds ear of corn and standard.	Inscr. barbarous. Male deity l., nimbate; in extended r. hand, fire; in l., sword; to l., [symbol].
126	121·2	AV ·8	PAONANOPAOO OHPKIKOPANO Upper part of king l., emerging from clouds, diad.; wears rounded helmet; holds ear of corn and elephant-goad.	ΦAPO Male deity l., head winged, nimbate; holds in r. hand, wreath; in l., sceptre; to l., [symbol].
127	122·5	AV ·75	Similar.	ΦAPPO Male deity r., head winged, nimbate; r. hand rests on hip; in l., sceptre; to r., [symbol].
128	121·7	AV ·8		[I. O. C.]
129	122·2	AV ·9		inscr. ΦAPO.
130	33·3	AV ·5		
131	27·	AV ·5		[I. O. C. Pl. XXVIII. 30.]
132	123·3	AV ·75	Similar	ΦAPO Male deity l.; l. hand rests on hip; in r., sceptre; to l., [symbol].
133	121·4	AV ·8		inscr. ΦAPPO. [I. O. C.]
134	122·1	AV ·8		„ OqAΦ. (sword at waist).

No.	Wt.	Metal. Size.	Obverse.	Reverse.
135	120·8	AV ·8	PAONANOPAOO OhPKIKOPANO Upper part of king l., emerging from clouds, diad.; wears rounded helmet; holds ear of corn and elephant-goad.	ΦAPO Male deity l., head winged, nimbate, standing on fire; holds in r. hand, fire; in l., sceptre; to l., .
136	120·	AV ·8	Similar.	ΦAPPO Male deity l., head winged, nimbate, standing on fire; r. hand extended; in l., caduceus; to l., .
137	122·4	AV ·8		[I. O. C. Pl. xxviii. 31.]
138	122·	AV ·8	Similar.	ωPON Male deity l., bearded, wearing modius and himation; r. hand advanced; in l., long sceptre; to l., . [Pl. xxviii. 32.]
139	122·2	AV ·8		[I. O. C.]

(β) *Bronze; type, King on elephant.*

No.	Wt.	Metal. Size.	Obverse.	Reverse.
140		Æ 1·	PAONANO PAOOO-hPKENOPANO* The king r., diad. and nimbate, riding on elephant; holds spear and elephant-goad.	AΘPO Male deity l., diad.; holds in r. hand, wreath; and in l., tongs; to l., .
141		Æ 1·15		
142		Æ 1·		

* This inscription cannot be read entire on any single specimen; and many specimens are blundered or barbarous: but the formula in the text seems to be the normal and usual one.

No.	Wt.	Metal. Size.	Obverse.	Reverse.
143		Æ 1·	PAONANO PAOOO-HPKENOPANO The king r., diad. and nimbate, riding on elephant; holds spear and elephant-goad.	APOOXP Female deity r., diad. and nimbate; holds cornucopiae; to r., .
144		Æ ·95		[I. O. C.]
145		Æ 1·	Similar.	Insc. obscure. Female deity* l., nimbate; holds in extended r. hand, wreath; in l., cornucopiae; to l., 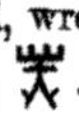. [I. O. C.]
146		Æ ·95	Similar.	HPAKΛO? Heracles r.; holds in r. hand, club; l. raised to head; to r., . [Pl. xxix. 1.]
147		Æ 1·05	Similar.	MAO Moon-god l., crescent behind shoulders; r. hand extended; with l. grasps sword; to l., . [I. O. C. Pl. xxix. 2.]
148		Æ 1·		
149		Æ 1·		
150		Æ 1·		
151		Æ ·85		
152		Æ ·8		(deity holds wreath and sword).

* Cf. the deity accompanied by the inscription ΔOXPO on gold of this king.

No.	Wt.	Metal. Size.	Obverse.	Reverse.
153		Æ 1·05	PAONANO PAOOO-ΗΡΚΕΝΟΡΑΝΟ The king r., diad. and nimbate, riding on elephant; holds spear and elephant-goad.	MAO Female deity l., nimbate; holds in both hands, cornucopiae; to l., .
154		Æ 1·	Similar.	MIIOPO Sun-god l., radiate; r. hand extended; with l. grasps sword; to l., . [I. O. C.]
155		Æ 1·		(inscr. MIIPO).
156		Æ ·95		„ „
157		Æ 1·	Barbarous inscr. King on elephant to l.	MPPO? Sun-god l., nimbate; r. hand extended; in l., sceptre; to l., .
158		Æ 1·05	PAONANO PAOOO-ΗΡΚΕΝΟΡΑΝΟ The king r., diad. and nimbate, riding on elephant; holds spear and elephant-goad.	OKPO Siva standing l., four armed; holds wreath, thunderbolt, trident, and goat; to l., .
159		Æ 1·		(Siva holds in fourth hand, vase). [Pl. XXIX. 3.]
160		Æ 1·05	Similar.	OKPO Siva standing l., two armed; holds in r. hand, trident; in l., vase and lion's skin (?); to l., ; to r., .
161		Æ 1·		
162		Æ ·9		[I. O. C.]
163		Æ ·85		
164		Æ ·95		
165		Æ ·95		

No.	Wt.	Metal. Size.	Obverse.	Reverse.
			(γ) *Bronze; type, King seated.*	
166		Æ 1·	ΡΑΟΝΑΝΟΡΑΟ ΟΟΗΡΚΕΝΟΡΑΝΟ* King facing, head r., seated cross-legged on cushions, body radiate; in l. hand, sceptre.	ΑΘΡΟ Male deity l.; holds wreath in extended r. hand; to l., .
167		Æ 1·	Inscr. King, head and body radiate, seated facing on throne.	Similar.
168		Æ 1·		
169		Æ ·8	Inscr. King nimbate, facing, head r., seated; holds in l. hand, sceptre.	ΑΡΔΟΧΡ Female deity l.; holds cornucopiae; to l., .
170		Æ ·8	Inscr. King nimbate, r., reclining.	ΑΡ]ΔΟΧΡ Female deity l.; holds in r. hand, sceptre (?); to l., .
171		Æ 1·	Inscr. King seated cross-legged on cushions, facing, head r., head and body radiate; l. hand raised.	ΜΑΟ Moon-god l., crescent behind shoulders; r. hand advanced; with l. grasps sword; to l., . [I. O. C. Pl. XXIX. 4.]
172		Æ 1·	in l., sceptre.	
173		Æ 1·	" "	
174		Æ ·95	" "	
175		Æ ·8	" "	

* On coins of this class the inscription is even more debased than on those of the last; sometimes, however, it ends ΟΟΗΡΚΕΚΟΡΑΝΟ.

No.	Wt.	Metal. Size.	Obverse.	Reverse.
176		Æ ·9	PAONANOPAO OOHPKENOPANO King seated cross-legged, facing, head r., nimbate; holds in each hand, staff or sword.	MAO Moon-god l., crescent behind shoulders; r. hand advanced; with l. grasps sword; to l., .
177		Æ 1·	Inscr. King, head and body radiate, half reclining, facing, on throne.	Similar.
178		Æ 1·		
179		Æ 1·		(inscr. retrograde). [Pl. XXIX. 5.]
180		Æ ·9		[I. O. C.]
181		Æ ·9		"
182		Æ 1·	Inscr. King, with head and body nimbate, seated cross-legged, facing, on cushions; in l. hand, sceptre.	MIOPO Sun-god l., radiate; r. hand advanced; with l. grasps sword; to l., . [I. O. C.]
183		Æ 1·		
184		Æ ·8	(king not nimbate).	(deity holds wreath in r.). [Pl. XXIX. 6.]
185		Æ ·95		
186		Æ 1·1	Inscr. King, with body radiate, half reclining, facing on throne, flames on shoulders.	Similar. (deity holds sceptre, not sword).
187		Æ 1·		
188		Æ 1·		(inscr. MIIOPO).
189		Æ ·85		
190		Æ ·85		(deity holds wreath in r.).

No.	Wt.	Metal. Size.	Obverse.	Reverse.
			PAONANOPAO OOϷPKEKOPANO King, with head nimbate and body radiate, seated facing, head r., cross-legged on cushions; holds in l. hand, sceptre.	NANA Nanaia r., nimbate; holds sceptre; to r., .
191		Æ 1·05		[I. O. C.]
			Similar.	OKPO Siva facing, nimbate, head l.; has four arms and hands, in which he holds a wreath, a thunderbolt, a trident and a vase; to l., .
192		Æ 1·05		
193		Æ ·9		
			Inscr. King, with head and body radiate, half reclining, facing, on throne.	Similar.
194		Æ 1·		[I. O. C. Pl. xxix. 7.]
195		Æ 1·		
196		Æ 1·		(Siva holds goat in fourth hand).
197		Æ ·9		(Siva grasps sword in fourth hand).

BAZODEO (VASU DEVA).

(a) *Gold.*

No.	Wt.	Metal. Size.	Obverse.	Reverse.
			PAONANO PAO BA ZOAhOKOPANO The king l., clad in conical helmet and suit of mail, diad. and nimbate; holds r. hand over altar; in l., spear; wears sword.	NANA Nanaia r., nimbate, head surmounted by crescent; holds sceptre, ending in forepart of horse, and patera; to r., .
1	122·5	AV ·85		[Pl. xxix. 8.]
2	122·2	AV ·8		[I. O. C.]
			PAONANOPA OBAZOΔhOK Similar.	OKPO Siva facing, having three faces and two arms; holds wreath and trident; to l., .
3	120·8	AV ·8		
4	122·3	AV ·8		(inscr. OPKO). [Pl. xxix. 9.]
			PAONANOPAOBA ZOAhOKOPANO The king l., clad in conical helmet and suit of mail, diad. and nimbate; holds r. hand over altar; in l., spear; standard behind head.	OKPO Siva facing, having three faces and two arms; holds wreath and trident; behind him, bull l.; to r., .
5	123·8	AV ·8		[Pl. xxix. 10.]
6	124·9	AV ·8		
7	123·5	AV ·85		(Siva one-faced). [I. O. C.]
8	124·8	AV ·85		(bull feeding).
9	123·4	AV ·8		„ (inscr. OPKO). „
10	122·8	AV ·85	(inscr. barbarous).	(Siva one-faced); symbol to l.

No.	Wt.	Metal. Size.	Obverse.	Reverse.
11	126·	AV ·85	PAONANOPAOBA ZOAHOKOPANO The king standing as before at altar; beside which, trident fixed in the ground.	OKPO Siva, one-headed, facing; holds wreath and trident; behind him, bull l.; to l., .
12	124·7	AV ·85		
13	121·2	AV ·8		
14	123·	AV ·9	to r., .	(inscr. OqKO; to l.,).
15	124·	AV ·85	„ .	„ „
16	116·4	AV ·85	„ „	„ „
17	31·	AV ·5		„ „ [I. O. C. Pl. xxix. 11.]
18	30·7	AV ·5		(Siva crosses his legs); to r., .
			Barbarous imitations.	
19	122·7	AV ·9	to r., .	[Pl. xxix. 12.]
20	122·5	AV ·9	„ „	to l., .
21	123·7	AV 1·	„ „; below, .	
22	125·5	AV 1·05	„ „ „ „	
23	120·8	AV ·95	„ „	to l., .
24	124·7	AV 1·05	„ „ „ „	[Pl. xxix. 13.]

No.	Wt.	Metal. Size.	Obverse.	Reverse.
			(β) *Bronze.*	
			PAONANOPAO BAZOAhOKOPANO* The king, standing as before, at altar; beside which, trident fixed in the ground.	OKPO Siva, one-headed, facing; holds wreath and trident; behind him, bull l.; to r., .
25		Æ ·9		
26		Æ ·9	to r., .	
27		Æ ·95	„ „	[Pl. XXIX. 14.]
28		Æ 1·		
29		Æ ·85		
30		Æ ·95	(inscr. barbarous).	
31		Æ ·95	„ „	
32		Æ 1·	(trident absent).	(inscr. wanting). [I. O. C.]
			PAOBA ZOΔhO King, standing as above, at altar.	Similar (?).
33		Æ ·75		

* Those legends are not complete on any specimen.

INDO-SCYTHIC, UNCERTAIN.

(a) *Gold ; without figure of King.*

No.	Wt.	Metal. Size.	Obverse.	Reverse.
1	66·7	AV ·6	Indian legend (see plate xxix. 15 ; the inscription seems to run on one side . . . . . *dideva-ta ?*). Greek city-goddess, clad in chiton and peplos, wearing mural crown, and holding a poppy-head.	TAYPOC Humped bull r. 𐨬𐨌𐨮𐨧 (*vrishabha*). [Pl. xxix. 15.]

SUPPLEMENT.

IMPORTANT TYPES NOT IN THE BRITISH MUSEUM.*

No.	Obverse.	Reverse.
	DEMETRIUS.	
1	Bust of the king r., diad.	ΒΑΣΙΛΕΩΣ ΔΗΜΗΤΡΙΟΥ Pallas facing, armed; holds lance and shield.
	[Pl. xxx. 1.]	AR Wt. 243· (Gen. Cunningham): an injured specimen (Wt. 219·3), recently acquired for Brit. Museum.
2	Head of the king r., in elephant's skin.	Same inscr. Pallas seated l., holding spear in r., and shield in l.
	[Pl. xxx. 2.]	Æ round, ·7 (Gen. Cunningham).
3	ΒΑΣΙΛΕΩΣ ΑΝΙΚΗΤΟΥ ΔΗΜΗΤΡΙΟΥ Bust of the king r., in elephant's skin.	[illegible] ..... [illegible] (*Māharajasa aparajitasa Deme.....*). Winged thunderbolt.
	[Pl. xxx. 3.]	Æ square, ·75 (Gen. Cunningham).

* In this list will be found the more important coins of the Greek and Scythic Kings which have been published, but are not represented in the British Museum. Mere varieties are not given, nor, in most cases, merely different denominations of already mentioned coins, unless when such denominations are higher than those of the British Museum Coins. To this Supplement belong three plates, the figures in which are in most cases due to Gen. Cunningham's valuable papers in the *Numismatic Chronicle*, and are reproduced by his kind permission. In one or two instances coins have been inserted here which were acquired for the British Museum too late for them to figure in their proper places.

No.	Obverse.	Reverse.
	PANTALEON.	
1	Head of the king r., diad. [Pl. xxx. 4.]	ΒΑΣΙΛΕΩΣ ΓΑΝΤΑΛΕΟΝΤΟΣ Zeus seated l.; holds in l., sceptre, in r., a figure of the three-headed Hekate. ℞ Wt. 232· (Gen. Cunningham).
	AGATHOCLES. *With name and type of Antiochus Nicator.*	
1	ΑΝΤΙΟΧΟΥ ΝΙΚΑΤΟΡΟΣ Head of Antiochus I. r., diad. [Pl. xxx. 5.]	ΒΑΣΙΛΕΥΟΝΤΟΣ ΑΓΑΘΟΚΛΕΟΥΣ ΔΙΚΑΙΟΥ Zeus striding to l., hurling thunderbolt; eagle at his feet: to l., wreath. ℞ Wt. 255· (Gen. Cunningham).
	ANTIMACHUS I. *With name and type of Diodotus.*	
1	ΔΙΟΔΟΤΟΥ ΣΩΤΗΡΟΣ Head of Diodotus r., diad. [Pl. xxx. 6.]	ΒΑΣΙΛΕΥΟΝΤΟΣ ΑΝΤΙΜΑΧΟΥ ΘΕΟΥ Zeus striding to l., hurling thunderbolt; eagle at his feet: to l., wreath. ℞ Tetradrachm (The late Sir E. C. Bayley).
	With his own types.	
2	Indian elephant r. [Pl. xxx. 7.]	ΒΑΣΙΛΕΩΣ ΘΕΟΥ ΑΝΤΙΜΑΧΟΥ Nike l., holding wreath and palm, standing on prow of ship. Æ round, ·9 (formerly Gen. Cunningham).

No.	Obverse.	Reverse.
	EUCRATIDES.	
1	Bust of the king r., helmeted.	ΒΑΣΙΛΕΩΣ ΜΕΓΑΛΟΥ ΕΥΚΡΑΤΙΔΟΥ The Dioscuri charging r., carrying palms.
	[*Rev. Numism.*, 1867, Pl. XII.]	ɅV Wt. 2593·5 gr. (20 stater piece, Bibl. Nationale, Paris).
2		ɅV Stater (Col. Strutt).
3	Bust of the king l., helmeted, but with shoulders bare; thrusting with spear.	As last.
	[Pl. XXX. 8.]	Æ Wt. 233· (Gen. Cunningham).
4	ΒΑΣΙΛΕΩΣ ΜΕΓΑΛΟΥ ΕΥΚΡΑΤΙΔΟΥ Bust of the king r., helmeted.	𐨨𐨱𐨪𐨗𐨯 𐨨𐨱𐨟𐨐𐨯 𐨅𐨂𐨐𐨿𐨪𐨟𐨁𐨡𐨯 (*Maharajasa mahatakasa Evukratidasa*). The Dioscuri standing side by side; hold spears and swords.
	[Pl. XXX. 9.]	Æ Wt. 34·5 gr. (formerly Gen. Abbott). On a coin of this class in Gen. Court's Collection, the inscription begins 𐨪𐨗𐨯 (Von Sallet in *Zeit. f. Num.* 10, p. 157).
5	Head of Apollo r., laur.	ΒΑΣΙΛΕΩΣ ΕΥΚΡΑΤΙΔΟΥ Horse l., standing.
	[Pl. XXX. 10.]	Æ round, ·7 (Vienna).
6	ΒΑΣΙΛΕΩΣ ΜΕΓΑΛΟΥ ΕΥΚΡΑΤΙΔΟΥ Bust of the king r., diad.	Indian inscr. as above. The pilei of the Dioscuri, surmounted by stars, and two palms.
	[Pl. XXX. 11.]	Æ square, ·55 (Gen. Cunningham).

No.	Obverse.	Reverse.
7	ΒΑΣΙΛΕΩΣ ΜΕΓΑΛΟΥ ΕΥΚΡΑΤΙΔΟΥ Bust of the king r., diad. and helmeted. [Pl. xxx. 12.]	[illegible] (*Māhārajasa rajadirajasa Evukratidasa*).. Nike l.; holds wreath and palm. Æ square, ·7 (Gen. Cunningham).

HELIOCLES.

No.	Obverse.	Reverse.
1	Bust of the king r., helmeted.	ΒΑΣΙΛΕΩΣ ΗΛΙΟΚΛΕΟΥΣ ΔΙΚΑΙΟΥ Zeus seated l.; holds Nike and long sceptre. AR Tetradrachm (formerly Major Hay).
2	[Pl. xxxi. 1.]	AR Drachm (The late Sir E. C. Bayley).

ANTIALCIDAS.

No.	Obverse.	Reverse.
1	ΒΑΣΙΛΕΩΣ ΝΙΚΗΦΟΡΟΥ ΑΝΤΙΑΛΚΙΔΟΥ Bust of the king r, diad.	[illegible] (*Maharajasa jayadharasa Aṃtialikidasa*). Elephant walking r.; wreath in raised trunk. Æ square, ·75 (Major Landon: now presented to British Museum).

ANTIALCIDAS AND LYSIAS.

No.	Obverse.	Reverse.
1	ΒΑΣΙΛΕΩΣ ΑΝΙΚΗΤΟΥ ΛΥΣΙΟΥ Bust of bearded Herakles r.; club on shoulder. [Pl. xxxi. 2.]	Inscr. as last. The caps of the Dioscuri, and two palms. Æ square, ·7 (Bodleian Library).

No.	Obverse.	Reverse.
	THEOPHILUS.	
1	ΒΑΣΙΛΕΩΣ ΔΙΚΑΙΟΥ ΘΕΟΦΙΛΟΥ Bust of the king r., diad. [Pl. XXXI. 3.]	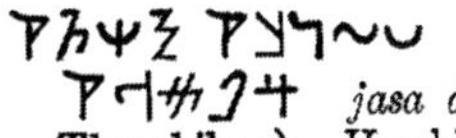 (*Maharajasa dhramikasa Ṭheuphilasa*). Herakles, crowning himself; holds in l. hand, club and lion's skin. Æ Wt. 36· (Gen. Cunningham).
2	ΒΑΣΙΛΕΩΣ ΔΙΚΑΙΟΥ ΘΕΟΦΙΛΟΥ Head of bearded Herakles r.; club on shoulder. [Pl. XXXI. 4.]	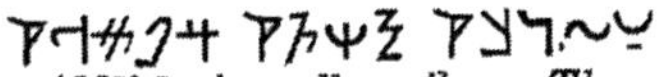 (*Māhārajasa dhramikasa Ṭheuphilasa*). Cornucopiae. Æ square, ·8 (Gen. Cunningham).
	ARCHEBIUS.	
1	ΒΑΣΙΛΕΩΣ ΔΙΚΑΙΟΥ ΝΙΚΗΦΟΡΟΥ ΑΡΧΕΒΙΟΥ Bust of Zeus r., diad.; sceptre on shoulder. [Pl. XXXI. 5.]	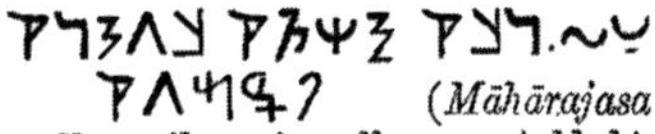 (*Māhārajasa dhramikasa jayadharasa Arkhebiyasa*). The caps of the Dioscuri, and two palms. Æ square, ·9 (Gen. Cunningham).
	APOLLODOTUS.	
1	ΒΑΣΙΛΕΩΣ ΣΩΤΗΡΟΣ [ΑΠΟΛΛΟΔΟΤΟΥ] Apollo seated r. on throne, holding out bow.	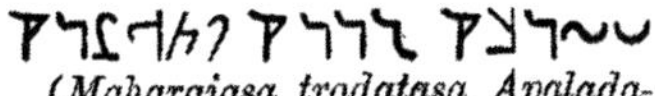 (*Maharajasa tradatasa Apaladatasa*). Tripod. Æ square, ·8 (Gen. Cunningham).

No.	Obverse.	Reverse.
	STRATO I.	
1	ΒΑΣΙΛΕΩΣ ΕΠΙΦΑΝΟΥΣ ΣΩΤΗΡΟΣ ΣΤΡΑΤΩΝΟΣ Bust of the king r., diad. [Pl. xxxi. 6.]	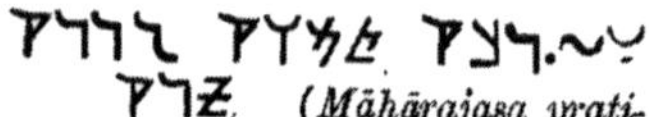 (*Māhārajasa pratichhasa tradatasa Stratasa*). Pallas l.; holding aegis and hurling thunderbolt. Æ Wt. 134· (Gen. Cunningham).
	STRATO II.	
1	ΒΑϹΙΛΕΩϹ ϹΩΤΗΡΟϹ ϹΤΡΑΤΩΝΟϹ ΥΙΟΥ ϹΤΡΑΤΩΝΟϹ Bust of the king r., diad. [Pl. xxxi. 7.]	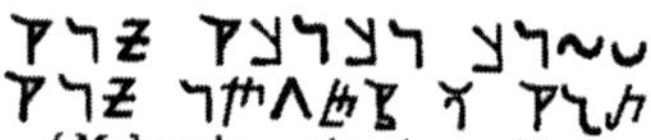 (*Maharaja rajarajasa Stratasa putrasa cha sampriyapita Stratasa*). Pallas l.; holding aegis and thunderbolt. Æ Wt. 36· (Gen. Cunningham).

This is Gen. Cunningham's reading of his specimen (engraved), and given on his authority.

No.	Obverse.	Reverse.
	MENANDER.	
1	ΒΑΣΙΛΕΩΣ ΣΩΤΗΡΟΣ ΜΕΝΑΝΔΡΟΥ Head of Pallas r., helmeted. [Pl. xxxi. 8.]	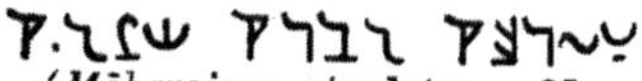 (*Māharajasa tradatasa Menadrāsa*). Owl r. Æ Wt. 28· (Gen. Cunningham).
2	ΒΑΣΙΛΕΩΣ ΣΩΤΗΡΟΣ ΜΕΝΑΝΔΡΟΥ Bust of the king l., wearing aegis and thrusting with spear.	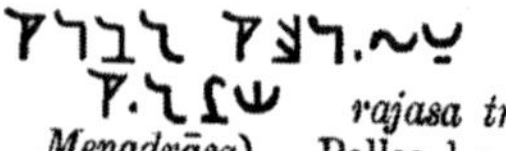 (*Māhārajasa tradatasa Menadrāsa*). Pallas l.; holding thunderbolt and aegis. Æ Didrachm (Published by Gen. Cunningham from a sealing-wax impression).

No.	Obverse.	Reverse.
3	**ΒΑΣΙΛΕΩΣ ΣΩΤΗΡΟΣ ΜΕΝΑΝΔΡΟΥ** Young male head r., wearing wreath.	(*Māhārajasa tradatasa Menadrāsa*). Dolphin r.
	[Pl. xxxi. 9.]	Æ square, 1·
4	Same inscr. Two-humped camel l.	Same inscr. Bull's head, facing.
	[Pl. xxxi. 10.]	Æ square, 1· (Museum As. Soc. Bengal).
5	Same inscr. Elephant l.	Same inscr. Elephant-goad.
	[Pl. xxxi. 11.]	Æ square, ·9 (Gen. Cunningham).
6	Same inscr. Boar's head r.	Same inscr. Palm-branch.
	[Pl. xxxi. 12.]	Æ square, ·8

Nos. 3 and 6 are said by Gen. Cunningham to be in the East India Museum. This is incorrect, as the coins of this Museum are now in the British Museum, and these types are wanting.

EPANDER.

No.	Obverse.	Reverse.
1	**ΒΑΣΙΛΕΩΣ ΝΙΚΗΦΟΡΟΥ ΕΠΑΝΔΡΟΥ** Bust of the king r., diad.	(*Maharajasa*] *jayadharasa Epadrasa*). Pallas l.; holds aegis and thunderbolt.
	[Pl. xxxi. 13.]	AR Wt. 19· (broken), (Gen. Cunningham).

DIONYSIUS.

No.	Obverse.	Reverse.
1	Apollo r., clad in chlamys; holds arrow with both hands.	(*Maharajasa tradatasa Dianisiyasa*). Royal diadema.
	[Pl. xxxi. 14.]	Æ square, ·6 (Col. Bush).

No.	Obverse.	Reverse.

ZOILUS.

No.	Obverse.	Reverse.
1	ΒΑΣΙΛΕΩΣ ΔΙΚΑΙΟΥ ΙΩΙΛΟΥ Bust of the king r., diad. [Pl. xxxii. 1.]	(*Māhārajasa dhramikasa Jhoïlasa*). Herakles, facing; holds in r., wreath; in l., club and lion's skin; on his shoulder, Nike holding wreath. AR Wt. 36·5 (Gen. Cunningham).
2	ΒΑΣΙΛΕΩΣ ΔΙΚΑΙΟΥ ΙΩΙΛΟΥ Head of bearded Herakles r., in lion's skin. [Pl. xxxii. 2.]	(*Maharajasa dhramikasa Jhoïlasa*). Club and bow-case, within ivy-wreath. Æ square, 1·1 (Lady Headfort).

ARTEMIDORUS.

No.	Obverse.	Reverse.
1	ΒΑΣΙΛΕΩΣ ΑΝΙΚΗΤΟΥ ΑΡΤΕΜΙΔΩΡΟΥ Bust of the king r., diad. [Pl. xxxii. 3.]	(*Māhārajasa apadihatasa Artemidorasa*). Artemis, clad in short chiton and chlamys, shooting l. AR Wt. 128· (Gen. Cunningham). A specimen much injured (Wt. 117·3), recently acquired for British Museum.
2	(king helmeted). [Pl. xxxii. 4.]	AR Wt. 36· (Gen. Cunningham).
3	Same inscr. Bust of the king r., diad. [Pl. xxxii. 5.]	Same inscr. Nike r.; holds wreath and palm. AR Wt. 37· (Gen. Cunningham).

No.	Obverse.	Reverse.
	PHILOXENUS.	
1	The British Museum has recently acquired a didrachm (Wt. 140·) of this king with the usual type and inscriptions (p. 56), but having on the obverse a helmeted bust of the king l., thrusting with spear.	
	NICIAS.	
1	ΒΑΣΙΛΕΩΣ ΣΩΤΗΡΟΣ ΝΙΚΙΟΥ Bust of the king r., diad.	[illegible] (*Mahārajasa tradatasa Nikiasa*). The king (or Pallas ?) helmeted, standing l.; holds palm over shoulder.
	[Pl. XXXII. 6.]	Æ Wt. 36· (Gen. Cunningham).
	TELEPHUS.	
1	ΒΑΣΙΛΕΩΣ ΕΥΕΡΓΕΤΟΥ ΤΗΛΕΦΟΥ Giant (Skythes ?), his body ending in three serpents; holds in each hand, hammer ?	[illegible] (*Maharajasa palanakramasa Teliphasa*). Helios radiate facing, clad in tunic and chlamys, holds long sceptre; beside him male figure wrapped in mantle, wearing wreath or horned: in field, mon.
	[Pl. XXXII. 7.]	Æ Wt. 37· (Bodleian Library).
	Mr. Oman having kindly procured a cast of this coin, we are enabled to give a more accurate description of it than has hitherto appeared. Mr. Bendall suggests the reading *pālanakshamasa* as a rendering of *εὐεργέτου*.	
	AMYNTAS.	
1	Gen. Cunningham possesses hemidrachms with the usual type of reverse, the seated Zeus; but having on the obverse respectively, (1) bust of the king in Macedonian causia; (2) bust of the king, bare-headed, thrusting with spear.	

No.	Obverse.	Reverse.

HERMAEUS.

1 Gen. Cunningham has a didrachm of the usual type (Wt. 153 grs.), with helmeted head of the king on the obverse.

No.	Obverse.	Reverse.
2	ΒΑΣΙΛΕΩΣ ΣΩΤΗΡΟΣ ΕΡΜΑΙΟΥ King on horseback r., galloping.	(*Maharajasa mahatasa Heramayasa*). Zeus seated l. on throne. Ʀ Wt. 31· (Gen. Cunningham).
3	ΒΑΣΙΛΕΩΣ ΣΤΗΡΟΣ ΣΥ ΕΡΜΑΙΟΥ Bust of the king r., bare. [Pl. xxxii. 8.]	(*Maharajasa rajarajasa?*] *mahatasa Heramayasa*). Nike l.; holding wreath. Æ round, ·7 (Gen. Cunningham).
4	(*Māhārajasa raja* . . . . [*Herama?*]*yasa*). Horse r.	Uncertain device, surrounded by a circle of unascertained Chinese characters. Æ 1· (Sir D. Forsyth), *Num. Chron.*, 1879, p. 276.

MAUES.

No.	Obverse.	Reverse.
1	ΒΑΣΙΛΕΩΣ ΒΑΣΙΛΕΩΝ ΜΕΓΑΛΟΥ ΜΑΥΟΥ Biga r., in which radiate figure holding sceptre or spear, and charioteer.	(*Rajadirajasa mahatasa Moasa*). Zeus seated l. on throne; thunderbolt in extended r. hand. Ʀ Didrachm (Bodleian Library), Wt. 121·
2		Ʀ Hemidrachm (acquired for Brit. Mus.), Wt. 27·6.

AZES AND AZILISES.

No.	Obverse.	Reverse.
1	ΒΑΣΙΛΕΩΣ ΒΑΣΙΛΕΩΝ ΜΕΓΑΛΟΥ ΑΖΟΥ The king r., on horseback; lance couched. [Pl. xxxii. 9.]	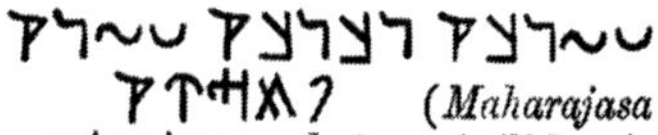 (*Maharajasa rajarajasa mahatasa Ayilishasa*). A city? l., holds in r. hand an object resembling a brazier; in l., palm bound with fillet. Æ Didrachm (R. Rochette, 1ère Suppl., Pl. II., No. 16).
2		Æ Hemidrachm (Grotefend).

AZILISES.

No.	Obverse.	Reverse.
1	'Standing figure to the r., with the r. arm extended horizontally, and holding a chaplet.'	'Figure in short tunic, with loose veil-like garments around the head, &c. Arian legend, imperfect, ... *jasa mahatasa Ayilishasa.*' Æ square (Thomas's Prinsep II., p. 212, No. 9, Sir E. C. Bayley).

VONONES AND SPALAHORES.

No.	Obverse.	Reverse.
1	'ΒΑΣΙΛΕΩΣ ΒΑΣΙΛΕΩΝ ΜΕΓΑΛΟΥ ΟΝΩΝΟΥ Hercules, with club and lion's skin; r. hand raised to the head.' [*Ariana Antiqua*, Pl. viii. 9.]	'Arian legend: — *Spahora bhrata dhramikasa Spalahorasa.* Minerva to the l., armed with shield and spear; r. arm extended.' Æ square (Thomas's Prinsep II., p. 204, No. 3, Mr. Brereton).

No.	Obverse.	Reverse.
	GONDOPHARES.	
1	Bust of the king l., wearing Arsacid tiara, diad.	ΒΑCΙΛΕWC ΒΑCΙΛΕWΝ ΜΕΓC ΥΝΔΟΦΕΡΗC ΑΥΤΟΚΡΑΤΟ King seated r. on throne, holding sceptre; behind, Nike crowning him.
	[Pl. XXXII. 10.]	Æ Wt. 58· (Berlin, *Zeitschr. f. Num.* 1879, p. 358).
	ZEIONISES.	
1	Barbarous inscr. The king r., on horseback; arm extended.	Inscription ending (*Jihāniasa*). The king facing; on one side, Nike; on the other, a wingless figure, crowning him.
	[Pl. XXXII. 11.]	Æ Didrachm (Thomas's Prinsep, Pl. XXVIII. 5).
	ARSACES DIKAIOS.	
1	ΒΑCΙΛΕΥΟΝΤΟC ΒΑCΙΛΕWΝ ΔΙΚΑΙΟΥ ΑΡCΑΚΟV The king, on horseback r.; r. hand raised.	Arian legend:—(*Māhārajasa rajarajasa mahatasa Ashshakasa tradatasa*). Type obliterated.* [On another specimen, Male figure to the left, holding a small figure in his right hand].
		Æ round (Cunningham).

* A coin of this class has a type thus described by Rollin and Feuardent, *Catalogue de Médailles*, No. 8296.—Figure militaire (?) diadémée debout, à g., tenant de la dr. une palme, la g. sur son épée (?).

ARSACES THEOS.

No.	Obverse.	Reverse.
1	ΒΑϹΙΛЄѠϹ ΘЄΟΥ . . ϹΑΚΟΥ Horse r. [Pl. xxxii. 12.]	Bow in case: fillet-border. Æ square, ·7 (Berlin, *Zeitschr. f. Num.*, Pl. v. 2).

KADPHISES II.

No.	Obverse.	Reverse.
1	ΒΑϹΙΛЄΥϹ ΟΟΗΜΟ ΚΑΔΦΙ-ϹΗϹ King r., holding club; seated in biga moving slowly to r. [Pl. xxxii. 13.]	Usual reverse; type, Siva standing (see p. 124). *N* Stater (*Ariana Antiqua*, Pl. x. 9).

KANERKES.

No.	Obverse.	Reverse.
1	ΡΑΟΝΑΝΟΡΑΟ Κ[ΑΝΗΡΚΙ] ΚΟΡΑΝΟ Bust of the king r., helmeted, holding spear, above clouds.	ΗΛΙΟϹ Helios standing, radiate; one hand advanced, the other grasping sword. *N* Wt. 30·8 (Rollin and Feuardent).

This coin, published by v. Sallet, is noteworthy as bilingual.

No.	Obverse.	Reverse.
2	ΡΑΟ ΚΑ]ΝΗΡΚΙ The king standing, at altar. [Pl. xxxii. 14.]	]ΓΟΒΟΥΔΟ Buddha seated facing, cross-legged; arms in posture of benediction. Æ 1· (Berlin, *Zeitschr. f. Num.* 1879, Pl. ix. 1).

INDEX I.

TYPES.

C.

D.

E.

K

L.

M

N.

O.

P.

W.

Z.

INDEX II.

KINGS, TYRANTS, &c.

INDEX III.

TITLES OF KINGS.

A. GREEK.

B. SCYTHIC, IN GREEK LETTERS.

C. INDIAN TITLES AND WORDS.

INDEX IV.

REMARKABLE INSCRIPTIONS AND LEGENDS.

TABLE

FOR

CONVERTING ENGLISH INCHES INTO MILLIMÈTRES

AND THE

MEASURES OF MIONNET'S SCALE.

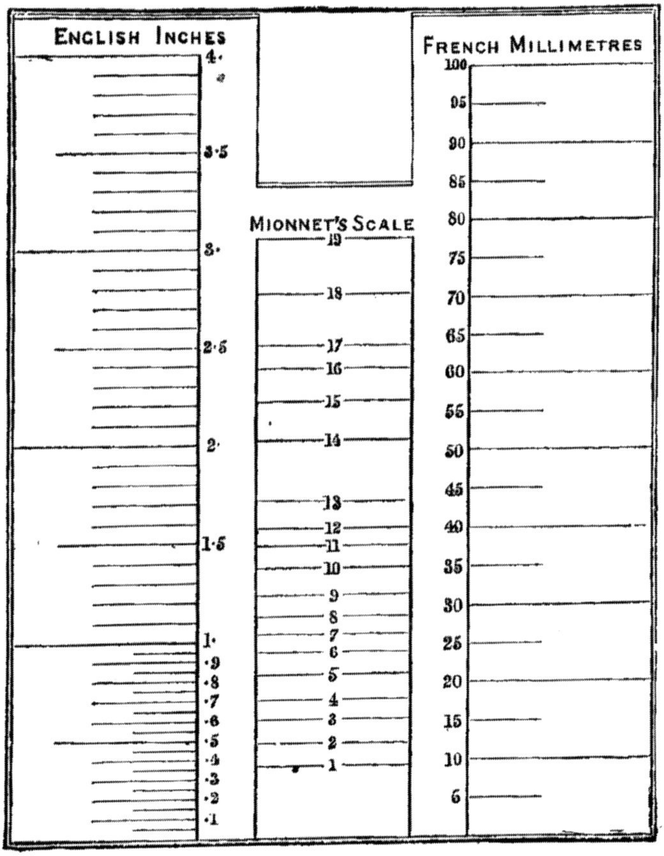

TABLE
OF
The Relative Weights of English Grains and French Grammes.

Grains.	Grammes.	Grains	Grammes.	Grains	Grammes.	Grains.	Grammes.
1	·064	41	2·656	81	5·248	121	7·840
2	·129	42	2·720	82	5·312	122	7·905
3	·194	43	2·785	83	5·378	123	7·970
4	·259	44	2·850	84	5·442	124	8·035
5	·324	45	2·915	85	5·508	125	8·100
6	·388	46	2·980	86	5 572	126	8·164
7	·453	47	3·045	87	5·637	127	8·229
8	·518	48	3·110	88	5·702	128	8·294
9	·583	49	3·175	89	5·767	129	8·359
10	·648	50	3·240	90	5·832	130	8·424
11	·712	51	3·304	91	5·896	131	8·488
12	·777	52	3·368	92	5·961	132	8·553
13	·842	53	3·434	93	6·026	133	8·618
14	·907	54	3·498	94	6·091	134	8·682
15	·972	55	3·564	95	6 156	135	8·747
16	1·036	56	3·628	96	6·220	136	8·812
17	1·101	57	3·693	97	6·285	137	8·877
18	1·166	58	3·758	98	6·350	138	8·942
19	1·231	59	3·823	99	6·415	139	9·007
20	1·296	60	3·888	100	6·480	140	9·072
21	1·360	61	3·952	101	6·544	141	9·136
22	1·425	62	4·017	102	6·609	142	9·200
23	1·490	63	4·082	103	6·674	143	9·265
24	1·555	64	4·146	104	6·739	144	9·330
25	1·620	65	4·211	105	6·804	145	9·395
26	1·684	66	4·276	106	6·868	146	9·460
27	1·749	67	4·341	107	6·933	147	9·525
28	1·814	68	4·406	108	6·998	148	9·590
29	1·879	69	4·471	109	7·063	149	9·655
30	1·944	70	4·536	110	7·128	150	9·720
31	2·008	71	4·600	111	7·192	151	9 784
32	2·073	72	4·665	112	7·257	152	9·848
33	2·138	73	4·729	113	7·322	153	9·914
34	2·202	74	4·794	114	7·387	154	9·978
35	2·267	75	4·859	115	7·452	155	10·044
36	2·332	76	4·924	116	7·516	156	10·108
37	2 397	77	4·989	117	7·581	157	10·173
38	2·462	78	5·054	118	7·646	158	10·238
39	2·527	79	5·119	119	7·711	159	10·303
40	2·592	80	5·184	120	7·776	160	10·368

TABLE

OF

The Relative Weights of English Grains and French Grammes.

Grains.	Grammes.	Grains	Grammes.	Grains	Grammes.	Grains.	Grammes.
161	10·432	201	13·024	241	15·616	290	18·79
162	10·497	202	13·089	242	15·680	300	19·44
163	10·562	203	13·154	243	15·745	310	20·08
164	10·626	204	13·219	244	15 810	320	20·73
165	10·691	205	13·284	245	15·875	330	21 38
166	10·756	206	13·348	246	15·940	340	22·02
167	10·821	207	13·413	247	16·005	350	22·67
168	10·886	208	13·478	248	16 070	360	23·32
169	10·951	209	13·543	249	16·135	370	23·97
170	11·016	210	13·608	250	16·200	380	24·62
171	11·080	211	13·672	251	16·264	390	25·27
172	11·145	212	13·737	252	16·328	400	25·92
173	11·209	213	13·802	253	16·394	410	26·56
174	11·274	214	13·867	254	16·458	420	27·20
175	11·339	215	13·932	255	16·524	430	27·85
176	11·404	216	13 996	256	16·588	440	28·50
177	11·469	217	14·061	257	16 653	450	29·15
178	11·534	218	14·126	258	16·718	460	29·80
179	11·599	219	14·191	259	16·783	470	30 45
180	11·664	220	14·256	260	16·848	480	31·10
181	11·728	221	14·320	261	16·912	490	31·75
182	11·792	222	14 385	262	16 977	500	32·40
183	11·858	223	14·450	263	17 042	510	33·04
184	11·922	224	14·515	264	17·106	520	33·68
185	11·988	225	14·580	265	17·171	530	34·34
186	12·052	226	14 644	266	17·236	540	34·98
187	12·117	227	14 709	267	17·301	550	35·64
188	12·182	228	14·774	268	17·366	560	36·28
189	12·247	229	14·839	269	17·431	570	36·93
190	12·312	230	14·904	270	17·496	580	37·58
191	12·376	231	14·968	271	17·560	590	38·23
192	12·441	232	15·033	272	17·625	600	38·88
193	12·506	233	15·098	273	17·689	700	45·36
194	12·571	234	15·162	274	17·754	800	51·84
195	12·636	235	15·227	275	17·819	900	58·32
196	12·700	236	15·292	276	17·884	1000	64·80
197	12·765	237	15·357	277	17·949	2000	129·60
198	12·830	238	15·422	278	18·014	3000	194·40
199	12·895	239	15·487	279	18·079	4000	259·20
200	12·960	240	15·552	280	18 144	5000	324 00

Pl. I.

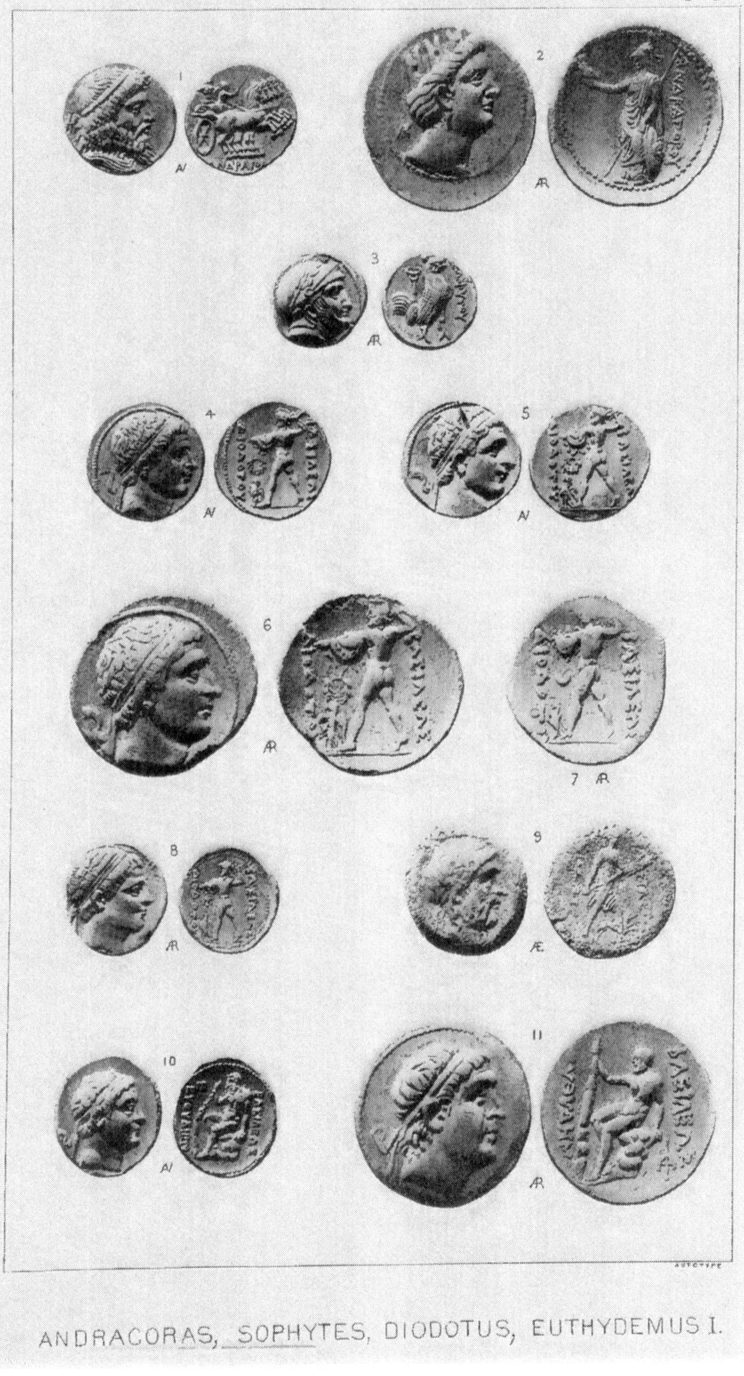

ANDRACORAS, SOPHYTES, DIODOTUS, EUTHYDEMUS I.

Pl. II.

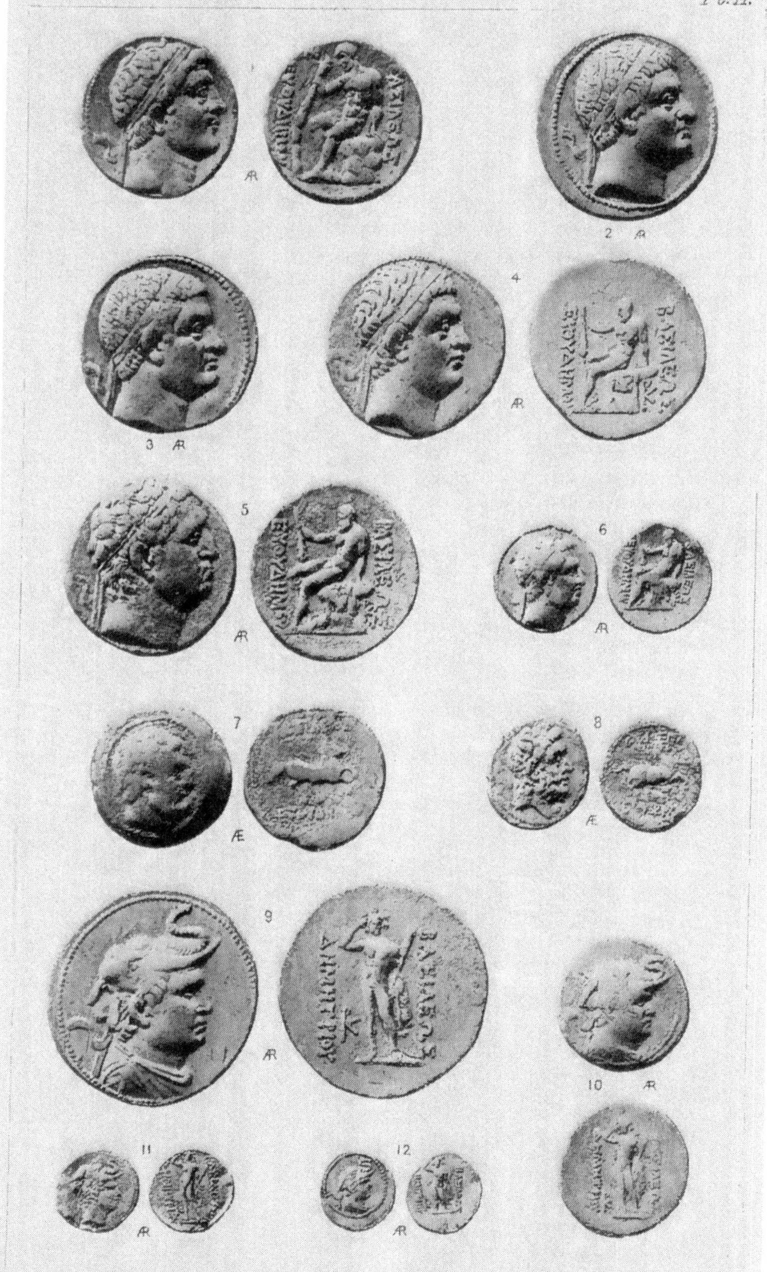

EUTHYDEMUS I, DEMETRIUS.

DEMETRIUS, EUTHYDEMUS II, PANTALEON.

Pl. IV.

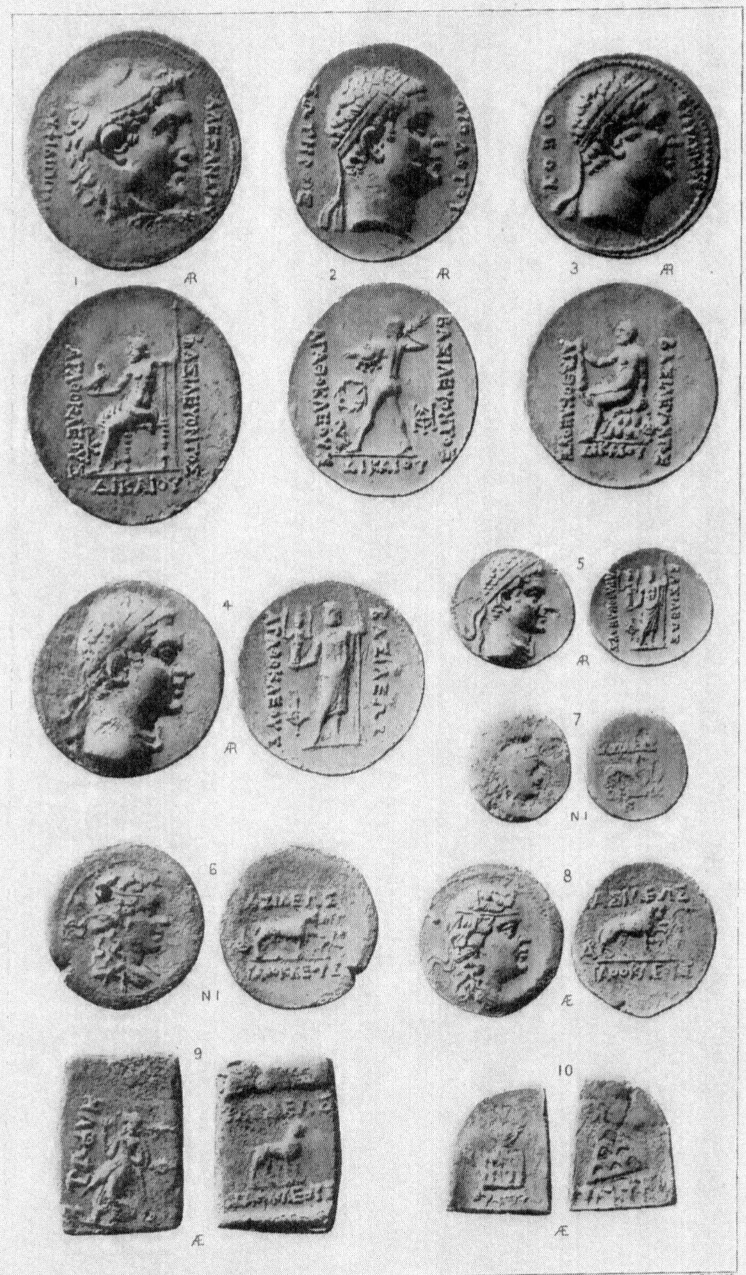

ACATHOCLES.

Pl. V.

ANTIMACHUS I, EUCRATIDES.

Pl. VI.

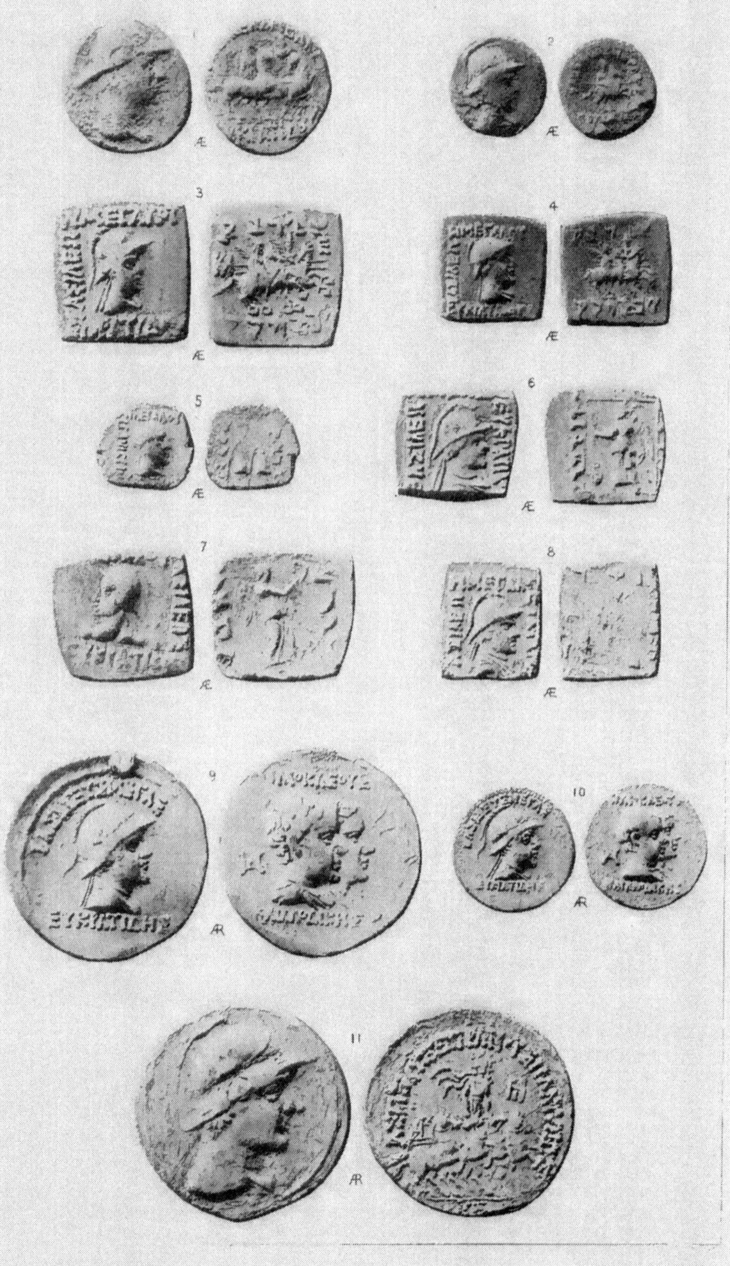

EUCRATIDES, PLATO.

Pl. VII

HELIOCLES, ANTIALCIDAS.

Pl. VIII.

ANTIALCIDAS, LYSIAS, DIOMEDES.

ARCHEBIUS, APOLLODOTUS.

Pl. V

APOLLODOTUS, STRATO I.

Pl. XI.

STRATO I, AGATHOCLEIA, MENANDER.

Pl. XII.

MENANDER, EPANDER, DIONYSIUS, ZOILUS.

Pl. XIII.

APOLLOPHANES, ARTEMIDORUS, ANTIMACHUS II, PHILOXENUS, NICIAS.

Pl. XIV.

HIPPOSTRATUS, AMYNTAS.

Pl. XV.

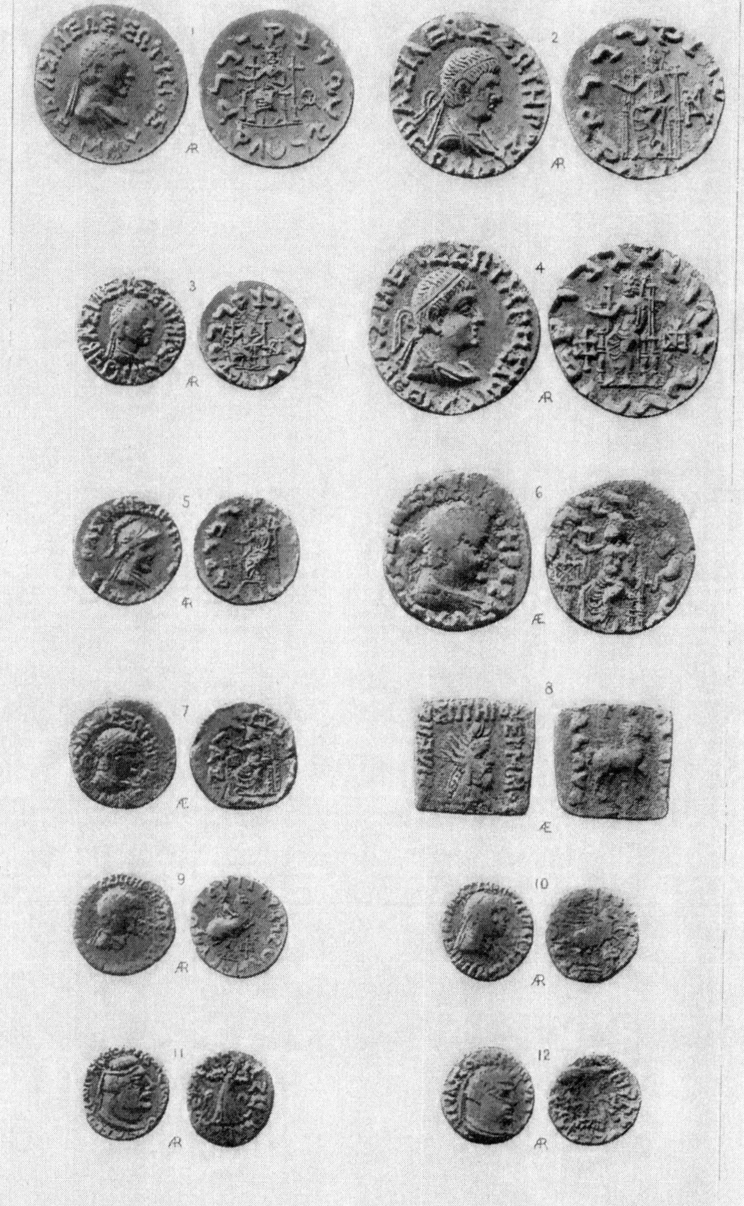

HERMAEUS, CALLIOPE, RANJABALA.

MAUES.

Pl. XVI.

MAUES, AZES.

Pl. XVIII.

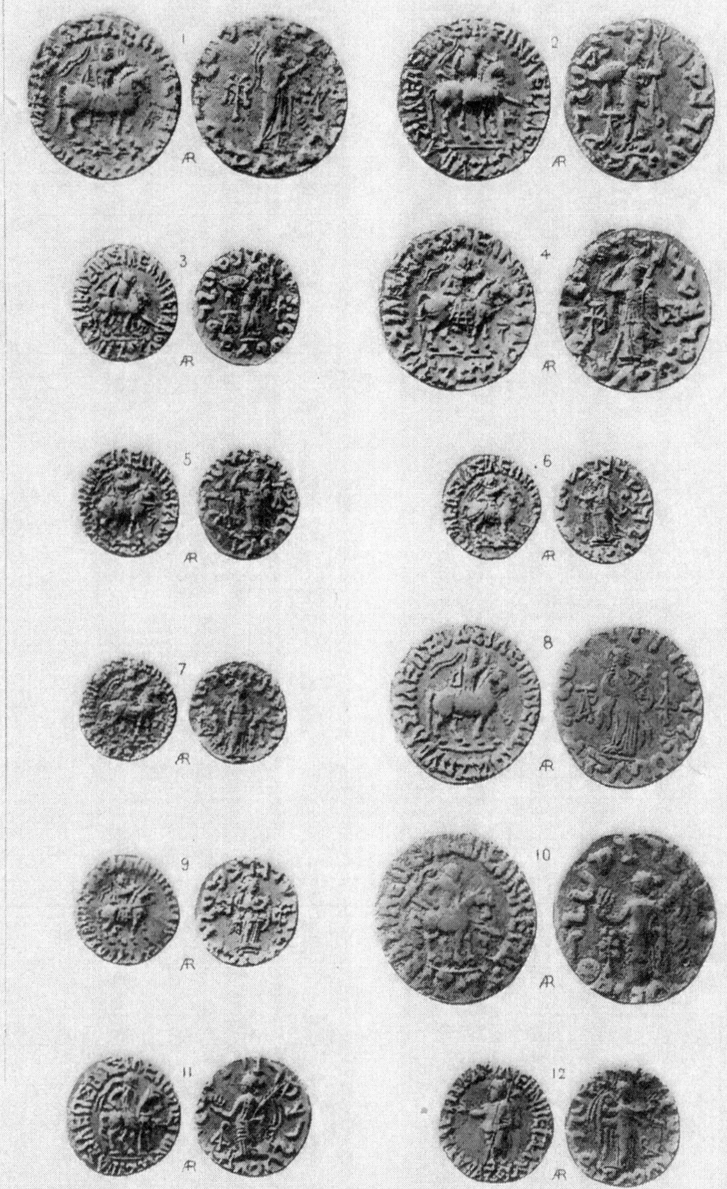

AZES.

Pl. XX

AZES.

Pl. XX.

AZES, AZILISES.

Pl. XXI.

AZILISES, VONONES, SPALAHORES, &c.

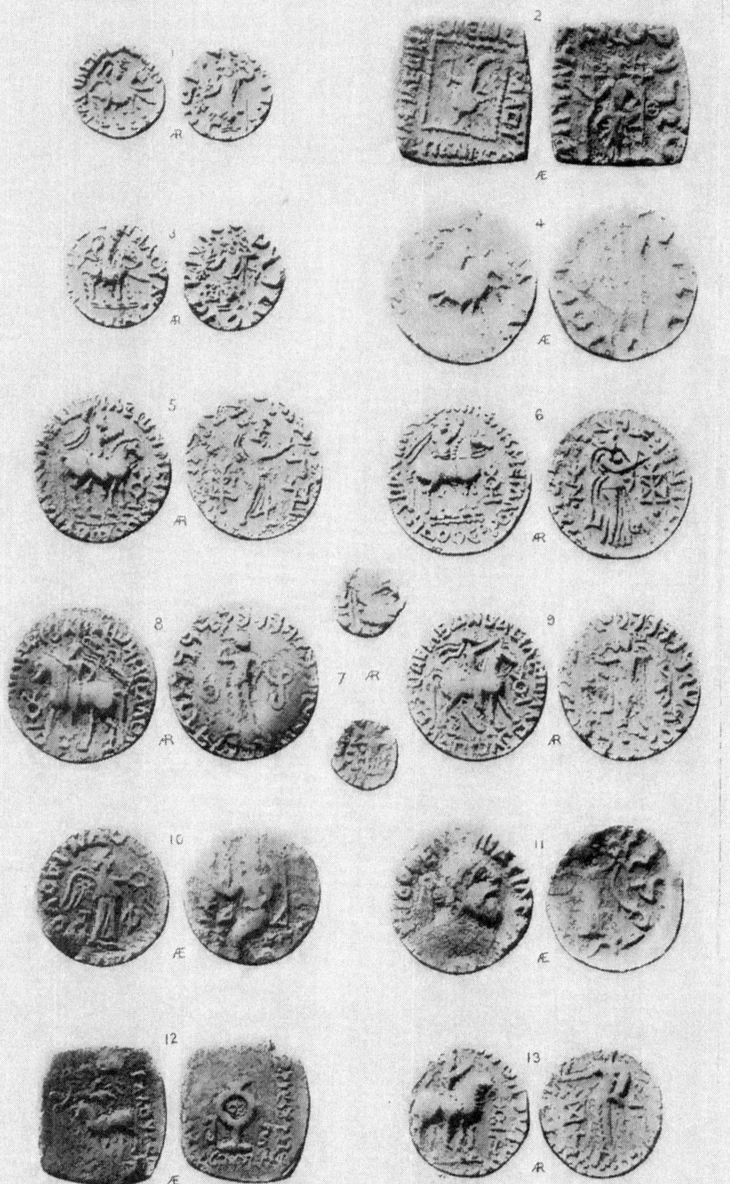

SPALIRISES &c. GONDOPHARES.

Pl. XXIII.

ABDAGASES, ZEIONISES &c. PACORES, ORTHAGNES, SANABARES.

Pl. XXV.

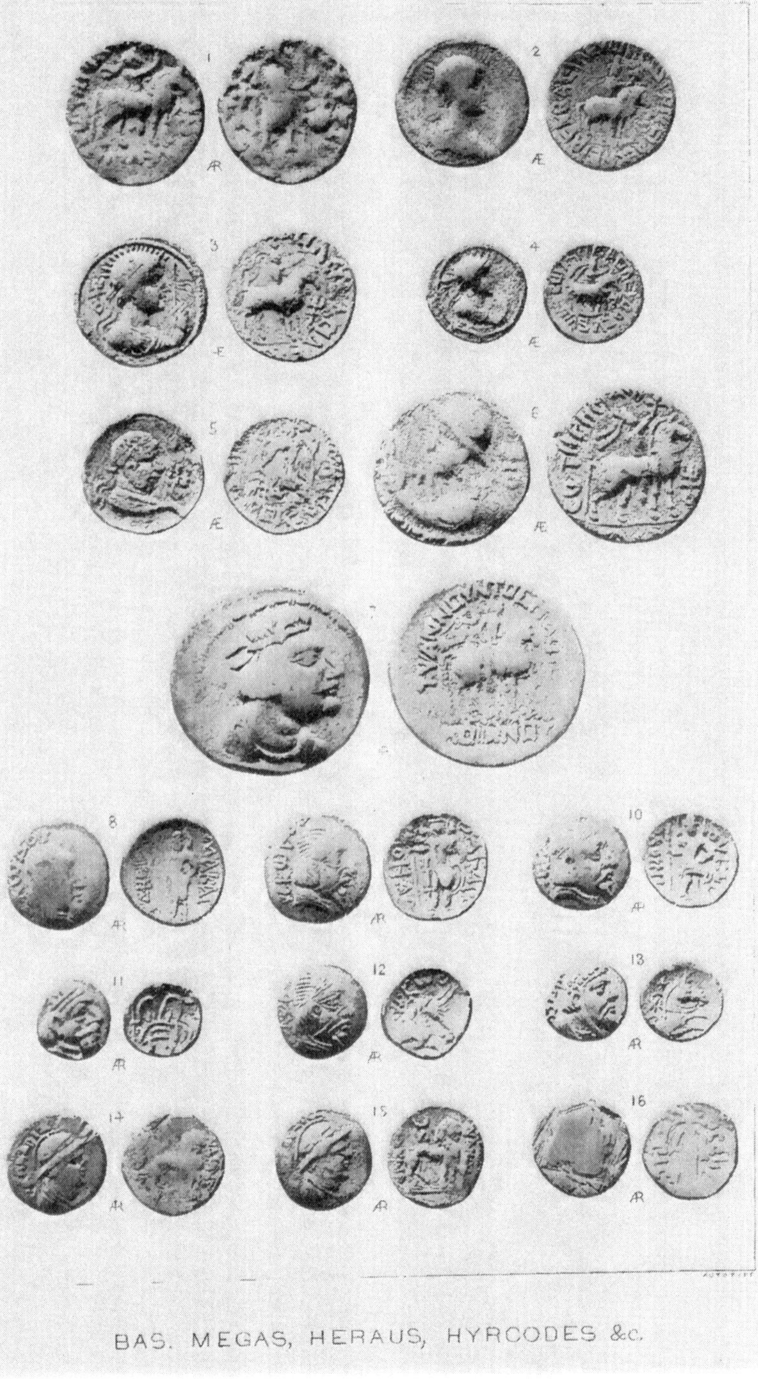

BAS. MEGAS, HERAUS, HYRCODES &c.

KADPHISES I, KADAPHES, KADPHISES II.

Pl. XXVI

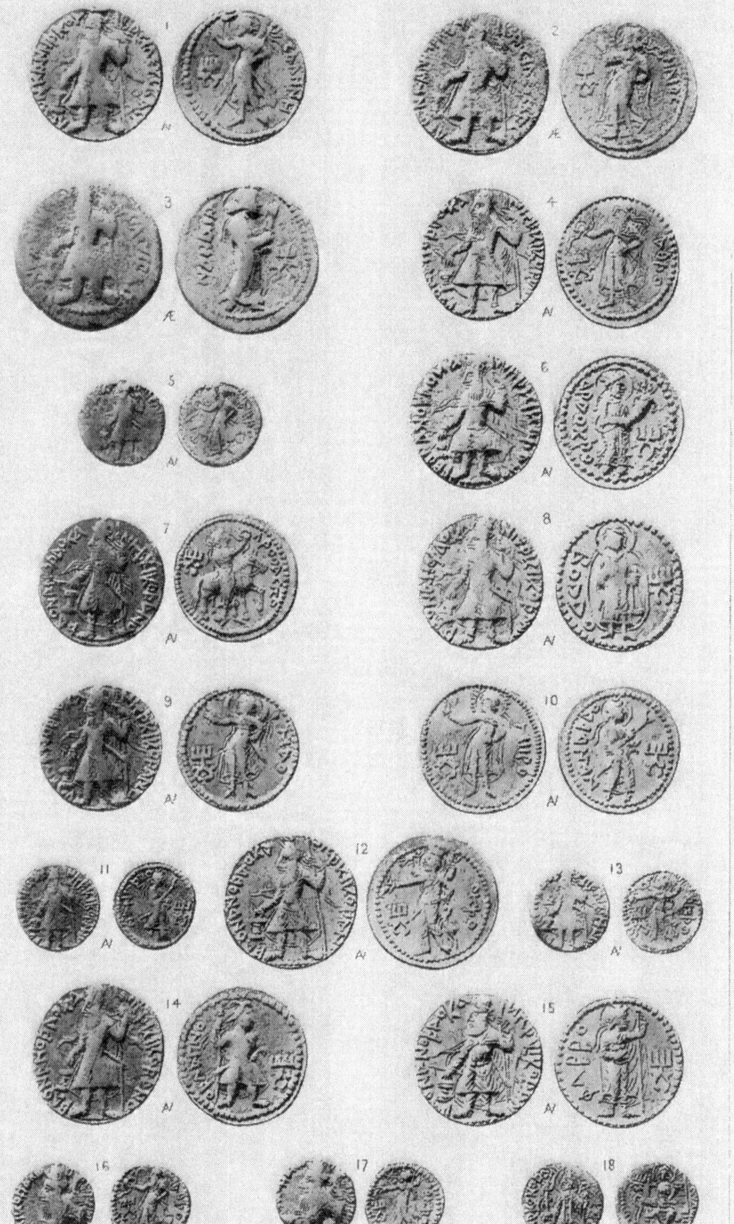

KANERKES.

Pl. XXVII

KANERKES, HOOERKES.

Pl. XXVIII.

HOOERKES.

Pl. XXIX.

HOOERKES, BAZODEO &c.

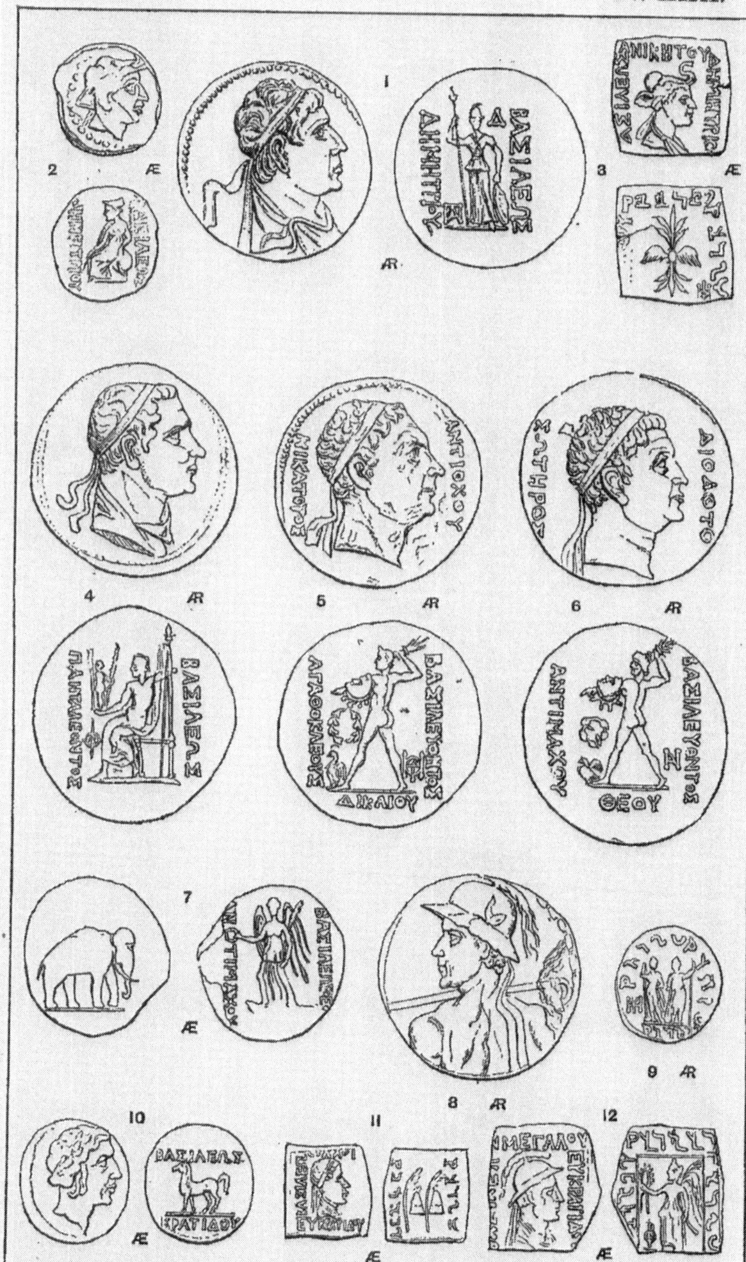

SUPPLEMENTARY. 1.

SUPPLEMENTARY. 2.

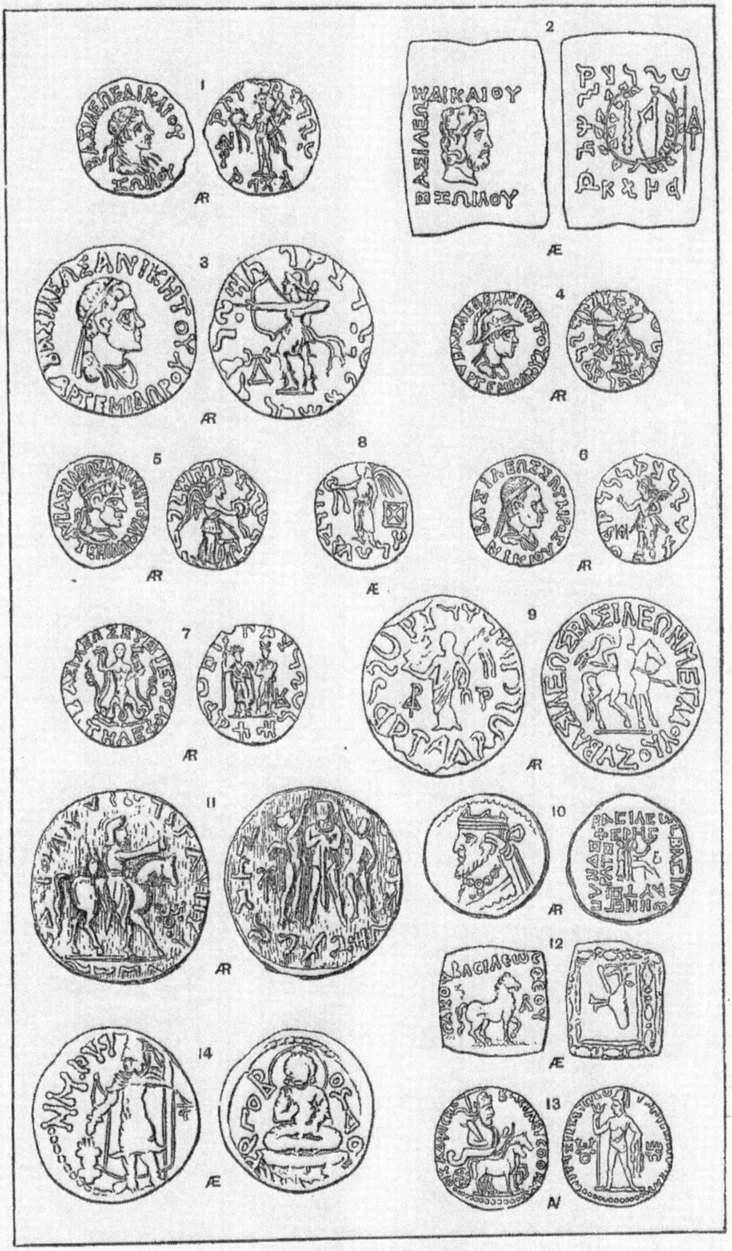

SUPPLEMENTARY. 3.